SEND FOR BENSON!

A Life of
Sir Christopher Benson

Send for Benson! is the last of Eric Stockdale's four somewhat unconventional contributions to the history of London, each one leading to the next. The first two were set in the eighteenth century: *'Tis Treason, My Good Man! – Four Revolutionary Presidents and a Piccadilly Bookshop*, published in 2005 by Oak Knoll Press and the British Library; and *Middle Temple Lawyers and the American Revolution*, co-written with Randy J. Holland, 2007, Thomson West. The third contribution was 'The Middle Temple since 1900', the 100-page final chapter of *History of the Middle Temple*, edited by R. O. Havery, 2011, Hart Publishing.

The present work is an account of the life of a remarkable man, Sir Christopher Benson (1933–), who in the past 40 years has contributed significantly to many of the improvements made in London, mainly as a property developer, but also in other roles, such as chairman of the London Docklands Development Corporation the Housing Corporation and Crossrail.

SEND FOR BENSON!

A Life of
Sir Christopher Benson

Eric Stockdale

OBLONG 2015

Published in 2015 by
Oblong Creative Ltd
416B Thorp Arch Estate
Wetherby LS23 7FG
UK

Send for Benson! A Life of Sir Christopher Benson

Text © 2015 Eric Stockdale

ISBN 978 0 9575992 7 7

AUTHOR'S NOTE
Every effort has been made to identify the sources of
illustrations used in this book and to obtain permissison
to reproduce them. The author offers his apologies for
any omissions or errors which remain in this regard.

Produced in the UK by Oblong Creative Ltd

Table of Contents

Acknowledgements

The author would like to acknowledge the help he received from the following, all of whom encountered Christopher Benson at one or more of the stages of his long and varied career:

Julian Benson, Lord Blyth of Rowington, Hamish Bryce, Michael Collier, Peter Costain, Sir Jeremy Dixon, David Edmonds CBE, Arthur Hayes, Sir Terry Heiser GCB, Cllr. Patricia Holland, Dr Carol Homden CBE, Dr Gwyn Humphreys, Bill Jack, Jeanne Kaniuk, Alan Lovell, Tony McGann OBE, Anthony Mayer CBE, Carole Nicholson, Susan Palmer, Laurence Rutman, Baroness Scotland of Asthal QC, Roger Squire and Brigadier Charles Wright.

Introduction

My first encounter with Christopher Benson's name was when I was working in the archives of the Middle Temple, as one of the authors of the official history of that Inn of Court. He figured in them as he had been elected an Honorary Bencher as far back as 1984, on the nomination of the Inn's Master Treasurer for the year, Sir Desmond Ackner, who was then a member of the Court of Appeal but was soon to become a Lord of Appeal in Ordinary, or Law Lord. Ackner was an extremely shrewd man, given to making sound decisions and good choices. He had asked Benson whether he would be prepared to give the Middle Temple Benchers (as the members of its governing body are known) the benefit of his free advice about its estate, and in particular, about the acquisition of further properties for use as barristers' chambers. That was an urgent need, as the Inn was bursting at the seams in its historic, but only site — in the Temple, between Fleet Street and the Thames Embankment. Benson's CV, which was included in the printed booklet giving the background of all the Benchers, showed that he was not only an experienced property developer, but that he had also undertaken a variety of other tasks, both in the commercial area and in the public field as chairman of several quangos. He had also acted, somewhat surprisingly, as the last Principal of the Inns of Court School of Law.

When I eventually met him there was no shortage of topics to discuss. I found he had a fund of interesting stories to tell about his very full and varied life and that he was a delightful raconteur with a self-deprecating sense of humour. Although he had started his working life at sea and had then to change it to that of a landlubber in the West Country, where he learned the craft of the chartered surveyor and property developer, his story turned out to be essentially London based. It is true that as chairman of the Housing Corporation he was able to give some crucial help to the beginnings of the regeneration of Liverpool; and that he was later able to help scientists at Bradford University to maximise the benefits deriving from one of their inventions and its development, but in the main his efforts were London centred.

Benson's story turned out to be, above all else, a part of London's history. When he was managing director and then chairman of the second largest property development company in the country, he oversaw the completion of many large-scale projects. Some were abroad and led to both challenging and amusing encounters, but their main focus was on the square of mile of the City, with others in Greater London. Unlike some of his predecessors in earlier days, he did not tear down precious old buildings and replace them with tasteless modern boxes. As a general rule he saw to it that good architects were employed to erect attractive buildings, whether office blocks or shopping centres. He showed a concern for the archaeology of the sites, and got his company to fund numerous rescue digs in London, providing £500,000 to the Museum of London for those purposes in one year alone. Similarly, when the Sir John Soane's museum in Lincoln's Inn Fields, one of London's treasures, needed extensive funding for repairs and renovation, Benson arranged for his company to donate £1m towards the £2.5m target and encouraged the government to match that sum with a similar grant.

When the rebuilding of the Royal Opera House in Covent Garden became a distinct possibility, Sir Claus Moser, its chairman, invited Benson to become a director and to chair the development board. Although Benson remained involved only for the first few years of the ambitious enlargement and improvement scheme, both of its distinguished principal architects vouch for the value of his input.

It was doubtless because of his experience as a successful developer of town centre properties, often at the request of a city or town council, that he was asked to act as the chairman of the London Docklands Development Corporation for nearly five years. While in that post he played an influential part in the early days of the Canary Wharf development, as well as in the continuing improvement of the infra-structure of the area, and the provision of housing and other facilities for the residents of what had become a large neglected area after the closing of the docks. Without the efforts of Benson and his many colleagues and collaborators in Docklands, London might well not have succeeded in becoming or remaining one of the world's great financial centres, and could have failed in the hotly contested competition to be awarded the 2012 Olympic Games.

Britons are very proud of their rights of assembly and of free speech but from time to time, like the London supporters of John Wilkes in the eighteenth century, they go over the top. Both the rebuilding of the Royal Opera House and the redevelopment of the London Docklands were bitterly opposed on what Benson felt were ill-considered grounds. They were, however, a part of traditional London life.

Ken Livingstone, the Mayor of London, invited Benson to serve on Transport for London, and after a year, asked him to be the first chairman of the company formed to plan Crossrail. That was a job that was tailor-made for him, in view of his previous experience in Docklands. Unfortunately, he became increasingly exasperated with the delays caused, in his opinion, by the Secretary of State, so after three years their relationship came to an end. Fortunately, Crossrail is making good progress, building on the sound early work of Benson and his team of highly skilled engineers and other professionals.

After Benson had concluded his term as chairman of the London Docklands Development Corporation, Sir Terry Heiser, the Permanent Secretary of the Department of the Environment, wrote in a farewell letter: 'But I want to say that I have no doubt that what is happening now in Docklands will figure in histories of the metropolis which will be written in the years to come. So will you.' Although Benson insists that he is not entitled to make any such claim, I suggest that he has earned the right to be considered as one of the men who have helped to make substantial changes to the face — and life — of London, changes for the better.

Eric Stockdale

CHAPTER ONE

The Call of the Sea

Christopher Benson was born on 20 July 1933 at Wheaton Aston in Staffordshire, the son of Charles Benson and his wife Catherine, known as Katie. Charles had served in the 1914–18 War as a despatch rider and had then qualified as a licensed dentist. Katie was a state registered nurse and by the time she stopped nursing to have her two children, she was a ward sister. After returning to work she became a matron of a fever hospital in Lancashire.

When Christopher was still very young the family moved to Waddington, near Clitheroe in Lancashire, but soon returned to Wheaton Aston. His father was no longer able to find work locally and had to commute to Derby to another practice. In 1939 they all moved to Worcester. Christopher and Margery, his elder sister, were entered at Hallow Infant School and to attend it had to walk together, four miles each way. Fortunately, the next school was nearer home, but Christopher's record in all subjects there was poor. His parents could not have been surprised when he failed to get into the local grammar school at the age of eleven; he attended the Worcester Cathedral King's School instead.

Christopher continued to fail in mastering academic subjects and he did not improve his chances by playing truant quite often. He later summed up his record at that school concisely: 'I played rugby and truant.' Like many another unsuccessful scholar, he enjoyed various sports and at the King's School and later, became very proficient in different ones. He took like a duck to water and became a good swimmer, diver and water polo player. He also became a good boxer and rugby player, nearly always as hooker. One of Christopher's teachers could tell that he had something about him that deserved encouragement. He was a former naval officer called Pedder and suggested that the Royal Navy might suit him.

Christopher was only twelve when the war finished in 1945 but he remembered seeing the red glow when Birmingham was set on fire by incendiary bombs during earlier bombing raids. Like many boys he grew up with an admiration for the Royal Navy, which was in action virtually every single day. His parents' medical background made him think that being a naval surgeon would make an interesting career. The more Christopher thought about the Royal Navy, the more he liked the idea, so much so that he eventually applied for admission to the Naval College at Dartmouth. He went to Malvern for the entrance test and predictably failed in this, his first attempt to get started on the long haul required for anyone hoping to be a Royal Navy officer.

Charles Benson realised that his son was serious about the sea and so when he was still thirteen took him to visit two of the training ships available for boys. The first was *HMS Conway*, located permanently in the sea in the Menai Straits; the second was *HMS Worcester*, moored alongside the famous three-masted *Cutty Sark*, at Greenhithe on the Thames in London. This was Christopher's first view of the London Docklands that were to play an important part in his later career, when he became the second chairman of the Development Corporation. The boy chose the ship belonging to the Thames Nautical Training College in the sheltered London river in preference to the one in the wilds. One of this ship's unusual attributes was her own swimming pool ashore — a matter of some importance for a keen swimmer.

The *Worcester*, built to look as though she had a wooden hull though it was in fact made of steel, had served as a submarine mother ship at Scapa Flow. Her commander, Captain G. C. Steele VC, was well qualified for his job. He had started his naval life as a cadet with the P&O shipping line and had then been on active service with the Royal Navy. He had earned the highest gallantry award for his heroism after the end of the 1914–18 War, in 1919, during an ill-considered and quixotic British gunboat attack on the new Soviet fleet at Kronstadt, the harbour protecting Petrograd. Benson remembers him as a gentle but firm man, who applied naval discipline. He was well supported by the chief officer, a Merchant Navy captain, R. M. Richardson.

When Benson joined the ship there were two cadet streams: one for boys destined for the Royal Navy, the other for future Merchant Navy candidates. He chose the first but a year after his arrival, much to his disappointment, the Royal Navy stream was discontinued, leaving him with no choice but to continue his training with a view to becoming a Merchant Navy officer. He was very unhappy during his time aboard. One of the regular tasks of the cadets was the coaling of the vessel. Although she was not going anywhere, she required a great deal of coal in her bunkers for heating and hot water. Benson was never afraid of hard work, but he had the sneaking feeling that there ought to have been some mechanised way of dealing with the fuel supply.

He had been in the school band at King's, playing the bugle, and was happy to be appointed ship's bugler. Apart from that he was sustained by his sporting success. For the three years that he was a cadet he spent a great deal of time rowing and became a proficient oarsman. As he put it, 'A boat was our main

Bugler boy Benson

means of transport; we rowed everywhere.' At the age of seventeen he became the Worcester county men's diving champion and played water polo in a men's team. He improved in his other sports also. As hooker of Worcester's rugby team he helped it to defeat the team from *Conway* for the first time, and also the one from the Nautical College, Pangbourne. The first promotion possible for a cadet was to the local rank of badge cadet. Benson claims that he only achieved that honour because of his sporting prowess — a recognition in the best traditions of all the armed services. However, he was probably too modest in making that claim, as when he passed out shortly after his sixteenth birthday, he was the only senior badge cadet on parade. His extensive training also enabled him to apply successfully to be gazetted as a midshipman in the Royal Naval Reserve.

Benson, like Captain Steele before him, was taken on as a cadet by P&O. He was meant to join one of their ships on her return from the Mediterranean, but she was delayed for repairs in Genoa. Very thoughtfully P&O released the young man from his obligation to join that ship and suggested that he should try for a cadetship with the Union Castle line instead. That line had a vacancy for him

3

Coaling ship

and he sailed under its flag for the next two years, when he was sixteen to eighteen years old.

His first ship was the *SS Sandown Castle*, a small tramp of 11,500 dead-weight tons built in 1922, which Benson described as 'a rust bucket'. He was qualified to describe her in that way, as he spent many an unhappy hour working on her paintwork, often under an African sun. He joined the ship in the Royal Albert dock in London in January 1950. His father accompanied him to the gangway but was not permitted to come aboard with his sixteen-year-old son. The mate said, 'Wave goodbye to your Daddy, laddie,' and ordered young Benson below to supervise the stowage of spirits in the number three hatch. Both father and

4

son fought back the tears at this unexpectedly curtailed farewell, which meant, apart from anything else, that they could not use their tickets for a West End show that evening. It was brutal — but probably regarded by the mate as the best way to start making a man of the boy. Benson was left down below for some forty-eight hours, but fortunately the stevedores stowing the cargo and ship's stores took pity on him. They showed him how to drop a case of Scotch 'accidentally', and shared their food and drink with him. He still remembers those men with affection.

When the ship sailed the captain allowed his new cadet on the bridge while she cleared the Thames. Benson was so tired by the whole experience, that he did not even notice the *Worcester* or *Cutty Sark* when the ship steamed past them. He soon learned that cadets were expected to work hard and to study at sea. They were not only given endless cleaning and paintwork duties but also took their turn at the wheel and on lookout.

The first port of call was Marseilles, where Benson stayed aboard. The next was Genoa, where the four cadets were allowed to go ashore in uniform, one at a time. Benson had been given a Rolex by his father as a reward for his three years in training and stopped to looked at the watches in a jeweller's window. A civilian sidled up to him and attempted to pick him up, with a promise of a good watch if he came with him. Benson said that he already had one, did not need another, and had to get back to his ship. He was told that he would be taken back there in time. Fortunately, a police officer hove in sight. Benson told the civilian that he would go and ask the officer how best to get back to the ship. That did the trick: the man vanished within seconds.

The rest of the voyage through the Mediterranean and the Suez Canal proved interesting though uneventful, but off the coast of Kenya Benson sustained a bizarre injury. He shared a cabin with another cadet and had 'won' the top bunk. On his return from duty on the middle watch, a four-hour stint from midnight to four in the morning, he found that his large cabin mate was sleeping in the top bunk. Benson told him to get out and sleep in his own lower bunk but his colleague more than once refused to move. Benson then warned him that if he was still there when he returned from having a shower, he would turf him out. On finding his bunk still occupied by his colleague on his return, Benson tried to haul him out of it, but was savagely bitten on his upper arm by the reluctant mover. The wounded cadet soon found that he also had a swelling in his armpit after being bitten and so reported to the third mate who, in the absence of a doctor, was in charge of the medical kit.

The mate was understandably puzzled by the injury and felt it was too serious for him to deal with, other than with disinfectant and a bandage. He asked

Benson how he had sustained this odd wound. Knowing that it was not done to rat on a shipmate, the wounded cadet replied, with a considerable degree of truth, 'I was bitten by a rat.' That information doubtless made the mate and the captain nervous about the possibility of a rat passing on Weil's disease, so the young cadet was escorted to hospital in the small Kenyan port of Tanga and abandoned there when his ship sailed shortly afterwards. Fortunately, a sensible nurse's simple treatment did the trick and the patient was soon dispatched by plane to catch up with his ship in Dar es Salaam. It was a great thrill for the sixteen-year-old to fly for the first time — a thrill that doubtless contributed to his later obtaining a fixed wing pilot's licence and then one to fly a helicopter.

While in Dar es Salaam, when Benson and a colleague had some free time, they took a boat and rowed around the harbour, sightseeing. There were many dhows around and they were beckoned onto one of them. The crew offered them dates, which seemed to be their cargo, and crowded around the two lads enthusiastically. Benson and his colleague decided they had better get back to their ship without delay. On arrival the mate told them off for their folly in boarding a strange vessel and warned them to be more careful in future.

When on the east coast of Africa Benson formed a healthy respect for the local dockers. One evening when he was in a hold supervising the unloading of cargo, he pulled out his handkerchief. His good Dunhill lighter had got entangled with it and fell down a crevice in the cargo, so he did not expect to see it again. Next morning the day shift supervisor handed him his lighter. The evening shift had not gone home until they had moved enough cargo to reveal the missing item.

When his ship was berthed in Capetown, a very old African stevedore regularly passed a bunch of grapes to him through the porthole of his cabin as a gift, even though being caught in the act might have landed him in trouble. He saw the other side of the coin when he went ashore there during that stay — ironically for a medical appointment. A white man addressed him in Afrikaans; when Benson started to explain that he only spoke English, he was knocked down by a punch to the chin and kicked as he lay on the ground. His bilingual attacker then called him a 'f---g English bastard'.

During that first voyage Benson did not keep a diary, save for a record showing only the sailing times, distances covered and ports visited. His first trip took 144 days, quite an experience for a sixteen-year-old. Fortunately, on his second voyage he kept a more detailed diary, one which gives an interesting glimpse of the rites — and wrongs — of passage, including the young man's progress in turning himself into a real sailor, with too much drink and tobacco. On that occasion he sailed in the *MV Rochester Castle* from Hull on 25 June 1950, bound initially for Philadelphia and New York.

Four days later Benson wrote in his diary: 'I have come to the conclusion that it is not the long hours we work (we don't) but the few hours we sleep that gets me down. The sea, for an officer especially, is an exceptionally lazy life.' On Independence Day the ship entered the Delaware and made her way to Philadelphia. He enjoyed his shore leave there on 5 July until torrential rain soaked him and a colleague to the skin. They went to a cinema to see a double feature and to dry off and missed the last dock bus. 'We had to walk about eight miles. We arrived back to the ship and turned in at 1.52 am. We turned out at 6 am and turned to, to prepare the ship for sea. We left at twelve noon and after lunch I turned the cabin lights out and closed the door in order to make the bosun and mate think I was working somewhere, however the mate caught up with me at 4 pm and I had to work the ship till tea at 5 pm. As a punishment I had to tend the pilot and flags till about 10 pm. Actually it was not much of a punishment as I should have had to have done it anyway.'

Four days in New York enchanted Benson as much as most visitors. He made the most of a marvellous club for young seaman on West 23rd Street, the British-American Apprentices Club, where there was always a warm welcome. On 11 July he wrote: 'Worked the ship until lunch. Then went to stations for departure New York. I feel as bad about leaving NY as I did about England. We passed the Statue of Liberty and the skyscrapers of lower Manhattan looked so inviting that, whatever happens, I swear an oath to revisit NY.'

The following day, the first of an eighteen-day passage to Capetown, proved a bit of an anticlimax, which the young man described humorously. 'Turned out at 6.45 am. Scrubbed and washed down all the decks. Scraped and red-leaded paintwork round the ship. Got covered in red-lead. Have come to the conclusion that red hair does not suit my complexion.' On 20 July Benson celebrated his seventeenth birthday by sharing a few bottles of beer with his fellow cadets.

After some days in South African ports the ship returned to home waters via the Canary Islands, where Benson checked in a cargo of bananas. Going to sea was not a way to avoid examinations. On 28 August he noted: 'Turned out 4 am and took first wheel until 6 am, then worked on deck till 8 am. 10 am went to the saloon and started Seamanship exam till 12.30. Lunch 2 pm. Mathematics exam till 4.30. Went on the wheel at 6 pm and got a shock: there were about thirty fishing vessels advancing on us; we had a fine time dodging them. Turned in 10 pm.' On a number of following days he had to take more examinations on board as well as taking his turn with normal duties. After calling in on Dublin and Belfast the ship returned to Liverpool on 10 September 1950.

Unfortunately Benson abandoned his diary for his next and longest voyage in the *Rochester Castle*. It was a round-the-world trip: south via the Suez Canal, then on from South Africa to New Zealand, the Pacific and the Panama Canal, finally crossing the Atlantic from New York. During that voyage he experienced a cross-section of climates and concluded that the North Atlantic in winter was not for the fainthearted. Standing lookout watch on the open deck of the fo'c'sle, he would at times have to be lashed to the rail so as not to be washed overboard. His signalling equipment at times like that was not much use: he had a fo'c'sle bell. One ring of the bell indicated a ship to port; two, to starboard.

The ship spent some two weeks in November and December tied up in Napier. Benson was allowed to have shore leave, which he wanted to spend seeing something of New Zealand, but he had not got enough money. Fortunately he was able to earn some, as the cadets were allowed to work — and be paid — for working as stevedores in the hold for their employers, as well as on shore for a local wool warehouse. With their earnings, Benson and his three fellow cadets had enough money to rent a car to take them on a short tour to Lake Taupo, but none of them had a driving licence. Benson had owned a motorcycle and had a licence for it since he was sixteen. He made inquiries in the town and was directed to the police station, where he explained his predicament. The police chief took him out in his car in the town and Benson managed not to crash it, so the kind officer passed him and gave him a licence for six months.

Benson loved the countryside he drove through and returned the rental car without a scratch on it. One evening he made for the swimming pool in Napier and found that it was club competition night. He asked whether he might compete and was invited to do so. He won the diving competition and was warmly congratulated by his hosts. He left New Zealand with very happy memories. Incidentally, Benson who knew what their work entailed even before doing it himself in Napier, always had a healthy respect for dockworkers and after a while at sea felt disgust for the way the London dockers were treated. Later he remembered, 'I was very hurt, and I noted it in my diary at the time, what a wicked way it was to treat human beings, to have them gathered like animals at the dock gates to be picked off or not for a job on the day.'

After the crossing of the Pacific, the Panama Canal was an amazing experience, especially after the much tamer Suez Canal. On entering it the crew were all warned to be careful not to throw anything into the water or to make any pointing gesture. The canal was at the time still in the hands of the United States, with American soldiers guarding the shores and the installations. If anyone threw anything into the water it might be assumed to be a bomb. The troops were likely, they were warned (possibly as a leg pull), to shoot first and ask questions afterwards.

As they passed through the Canal at night, another ship passed by, lit up like a Christmas tree. The Panama pilot said: 'Just look at that, the goldarndest passenger list you ever did see. From forrard to aft it's prostitutes and priests, murderers and reformers!'

As his eighteenth birthday approached Benson decided to leave the Merchant Navy as he still hankered for the discipline and other attributes of the Royal Navy. He could have avoided National Service by continuing in the Merchant Navy, but he was very happy to join the Royal Navy for compulsory two years' service, like other eighteen-year olds. He joined at Victoria Barracks in Portsmouth, *HMS Victory*, and was trained as an ordinary seaman. In view of his time as a cadet, and especially his two years at sea, he was sent for an interview by the Commissions Board, presided over by a rather testy Captain Orpin. This third attempt to undergo training to become a naval officer also proved unsuccessful. The captain clearly did not like the candidate or the Merchant Navy, telling him that he would 'never be considered for a commission again.' Not only was the candidate deeply disappointed but so was Chief Petty Officer Gaffney, a big, gruff but incredibly kind Welshman, who was in charge of his training squad and had clearly been impressed by the rather unusually well-qualified young man. He told the squad as a whole, 'We will make a pig of Benson.' That was not an insult (save for officers) as pig was the sailor's term for an officer.

Benson became the unofficial leader of the squad, which quickly succeeded in being better than all the others made up of new entrants. At the end of the training period he won the Bosun's Call, as his pipe was known, as the best recruit. More important was the fact that he also obtained an Admiral's recommendation, which required the Commissions Board to consider him once more as a potential officer. The candidate was dismayed to find that Captain Orpin was in the chair again. He made his distaste for the candidate clear, stating that despite his seagoing experience, he would not have him in the Seaman Branch but only as a candidate for the Aviation or the Supply and Secretarial Branch (now Logistics). Benson, delighted that, thanks to the Admiral, his fourth attempt to embark on an officer's training was succeeding, chose the latter. He later regretted having turned down 'the chance to learn to fly with the best instructors in the world'.

The officer's training course was at *HMS Ceres* at Wetherby in Yorkshire, a shore establishment some way from the sea. Officer cadets in the Royal Navy were classified as upper yardmen, a reference to the days when the best able seamen manning the topmasts of the sailing ships were considered for promotion. Benson enjoyed his training and found naval law particularly interesting, so much so that he thought about possibly training as a barrister one day. At some stage he wrote to one of the Inns of Court for information about studying for the Bar. He passed out as a midshipman, not yet an officer and not quite a gentleman, as the Royal Navy only promoted to sub-lieutenant at the age of twenty-one. It had been a very long haul for the thirteen-year-old boy, but he had made it at last.

Lossiemouth in Scotland, a Fleet Air Arm base, made a pleasant place for his first posting. For some eighteen months Benson enjoyed his work and the company there, especially the female naval air mechanics and the Steamboat Inn. He welcomed the discipline, which compared well with what he considered to be the organised chaos of the merchant service. The facilities for sport were good; among other pursuits, he played as hooker in the Royal Navy Scotland rugby team and had hopes of playing in the Royal Navy fifteen. He had also been told that he might be transferred to the Royal Yacht *Britannia*. Then disaster struck.

Shortly after Christmas 1953 Benson enjoyed a pleasant evening in a nearby sailing club, in the company of his girlfriend Ruth and a colleague, Richard Hardy. By then he had an open MG, which he shared with his sister. After a drink in the club he drove it back to Lossiemouth with his girlfriend beside him and his friend squeezed in behind them. He was quite fit to drive. Contractors were working on the naval base; in the dark Benson drove along what he thought was a newly constructed main runway. In fact, it was merely the perimeter track being used by the contractors, that ended with a large mound of soil and debris, which the MG mounted at a fair speed. It overturned and landed on its driver's head. The passengers were also injured, fortunately not as seriously.

That incident nearly cost Benson his life; it certainly cost him his naval life. Once he regained consciousness and became aware of the gravity of his injuries, he realised that the future looked bleak. He had multiple skull fractures, all hairline, and extremely serious facial damage. He had a collapsed lung and had lost the sight of one eye and his hearing in one ear. His eye recovered its sight, but the ear was left with persistent tinnitus. Fortunately for him, he had two strokes of good luck. The first was that the Royal Navy, in the tradition of looking after its own, behaved extremely well in the provision of medical support. The other was really quite extraordinary.

After being taken to a hospital in Elgin, Benson was transferred to the 200-year-old Royal Naval Hospital at Haslar in Hampshire. From there he was taken to Rooksdown House in the grounds of Park Prewett hospital in the same county; this was the clinic of New Zealander, Sir Harold Gillies. Gillies was one of the great men in the history of medicine. In the 1914–18 War he had served in the Royal Army Medical Corps in France and had observed some early attempts to deal with the terrible facial injuries suffered by thousands of soldiers. He persuaded the Army to set up a special unit in an Aldershot military hospital and started to reconstruct the faces of some of the most seriously injured men. He also trained other surgeons to undertake similar plastic surgery. In 1917 Queen's (later Queen Mary's) Hospital was opened in Sidcup in Kent to provide facilities for the new specialism of plastic surgery, largely devised by Gillies. Together with his colleagues he treated thousands of men, using some completely new techniques, such as attaching flaps of the patient's skin, called pedicles, to injured areas for grafting purposes. Some of the patients needed many operations to deal with their injuries.

After the war Gillies wrote a textbook, *Plastic Surgery of the Face*, which was published in 1920. Ten years later his valuable work was at last officially recognised and he was knighted. Gillies fortunately also trained his nephew Archibald MacIndoe in the same specialty. During the 1939–45 war MacIndoe was able to help numerous RAF pilots with plastic surgery, after they had sustained terrible burns in action.

Benson was extremely lucky that Gillies, whose seventy-first birthday was on 17 June 1953, was still practising. His facial injuries had been so severe that even his mother, an experienced nurse, walked past his bed without recognising him when she first came to visit him in hospital. Some months later when Benson plucked up the courage to go to a local hunt ball, a former girl friend, slightly sozzled, said, 'Jesus Christ, why do they let people like that in here?' Over a period of two years Gillies worked on the restoration of his head and face, fortunately with great success. Largely as a result of his gratitude for what his surgeon had achieved, Benson has supported the charity Changing Faces, set up to help people with facial deformities. Since 1993 he has acted as one of the charity's patrons. Benson still shudders to think what his life would have been like without the help of Harold Gillies. Thanks to him, although his life in his chosen career was over, he was able to think about alternative ways of earning a living.

CHAPTER TWO

A New Profession

A contractor's pile of rubble had turned both Benson's car and his life upside down. He had to find a new profession as soon as possible, one that he could embark on as soon as his facial reconstruction had been completed. It is ironic that the rubble should have led to his having a very successful career in the construction and development world. However, before Gillies had finished his remarkable treatment, Benson felt unable to face the world and tried to hide away by buying, with parental help, a small secluded sawmill in Worcestershire that was advertised for sale. He phoned the vendor's agent and made an inquiry about the property. The agent realised that he was speaking to a young man and asked him why he was going to bury himself in the woods. Benson explained his reason briefly and was told: 'I won't sell it to you. Get on with your life.' His curt advice was taken by the unseen stranger.

Charles Benson had practised as a dentist in Worcester for more than fifteen years by that time and knew many professional people in the city. He had some years earlier taken his son to meet a solicitor and a chartered auctioneer and estate agent, to try and get him to think of a career other than the sea. He now sent him to see Jeffrey Bullock of Bentley, Hobbs and Mytton, the second oldest firm of agricultural auctioneers in the country. Bullock had served as a lieutenant-commander in the war and was the senior partner. He took the young sub-lieutenant on as an articled clerk for three years and became a good mentor for him. He also recommended a helpful correspondence course.

Benson enjoyed his time learning his new profession. He loved seeing the countryside and visiting the various farms to make a survey and assessment of value and to check the animals on them. His area covered a beautiful part of the country, not only his home county of Worcestershire but also Herefordshire initially. He had the use of the MG, which had been rebuilt in Scotland, with one crucial suspension part wrongly installed. Fortunately, the MG factory at Abingdon had remedied that, so that the car went like the proverbial bomb. Sharing the MG with his sister proved inconvenient for both of them, so after a while Benson bought himself a crashed Morris Minor and had it rebuilt. Its performance compared ill with that of the MG; its owner recalled, 'It was some-times overtaken by bicycles.' As an articled clerk Benson received no pay, but he was able to make some legitimate pocket money from the generous mileage allowance that his employers paid — even for a slow car. He lived at home and his father covered the rest of his expenses.

After a while Benson was expected to conduct the auction of small parcels of animals. If he failed to sell any particular lot, despite the use of the illegal ruse of 'trotting' the bidding, then he was stuck with the animals. On one occasion when he was trying to sell half a dozen pigs, there was no final bidder, so he found him-self their proud owner. Fortunately, his fellow articled clerk David Heathfield, and his sister Margery were willing to share the ownership. They enjoyed pig-keeping so much that the three of them gradually built up a joint business that owned a hundred pigs at one stage, kept in different vicarage pigsties around the county. They made a small profit from the venture. Margery was particularly pleased about that as she was not earning but training to be a radiographer at the time. She did not mind taking on her share of mucking out the pigs as she had always mucked out her own pony.

More important was the fact that Benson obtained a love of pigs and of farming generally. As soon as he was able to do so, many years later, he bought a farm and raised cattle and sheep. He added to it from time to time but it is now all arable land without any livestock. He has always had a farm manager but at one stage he spent much of his limited spare time working on the farm, rather than flying for pleasure. Benson has always enjoyed owning a piece of England and keeping it well as a trustee for future generations.

After three years in articles, in 1958 Benson completed his professional exami-nations. Like many another student with a full-time occupation, he had found studying hard. He later said of this period of his life: 'I think that was the hardest part of my life ever. We started early in the auction firm and finished late. It was quite hard to come home and study at a corner table.'

He was kept on by the firm after qualifying, but left some six months later. He had got on well with all the partners in the firm bar one. One of the predictable consequences of Britain's ill-considered attack on Egypt in November 1956, was that the Arab oil suppliers reduced their supplies, so that petrol rationing had to be introduced in the United Kingdom. The leisure motorist suffered most, as people needing their car for work purposes received a fairly adequate ration. Benson received his fair allowance of petrol coupons but was asked by one of the partners, who had his own allocation, to surrender them to him. The young motorist refused, saying that he needed them for his own car and his work. That partner never forgave him.

Some days later, when that partner may have been the worse for drink, the two men were together at the firm's auction ring at Bromyard market in Herefordshire. The partner made the following announcement to the farmers attending the auction: 'Gentlemen, observe the next lot: eleven animals in the ring. Ten of them are cattle; the other is Mr Benson, who has a very high opinion of himself. Gentlemen, we know that the ladder of life is very wide at the bottom and very, very narrow at the top. At the bottom, gentlemen, *they* eat cheese, but at the top *we* eat chicken. Gentlemen, Mr Benson will never eat chicken.' Rather shamefully, some of the audience laughed. The words were burned into Benson's memory and played a major part in his decision to move on.

Benson went for an interview to Newtown, Montgomeryshire, where he was offered a job by the senior partner, a man called Wilson-Wright, who asked him whether he had any other appointments. When Benson told him that he was going to see John Jeffery & Son of Shaftesbury and Salisbury, he was advised: 'If they offer you a job, take it. I was trained by old John Jeffery; he is the best livestock auctioneer going.'

When he was interviewed in Salisbury by Robert Jeffery, Benson took an instant liking to him and accepted his offer of a job. He moved at once to Salisbury and found lodgings there. He worked closely with Jeffery and learned a great deal from him and his father John, as well as from an assistant auctioneer, George Creasey, later to be his best man. Two clerks also taught him a great deal: Phil Spencer, who was brilliant on agricultural valuations and deadstock (farm machinery), and John MacGregor, an expert on livestock, especially cattle.

Benson especially enjoyed the livestock auctioneering, saying later: 'I found this to be tremendous fun; very exacting, very exhausting, with auctions almost every day of the week, which could consist of five or six twelve-hour days. Also it was very good human relations training, explaining to an irate farmer why his prize sow had only made so much money, when he adjudged that it was worth two or three times the amount.'

Although very happy with the firm, Benson could see no prospects of a partnership, so after a while started looking for other opportunities. Shortly before he left the firm he met a surveyor called Geoffrey Fenn, who worked for the highly successful builder and developer Bernard Sunley. Benson mentioned that Salisbury City Council was going to build one large livestock mart (as the market was known locally) to replace the three existing ones in the city, including the one owned by the partnership. Fenn expressed an interest in a redevelopment and suggested that Benson should explore the possibilities. He in turn told his mentor, Robert Jeffery, about that suggestion, who told him, 'Get on with it.'

The young auctioneer and estate agent made a careful examination on foot of every single shop and other building or empty site surrounding the old mart, making inquiries about possible sales. From some of the adjoining owners he obtained an option to purchase for Sunley. In due course his firm sold the mart to Sunley, who also acquired the properties with options on them. Benson received his reward soon afterwards. Fenn left Sunley to work for Arndale Developments Ltd, a successful company run by its founders, Arnold Hagenbach and Sam Chippendale, and then recommended him as a bright young developer.

Arndale took him on part-time for six months, during which he worked mainly with Fenn on various town centre developments in the south of England. He found that he loved shops and town centres: he enjoyed looking at the buildings from top to bottom, trying to get a really good picture of each one and its potential. Apart from learning from Fenn, Benson also received useful tips from a friendly Chippendale about the way to assess the potential of town centre properties. Walk round the front and back wherever possible, he was advised; keep your eyes open for clues indicating unused premises and jointly owned ones; then make your own map. Do not rely on aerial surveys or printed maps. Benson commented later, 'Sam believed, as I do, that town centre development is about putting hearts back into towns.'

During his search for suitable developments sites in Tunbridge Wells in Kent, Benson discovered that the Marks & Spencer property director had acquired a plot behind their store in that town. That proved to be a complete block on any prospect of developing the adjoining sites that were available, so Benson made inquiries to find out whether there was any prospect of a sale by the store — but was sent away with a flea in his ear. He was not so easily shaken off, however, and looked for an alternative approach. He eventually found a spare lot behind the Marks & Spencer store in Barnstaple in Devon. On his recommendation Arndale acquired the Devon lot and Chippendale negotiated with Marks & Spencer what amounted to an exchange of the two back lots. As it happened, Arndale decided not to proceed with the development. Four or five years later, by which time Benson was with MEPC, he managed to collect up almost the same sites and developed the shopping centre in Tunbridge Wells that he had wanted Arndale to build.

After six months Arndale offered him full-time employment and he grasped the opportunity. That company had a great deal of work available and it made a pleasant change to have a decent salary at last. Benson's main contribution after going full-time with Arndale was his work on the redevelopment of Poole town centre and then on a similar project in Basingstoke, after Arndale had been taken over by Barry East's Town and City Properties. During that time he worked well with the principal architect, Derek Jones of Leslie Jones & Partners of Poole. They were later able to cooperate on a number of other projects.

Unfortunately, although he was a brilliant developer, Chippendale had the bad habit of changing plans far too often. Shortly before construction work was due to begin on the Poole scheme, Chippendale told Benson that he wanted to make some fundamental changes to the plans. When the younger man protested and said firmly, 'Sam, we are going to build it — there are no rubber walls', Chippendale swore and said, 'Right, get on with it and I will come to its funeral.' Benson replied that he would leave the company a week before the opening of the development. He received no invitation for that event. Fortunately, Benson was able to attend it as the escort of the invited Mayor of Salisbury, having had the foresight to marry her.

Benson had some years earlier been very impressed by the youngest Salisbury city councillor, Margaret Josephine (Jo) Bundy (now OBE, JP, DL). Though not an adherent of any political party, he had joined the local branch of the Young Conservatives, which Miss Bundy chaired, just to see more of her. His proposal of marriage was accepted some two years later. As his income as an employed auctioneer was not great, he borrowed £400 from his father so he could get married to Jo and have a honeymoon. His father made it a condition of the loan that it should be paid back in a month. Whether he thought his son should work overtime instead of having a honeymoon was not made clear. The young couple got married on 4 June 1960 and in due course had two sons, Charles and Julian, now both practising barristers of the Middle Temple, Charles being a Queen's Counsel.

Benson had been well paid during his time with Arndale but he decided it was time to risk starting out on his own without the security of a pay cheque. He had earlier resolved to set up on his own once he had saved up £10,000 – but he did not reach that target, as Chippendale's attitude had speeded up his plans. Although they now had two sons to support, Jo encouraged him to go it alone. A phone call from another Arndale director, on the day after he had left the company, confirmed for Benson that his decision was the right one. 'Chris, you have been seen in Chippenham looking at property', said the irate caller. 'If you buy anything in any town where you have been involved with Arndale, we will break you!' It was disappointing to receive a threat from a former colleague, but it was an empty one, since Benson was entitled to ply his trade anywhere. To be fair to the Arndale director concerned, he later apologised to Benson for his behaviour.

During a short holiday on Tenerife in 1969 with friends, Benson enjoyed swimming and playing around in the pool. One of the friends commented that he looked like a dolphin in the water. Poole had that animal in its coat of arms, so Benson decided that his new ventures should be called Dolphin Developments Ltd and Dolphin Property (Management) Ltd and that they should have a logo similar to the one used by Poole. For good measure, his and Jo's farming interests were later named Dolphin Farms Ltd. When in due course he received a knighthood, the dolphin rampant was elevated onto his coat of arms.

The next two years saw Benson spending many, many hours pounding the streets of town centres, mainly in the south of England, so much so that he spent too little time with his family, a matter that he now regrets bitterly. He was also sorry that he felt obliged to send the boys to a boarding school. He looked for and found numerous opportunities for redevelopment schemes, some small, others large. Some involved merely a single shop, others a new office block, supermarket, shopping centre or industrial estate. The finance for these projects came mainly from the Sun Alliance insurance giant, represented by surveyor Trevor Ashby and his boss Michael Dew (still a close friend), to whom Benson had been introduced by the surveyors Conway, Relf and Sabey. Benson could not have coped with his own paperwork and relied on the first of his many loyal female aides. Miss Richmond, an Australian, dealt with all his correspondence. He usually dropped his draft letters, on a tape, through her letterbox late in the evening, and collected them early next morning, immaculately typed.

The first successful venture was in Salisbury, where he found a shopkeeper who wanted to sell his premises and lease them back. Sun Alliance agreed to buy the property at the asking price. Benson thought that at most he might be paid an introduction fee by the company, but instead of that, he was delighted to learn that they intended to split the significant difference, between the price they had paid and their own valuation figure, with him — on a 50/50 basis. That half share proved large enough to keep him going for his first year on his own. It did more than that: it secured his loyalty. He later put it this way: 'So everything else I ever did, I always went back to Sun Alliance. They were never a pushover but always very fair. I was tickled pink many years later to be asked to go on the board, and then to chair it.'

For some two years the self-employed Benson managed to do the work of two or three men. He was helped a little sometimes by being able to fly between potential sites. He obtained his pilot's licence and bought his first plane in 1970. After he had rented a helicopter to enable him to attend two important meetings in two different towns on the same day, he decided to learn to fly that also. Having obtained the appropriate licence in 1973 he then bought and used a helicopter for his work. He had successful projects, of different sizes, in the following towns, as well as in Poole once more: Bridport, Ferndown, Romsey,

Helicopter pilot

Amesbury, Tewkesbury, Salisbury, Winchester, Cheltenham, Caerphilly, Port Talbot, Worcester, Truro and Sunbury-on-Thames.

The second venture in Salisbury provided a surprise. An empty old pub in the Market Square became available for redevelopment. Its name was proclaimed boldly in a large lozenge on its facade: Duchess of Albany. When Benson examined the interior he was startled to find that there were no interior walls. An earlier builder, or possibly do-it-yourself publican, had merely fixed the floors to the two neighbours' party walls and had hidden his outrageous work by covering those walls with painted canvas. Fortunately, the building was worth saving, so Benson inserted walls and floors, as well as a new setback top floor. He had saved the name lozenge and reinstalled it, freshly repainted, on the front when the building work was completed. Having originally welcomed the City Council's plan to replace its three central marts with one large one in the outskirts — a plan that had enabled him to show his skills as a developer — Benson came to regret it. He felt that the city centre had lost something important, in terms of colour and jollity, when it moved the farmers and their wives out from three central locations to the more distant large one.

The events during the Caerphilly project for a new supermarket for Tesco, overlooking the castle, give a flavour of the Principality's nationalism at the time. Construction proceeded very slowly and that was partly explained by a number of incidents of sabotage; sand and sugar had been put in gear boxes and fuel tanks of machinery belonging to his builder. Benson went down to see what could be done.

When he arrived at the site for a meeting with the builder, he found a painter up a ladder painting the fascia. When Benson left that meeting a little later he found that the both the painter and his ladder had gone, though the job had not been completed. When he found the painter he complained that while he was having a smoke, someone had cut six feet off his ladder. Benson asked a police officer standing opposite the building whether he had witnessed this criminal damage, but he replied that he 'didn't see nothing.'

Benson knew the county councillor for the area and expressed his views about the situation. 'What do you expect,' asked the local politician, 'when you choose a foreign contractor?' After a tender competition the building contract had been awarded to Moss of Cheltenham — a town only a short way, but over the border, in England.

A major scheme in Port Talbot provided some hard lessons. Benson had explored the possibility of developments in Port Talbot and other Welsh towns with the agent and friend, Peter Hales of E. J. Hales & Partners of Cardiff, and had become acquainted with an architect who introduced him to officers and members of the local authority. They seem to have liked Benson's approach and style and asked him to plan and develop a shopping centre on a prominent site alongside the River Afan. Benson explained that he was basically a one-man show, without the resources to undertake such a major scheme. He was told to try and find the resources and then the scheme would be awarded to him, in partnership with the local authority.

Benson still could not see how he could finance it himself at that early stage of his self-employed career. He went to see Len Jarrad, the senior partner of the surveyors Hillier Parker May and Rowden, who introduced him to Robert Potel, the chairman of Star (Great Britain) Holdings, a large and successful company. Potel approved of Benson's scheme and agreed on the choice of a local architect to draw up the plans. They jointly set up a limited company to execute it, with the composite name of Star Dolphin, Benson agreeing to accept less than a half share of the profits. On one occasion when they met, Potel said, in a condescending tone: 'I always enjoy having tea with you, Christopher, as I regard you as my property foot in the gutter.' Benson thought that the comment at any rate confirmed that he had both feet on the ground, but he should have realised the danger of dealing with a man who could make such a remark to a young colleague.

After many months of planning Potel, Benson and another director of Star met with the Port Talbot authorities in the town hall to sign the contract. As they were on the verge of signing, Potel flabbergasted Benson by announcing, 'We are reducing your share to 10%, as my colleague tells me we could have secured the scheme without you.' He added that Star would be doing the project management instead of him. Later he was told that due to internal financial restructuring, Star would have to buy him out for a nominal ten pounds. Benson knew he was stuck with this outrageous outcome as he had not the resources to stand up to a giant. He stresses, however, that this conduct was most unusual. Throughout his many years in the property development world, he found that nearly everyone he encountered behaved honourably. He almost always felt free to talk to rivals frankly: he rarely feared that they would take advantage of information that he had given them about future plans, or that they would try and get out of obligations they had undertaken.

The Port Talbot scheme went ahead and Benson at least had the consolation that when the development was formally opened by Princess Anne, it was named the Afan Centre with Dolphin Square and not Star Square in the middle. Years later, as managing director of MEPC, he derived some satisfaction from buying Star, by then renamed the English Property Corporation, from the Canadian corporation Olympia & York. He then visited Dolphin Square, which was among the properties acquired. He found out that his brainchild was worth far more than he had earlier been led to believe, and was also able to recommend and execute some improvements there.

Benson's hard work and success did not go unnoticed. Trevor Donaldson, a partner in Donaldson's estate agency, introduced him to Hugo Ferrand, chairman of the Law Land Co Ltd, one of the oldest development corporations. Ferrand invited him to join him as assistant managing director and Benson accepted. He had retained a stake in all his developments and so had a portfolio of considerable value. Law Land took it over and paid for it with an appropriate number of shares. He soon found that his working life had gone from one extreme to another. Having worked much too hard for two years as his own boss, he now found that it was irksome to have too little work to do. The Law Land board seemed content to rest on its considerable laurels, whereas he was still raring to go and undertake new developments.

Benson joined Law Land in September 1971 and left it in early November 1973. He was looking forward to having a break while looking around for his next move. As luck would have it, shortly before his departure he was approached by

Peter Anker, the managing director of the Metropolitan Estates and Property Corporation, or MEPC as it was to be renamed shortly afterwards. Anker had suggested a possible merger of the two large companies but nothing came of his approach. However, during the negotiations he dealt with the bright assistant managing director and must have decided to make some enquiries about him. Benson received a call from Anker inquiring whether he would care to join the second largest property company in the country as its development director. He had no hesitation in accepting that offer, and on 4 December received a letter of confirmation of his appointment from Kennedy Kisch, the deputy chairman, as Anker was ill at the time. Kisch mentioned that his board had unanimously approved the appointment on 20 November; among the terms was the 'opportunity of exchanging your investment in the Law Land Company for a holding of equivalent value in MEPC Ltd.' Benson was to stay for nearly twenty years with MEPC; the value of his shareholding was to increase substantially. His part in that growth in value will become apparent.

CHAPTER THREE

The Greatest Challenge

It is difficult to think of a worse time for Benson to join a major property investment and development company as its developments director than January 1974. In November 1972 the Conservative government had been alarmed by the danger of galloping inflation and had introduced a freeze on business rents for existing properties. When developers and their financial supporters understandably concentrated on building new properties that would escape such an imposition, the government responded in December 1973 with a new development gains tax to cover first lettings. It followed that rental income and property share prices went down. Then came one of our winters of discontent, made inglorious by various strikes, from miners' to gravediggers', leading to power cuts, a three-day working week and unburied bodies. The general election in February 1974 brought into power a Labour government that was happy to extend its predecessor's anti-capitalist legislation.

On the international stage, in October 1973 Egypt and Syria had attacked Israel. Predictably the attackers were supplied with sophisticated weapons by the Soviet Union and the defenders by the United States, so that high casualties on both sides were guaranteed. Despite a theoretical cease-fire, the fighting did not stop until three days after Benson had joined his new employer in January. Inevitably, the war was followed by the Arab oil producers reducing the supply of oil and simultaneously raising its price. The United States was their major target but the United Kingdom was seriously affected in different ways. The only major disaster that did not strike the property world in 1973 and 1974 was any major earthquake in England. A lesser man than Benson might have been put off his stride by the general situation and specific company related difficulties that he had to face in his first years with MEPC. He managed to work his way through most of the difficult challenges that confronted him and so was in due course able to answer knotty questions, similar to the classic one, 'Apart from that, Mrs Lincoln, how did you enjoy the play?'

By the time that Benson joined MEPC it was already a giant in the property world and the second largest British company in that field. Its founder was

Claude Leigh, who had started building up a portfolio of companies owning properties in London immediately after the First World War. In the 1930s he began building houses and blocks of flats in the city, the best known of which was the one designed for him by the architect T. P. (later Sir Thomas) Bennett: Dorset House in Gloucester Place, close to Baker Street station. His success enabled him to buy a superb Georgian mansion as his country home, Foliejon Park in Berkshire. It was grand enough for the Foreign Office to ask him to lease it for the remainder of the Second World War to a good friend of Great Britain, King Haakon of Norway, thousands of whose compatriots were fighting along-side British sailors, soldiers and airmen.

The various bombing raids on London demolished or damaged thousands of properties, but many of them could slowly be repaired after 1945, with the help of War Damage compensation funds raised by a wartime compulsory insurance scheme. In 1946 Leigh's different companies were placed by him into a new public limited company, named Metropolitan Estate and Property Corporation, with assets valued at that time at £6.5 m. In the 1950s Leigh extended the company's reach by acquiring buildings outside London, first in Manchester and later elsewhere; and by the acquisition of properties in Canada. Mergers and acquisitions vastly increased the holdings of the company.

In 1961 Leigh retired from being chairman and managing director and he died in January 1964. By then MEPC was worth £54.6 m. In the next decade the company managed extremely well despite the loss of its founder. For all those ten years the chairman was Charles Hardie and the managing director Richard Sheppard. Michael Hanson was later commissioned by Benson to write a useful history of the company. In it he quoted Hardie's tribute: 'With due respect to Claude Leigh, Richard Sheppard built up MEPC. He did a very good job in property investment, borrowing money at six per cent and buying secondary properties to show an eight per cent yield with no risk at all, but when you could no longer borrow money at six per cent it became necessary to create good investments by means of development.'

In 1968 MEPC was able to take over The Metropolitan Railway Surplus Lands Co Ltd fairly cheaply, as that company had overextended itself with a large office development project in Middlesbrough, much of which it had pre-let at an inap-propriate low rent. That acquisition enabled the company to build along the London suburban railway line so loved and praised by the poet John Betjeman. In the following year MEPC invested £11 m in the acquisition of valuable properties in London, Manchester and Leeds, opening the door to future developments in all three cities. In February 1970 the company made a successful takeover bid for London County Freehold and Leasehold Properties Ltd (LCF), which owned of thousands of quality flats in London, and other properties in England, Canada, Australia and Zimbabwe, as well as managing residential property for the copper mines in Zambia. As a result of this takeover the worth of the company's property assets jumped up to £242 m, but the flats were immediately sold on.

Sir Charles Hardie, as he had become the year before, retired in 1971 and was replaced by Sir Henry Johnson, a former British Rail chairman. Richard Sheppard gave up the job of managing director in the following year after fifty-one years with Leigh's companies, but he remained on the board for a further three. His successor as managing director was Peter Anker, who had played a major role in the build up of the company's presence in Canada. As a result of those latter changes, when Benson joined the board in January 1974 he was at first required to work under the Johnson/Anker team. However, that did not continue for long as the chairman had a stroke later that year and announced that he intended to retire at the end of March 1976. Nearer that time he announced that his choice to succeed him was Sir Gerald (or Joe) Thorley, whose distinguished history included simultaneously chairing the British Sugar Corporation and Allied Breweries.

Thorley was one of those very unlucky soldiers who had come out of France via Dunkirk in 1940 and then in early 1942 had been imprisoned by the Japanese after the fall of Singapore. Those experiences may have excused his swearing like a trooper (despite being an artilleryman), but Benson found his constant use of the f-word rather tedious. However, he liked Joe Thorley very much and worked well with him. He has recently said of him that Thorley did not suffer fools gladly and disapproved of bad timekeepers, as he himself was always in the office early. He added: 'Joe would go to the stake for a friend. He was immensely loyal. He had no vices and everyone admired him.' Thorley had started his working life in his family's brewery business, Ind Coope, and liked his beer. Without consulting his watch he always knew when it was 11 am and time for his daily pint. (The Benson family still refers to 'a pint of Sir Gerald'.)

Thorley was voted into the chair on 1 April 1976 and also acted as caretaker managing director, Anker having been persuaded to give up that post so that he could go back to Canada to do more good work there. Thorley said that he would not take his salary until he had returned the company to profit. On 1 July Thorley came into Benson's room and asked, 'Can you do it?' 'Do what?' The chairman replied, 'Be bloody managing director, that's what.' Within the hour the new man had to present the MD's report to the board of directors, but that did not prove to be a problem. 'We were all very well clued up,' he explained to the writer.

What Benson was not entirely clued up to was Thorley's sense of humour. MEPC had instituted residential staff conferences and one was held at Selsdon

Park, where the newly appointed managing director was to deliver the keynote address. Thorley kept the unsuspecting Benson up virtually all night, drinking. Next morning Benson, very much the worse for wear, foolishly made the speech without his prepared notes, and later could not recall a word of what he had said to his eager audience. For years after that incident, Alan Pearson, a great MEPC character, would occasionally tap the side of his nose and say to his boss, 'Don't forget what you promised at Selsdon.'

At about this time one of the financial journalists started writing about a boardroom battle or split, but he was mistaken: there was none. David Davies, the finance director, who had joined the company shortly before Benson, had wanted to be appointed managing director, but he did not resent the choice of the chairman, who also made both of them vice-chairmen of the company. Benson and Davies had no difficulty in working together. They made a point of dining together regularly to discuss any outstanding matters; if there were none they where happy to talk about the opera or ballet. Benson emphasised that the company did not pay for any of these events: they took it in turn to pay for the meal.

Not long after becoming managing director, in an interview with a representative of *The Property Journal*, Benson modestly said of MEPC: 'It has been the most easy company for anyone to have the good fortune to manage. That is because the people here are of such high quality. Joe Thorley, the chairman, is a great example; his years of experience in industry are available to me and my colleagues. He has any easy approach and encourages frank discussions.' This kind of statement, with minor variations, became almost commonplace with Benson, who meant every word of it. Throughout his career, and throughout his interviews with the writer, Benson was always quick to say something on the lines of: My staff were excellent; they made my life comparatively easy.

Benson worked as Thorley's managing director for nearly eight years, until the latter's retirement at the beginning of 1984. As Hanson put it, 'Together, they slowly pulled MEPC round and prepared it for the next boom.' However, before all else, Benson was required to do some fire-fighting to deal with the most urgent problems. Fortunately, he had the expert assistance on financial matters, whenever he needed it, of David Davies. They needed to act as speedily as possible, as the debt burden of MEPC had grown dangerously heavy. A run of good years may have made one or two of the directors careless about new acquisitions, being too sanguine about their prospects and paying too much for them. It was important that Benson and Davies should reduce the debt burden, partly by selling some of the company's estate, and that they should look very critically at any current developments and assets. Benson describes himself as a lone wolf: he preferred to travel on his own and only went anywhere with Davies when that was essential.

The situation in Brussels was extremely serious. An over-enthusiastic director had earlier been in the city, looking for investment or development opportunities, when his taxi broke down. He was rescued by a man in a Rolls-Royce who just happened to have a ready built thirty-storey office block with some shops for sale, a little outside the city centre. It was optimistically called the Manhattan Centre but very little of its 430,000 square feet had been let. There was a hotel on two floors, later converted to office use, and a bank, together with an official Tunisian travel bureau. When doubts were expressed about the integrity of the vendor, the director had repeatedly assured his colleagues, with little or no justification, that he trusted the man. Once the board members had decided to buy the Centre, they concluded it would be a good idea to snap up the multi-storey car park on the adjoining site for conversion to a shopping centre. It turned out they had succeeded in buying two pups for the price of two.

Benson had still been with Law Land when the first of these two purchases had taken place, and had been in Brussels for that company several times while it successfully developed a much smaller office block there. Richard Ellis, the surveyors that he dealt with, had an office opposite the Manhattan Centre. Their representative told Benson conversationally one day that it was 'a heap of rubbish.' Flying back from Brussels shortly afterwards, Benson noticed a party of half a dozen Englishmen on the plane, clearly celebrating their acquisition of a valuable property there. Once he joined MEPC he recognised three of the directors from the airborne party, who had clearly been celebrating their purchase of the Manhattan Centre.

As soon as Benson saw the two properties he realised that they were in a poor location and difficult to let, other than at a low rent to poor tenants. He noticed a woman in a leather coat who was paying in a large number of crumpled bank notes at the teller's window of the bank. She pulled out fistful after fistful from her coat pockets. At one point the coat fell open and he saw that she was naked under it. This wonderful site (yes, site not sight), apart from other shortcomings, was also in the red light district. Inspection of the adjoining car park confirmed that his misgivings about that were correct: the ceiling height of each floor was too low for any shop development. It remains a car park to this day. The vendor had guaranteed the rental income of the main block, but by then was bankrupt. He was a great financial escape artist. Having earlier slipped out of Egypt, he fled to Switzerland. Benson and Davies, together with a lawyer from the Paris office of the company solicitors, spent some fruitless time trying to pin him down in

Zurich. (The size of the wasted legal fees made Benson think that he was in the wrong job and should have pursued his earlier idea of a legal career.)

In June 1975 Benson was told that the Tunisian tenants in the Manhattan Centre owed some £48,000 rent, so he decided to see them about those arrears. When he got to their office he found that they had done a moonlight flit. He was a little surprised at this as the manager was the son of a very senior political figure in Tunisia. Keen to get an explanation he immediately flew to Tunis from Brussels, after sending a message to warn him of his imminent arrival. He was met at the airport by two men who asked for his passport so that they could collect his baggage. They drove him to a good hotel and escorted him to his room, which contained his luggage but not his passport. They then locked him in; he was not surprised to find the telephone cut off, but dismayed that he could not notify the British consul, the company or his wife about his false imprisonment.

After six or seven hours he was allowed out for a meal and then permitted to sit by the swimming pool — but the men refused to return his passport. Two days later his minders took him for a drive into the desert and he wondered whether they were going to dispose of their problem. Instead they took him to an old castle used as a carpet factory, where he was persuaded that it would be a good idea for him to buy a very expensive carpet. He thought he had better accept their advice — and still has the carpet.

When he asked for his passport once more, he was told that he would first have to sign a declaration that no Tunisian corporation or person owed a franc. He replied that he would have signed such a document earlier if asked: he had only come to find out why they had done a flit. When the writer commented, on hearing this part of the story, 'You were a bit naïve expecting a satisfactory explanation,' Benson replied, 'Not half!' The story had a happy ending after five days in that his passport was returned once he had signed a release, and he was allowed to return home. What hurt him most of all, he added to his account of this international incident, was that nobody had missed him, not even his wife. As soon as he was able to do so, Benson cut the company's continuing losses by disposing of the Brussels car park at a low price. The office development continued to lose money until it was substantially let some time later, but it was not fully let until 1983. Benson was glad to see it sold in early 1987.

The situation in Paris turned out to be rather better. Before his arrival at the company, MEPC had bought La Maison de Suède à Paris, a former Swedish commercial showcase on the Champs Elysées, and a small hotel behind it. Both properties stood empty as the planning authorities declined to let MEPC convert the main eight-story building into a shop with offices over it, coupled with a small hotel at the back. They seemed to be waiting for another prestigious body to take possession. As luck would have it, a terrorist group made a mistake common to murderers: they attacked the wrong target. They seemed to have had a grievance with Sweden and, thinking it was still in use by the Swedes, bombed the empty building, blowing out the front. The sole occupant, the caretaker, was fortunately out shopping and no pedestrian was hurt. Rather foolishly, the Baader Meinhoff group claimed the 'credit' for this pointless explosion. After this incident the offer made by the English company suddenly looked more attractive to the Paris planners, who gave permission for its plan to be implemented. An ill blast blew the company some good.

Munich, on the other hand, turned out to be another disaster area. MEPC had bought an expensive site opposite the main railway station, but had failed to obtain planning permission for a shopping centre and offices totalling over 400,000 square feet. The company owned a large hole in the ground which was swallowing up large amounts in loan interest payments. On one occasion Benson was going to fly with David Davies to meet their German bankers, with a view to getting a further loan to help with the Munich debt, or carrying charges. Davies spoke fluent German but the bankers always spoke English when he was present. On the way to Heathrow Davies realised he had forgotten his passport, so Benson went on alone. He was greeted by the senior banker present in English, but as soon as he heard that Davies was unable to attend the meeting, he switched to German for the rest of the meeting, making Benson rely on an interpreter. He managed to get a further loan but had been made to work hard for it. As soon as it was possible he managed to get rid of the Munich loss-making venture.

Shortly after that, Benson was in Munich together with Hugh Cantlie, MEPC's German manager, who spoke the language fluently, having spent some time there in the Army. They checked in at the Vier Jahreszeiten hotel and Benson unpacked his clothes in his room. He met Cantlie downstairs, where they were approached by a man who said that he was there on behalf of Herr Doktor C, who was owed a large sum of money by MEPC in respect of the abandoned Munich develop-ment. Cantlie told him, in firm German, to come back next day, with evidence.

When Benson returned to his room a little later, he found that his bed had gone. At first he thought he must have gone into the wrong room, but then he saw his clothes in the cupboard. Mystified, he went to the reception desk, where he was not believed — even though he was clearly sober. He insisted on one of the reception clerks coming with him — and was then believed and given another room. When Benson told him this unlikely story, the writer, unable to wait for the denouement, asked whether Herr Doktor C had turned out to be the owner or manager of the hotel, as well as creditor, but the answer was No, there was no connection between the two mysteries.

Next morning Herr Doktor C was there in person, with two formidable women, said to be nurses from his clinic. He repeated the claim about his entitlement to a large fee, but produced no evidence. He was told to go away, in two languages. Cantlie made some inquiries from his military contacts and learned that the Herr Doktor was a war criminal. That was the last Benson ever saw or heard of him.

Benson's other German problem was in Frankfurt, where MEPC had a site for which planning permission had been granted for a twelve-storey office block. Unfortunately, careful recalculations showed that such a building could not make any profit unless a thirteenth floor could be added. There was a some delay and a huge amount of work by the MD of the German subsidiary board, Nick Barr, before permission was granted for that lucky extra floor, but once it arrived, building work started. The completed building was able to make a small profit.

One of the projects that MEPC had acquired with LCF was a major one in Sydney, New South Wales. Gordon Dashwood, one of the directors of that company, who joined the MEPC board after the takeover, had made a determined effort to build up the LCF holdings in the Commonwealth, especially in Canada and Australia. In Sydney he had embarked on a major development in the heart of the city. It was for a forty-storey office block of 415,000 square feet, large enough for the Stock Exchange to take three lower floors, and for a number of shops on two levels, with offices above. Unfortunately the main contractor, Mainline Corporation, was plagued by union problems and went into liquidation. The Stock Exchange sued MEPC for the failure to complete the building and to give possession to them as tenants. Litigation went badly for MEPC and they took the matter on final appeal to the Privy Council. At the door of the court in Whitehall, Patrick Neill QC advised Benson and his colleagues to settle the matter and they did so.

Dashwood went out to Australia as non-executive chairman of the subsidiary company there for a year. Benson ordered the construction on the Sydney site to be resumed, with Costain as the principal contractor, and the project was eventually completed successfully. This was to be the first many contracts executed by Costain for MEPC. Peter Costain told the writer that, having regard to the unions' stranglehold on building work in Australia, it was very courageous of Benson to ask him to complete the work. 'It was the most gutsy decision I have ever come across,' he said.

Sir Zelman Cowan, the Governor-General, opened the premises formally in 1979. MEPC general policy was to retain possession of its major developments for the significant rents they produced. That happened for some years with the Sydney Exchange Centre, but it was sold ten years later for £175 m, when the company was offered that very good price for it. The board thought that the proceeds of sale could be more profitably used for the funding of new projects in Australia. Robert Frost, an accountant with the Australian subsidiary's accountants, had earlier been recruited to head the company's work there and proved a great success. He very speedily used part of the proceeds of sale to acquire two properties in Sydney for £30.5 m, an office block and a high tech industrial complex. He later invested the balance in good income producing properties.

There were advantages and disadvantages in owning property abroad. The first was that currency fluctuations could lead to enormous variations in both income and expenditure. If the pound fell, the incoming rent from premises abroad was greater. At the same time the company's payments of interest and return of capital in respect of loans from foreign bankers went up significantly. A rise in the value of the pound would have a corresponding double effect.

The other disadvantage was that foreign governments from time to time introduced tariff-like measures that affected outsiders' property rights. The mildest intervention that Benson had to deal with was that of the Australian government, which introduced a Foreign Investment Review Board. MEPC quickly adjusted to the Board's requirements and continued investing in that country. More serious was the Canadian government's introduction of measures that handicapped foreign investors. As the climate for investing in that country was anyway chilling, Benson and Davies advised their colleagues that the time had come to sell the company's holdings there. They agreed and the resultant sale raised a total of £82 m, which was applied to the reduction of overseas debts. Davies had considered the Canadian dollar to be over-valued and due for a devaluation, so he ordered that the proceeds of sale should be converted into US dollars *immediately* on receipt by the company's bank. That was done hours before the Canadian dollar was drastically devalued. Davies had made for the company rather more than his salary for that year.

In April 1979 Benson made an extended trip to the United States, to assess the prospects for a British developer in different cities there. He visited San Diego, Los Angeles, San Francisco, Phoenix, Las Vegas, Minneapolis, Chicago, Dallas, Houston, New Orleans and New York, ruling out some of them for various reasons.

Dashwood's earlier investment in Commonwealth countries had included both North and South Rhodesia, which became Zambia and Zimbabwe. MEPC's holding in Zambia was not significant, but in Harare, the capital of Zimbabwe, the company owned a large and very attractive office building, Livingstone House. Benson, who could only get into the country by going as a tourist, regarded it as one of the finest buildings in Africa. Unfortunately, President

Mugabe did not like to see any currency leaving the country, so MEPC was not permitted to use local funds for Benson's visit. To show that he was a bona fide tourist, he felt obliged to visit the Victoria Falls, Kariba Dam and Hwange National Park — but sometimes such sacrifices are expected of company directors. With difficulty, the company eventually managed to sell the building in Harare, with other assets, to a South African business for a pittance. However, even the small amount of proceeds could not be transferred out of the country, so that there was a total loss.

Quite often when Benson had to travel to Australia during their fire-fighting days — either with or without Davies — he would make a point of returning over the Pacific, calling in on the substantial MEPC developments on Hawaii and then those in the mainland United States. One of the successful purchases by Anker was the Kahala Hilton hotel in Honolulu, which was sold after two years at a profit that could usefully reduce the debt capital. However, the purchaser, a San Franciscan called Bill Weinburg, took his time in completing the transaction and was given a deadline for signing by the following Friday. Benson was in Hawaii with Frost and a local lawyer, but Weinburg did not show up there; it turned out he was on his yacht at Acapulco, the famous Mexican resort. The trio decided that they had no option but to call on him, even though that required them to rough it at the sumptuous Acapulco Palace hotel for a day or two.

The purchaser signed on the Friday evening and paid a good price for the Honolulu hotel, but Benson thought it was probably worth more. Weinburg spent a few million dollars improving it, mainly by adding balconies to all the sea facing suites, and more than doubled his money in a year. Benson and his two colleagues went out for a final dinner in Acapulco, which they considered foul. When Frost and the lawyer, who had both eaten a suspicious meat dish, got to Los Angeles, they were so sick they had to be hospitalised. Benson, who had eaten a vegetarian meal, survived unharmed.

The story of one of the other Hawaiian assets was less happy. At Discovery Bay MEPC built a development comprising 667 apartments in two forty-two storey towers, sitting on a large podium of shops and offices, with garages below — over a million square feet in all. The main contractor, Mainline Corporation, was the same one that went into liquidation in Sydney and so failed in Hawaii also. A replacement builder was found to complete the work and sixty-two per cent of the completed apartments were sold fairly quickly.

However, Benson received a number of complaints about leaks in the roof of the podium, which had a swimming pool above it. He made a careful inspection of the whole development himself from top to bottom. At the top of the towers he found that the large glass panels making up the pyramidal roof were neither properly supported nor fixed. They could easily have slipped and killed someone below. On inspection of the rest of the building he found further evidence of jerry-building: one space that ought to have been properly filled with the appropriate building materials was merely stuffed with a large collection of haversacks. The short term consequence was that Benson ensured that the necessary remedial works were undertaken speedily. Once they had been completed, the podium development was satisfactory and produced a good return, so MEPC kept it.

The longer term result of his discovery of jerry-building, was that he resolved to see every large development personally on completion — even if good architects were employed, as they usually were, to certify completion. That decision led to an increase in his flying time. If a development was said to be completed in Perth, Western Australia, he would fly out specially, if no trip was imminent. That sometimes involved his undertaking two twenty-six-hour flights, with only one day on the ground in between. Oddly enough, he never resented the time he spent circling the globe, as he considered every journey necessary for the welfare of the company. He did, though, miss his family.

Benson also examined all the projects that were under way in England and Ireland. Peter Anker had a rather grandiose idea for London's Oxford Street. He thought it would be possible to copy the Canadian idea — designed initially to protect shoppers from the regular heavy falls of snow — of having what was virtually a wide underground street of shops. Anker's version was to run from Bond Street Underground station all the way to Marble Arch, with a spur under Oxford Street to Selfridges store. Benson realised that not only would the Grosvenor Estates, the dominant freehold owner in the area, have to participate, but also that the financial risks entailed could easily bring down the whole MEPC structure. He went to Selfridges to seek the views of its very experienced owner, Charles Clore. His opinion was that the idea was ridiculous. It was duly scaled back and the redevelopment was confined to the area immediately surrounding and covering Bond Street station. The result was a comparatively small but successful shopping centre named West One, which is still there. (When Benson was later involved in the projected rebuilding of the Royal Opera House, the scheme was helped on its way by Clore money. Clore himself had been a great philanthropist; his daughter Vivienne Duffield followed in his footsteps and, among many other benefactions, gave £25 m towards the rebuilding of the Opera House.)

When Benson was appointed managing director in 1976, one of his first tasks was to see how overheads could be brought down. As a consequence, it was his very unpleasant task to cut the staff. As the company, in view of the continued cold financial climate, was undertaking a very limited amount of building, he decided, with the approval of the board of directors, to let the whole Building

Services Division staff members go. They had little or no work. They were all highly qualified men and Benson was sorry to lose them, but they all managed to find suitable alternative employment. Benson so disliked the task and swore that this would never happen again, that he inquired of his fellow directors if there was anyone else who should go. They agreed that one senior member of the staff was no longer contributing a fair day's work and that he should be asked to leave.

That employee sued the company for unfair dismissal. At the hearing before the Industrial Tribunal in October 1978 he claimed that he had been dismissed solely because of racial discrimination. He was Jewish and asserted that Benson had picked him out for dismissal because he was an anti-semite, who did not want to offend potential Kuwaiti lenders. The tribunal found in his favour by a majority of two to one. Benson was very upset as the charge against him was completely untrue. To make the whole matter worse, the allegation was picked up by the press and once in their files, repeated on later occasions. Benson had worked very happily with Jewish colleagues and regularly wore the gold cuff links, depicting the traditional menorah candlestick, that he and his wife had bought on a visit to Israel. The loan under consideration from the Kuwaiti bankers was a relatively small one, to be used in Australia, and could easily have been obtained from another source.

Some of his Jewish friends were also outraged about the slur. Richard Seifert, the architect of a number of landmarks such as Centre Point and the MEPC development in Long Acre, Covent Garden, made a point of immediately inviting Benson to lunch at the Savoy hotel. In the restaurant he asked for a table in the centre of the room, explaining to his guest that he wanted to demonstrate to their fellow lunchers that there was one well-known Jew who did not accept the allegation of anti-semitism.

For the next few weeks Benson was aware that there was often a well-built man hovering near him. He recognised him as a banking advisor to the successful Jewish property developer, Sydney Mason of the Hammerson Group. When he next saw Mason, who was a friend, Benson asked him about his shadow. Mason told him that in view of the foul allegation made against him, he thought it possible that some idiot might attack him. That was why he had, off his own bat, provided a discreet minder for a few weeks, one who was content with his unusual role.

Some time after this incident Benson suggested to Mason that a merger of MEPC and Hammerson would prove a perfect fit and, incidentally, create the country's largest property company. Mason was attracted by the idea, especially when Benson suggested that the Hammerson name could be used for the new entity and that Mason could be the chairman of the board. However, Mason did not like the suggestion that, formally, MEPC should take over his company. Benson's reason for that was that Hammerson had only a few shareholders, whose consent should be easily obtained, whereas MEPC had a much wider constituency, with greater inherent difficulties, including the longer time needed for all the consents. Mason balked at this last suggestion and turned the proposal down, basically on the grounds that the founder of his company and his mentor, Lou Hammerson, would 'turn over in his grave'. Years later he told Benson that he had been right and that the proposals should all have been accepted by him and the Hammerson group. (In 1997 James Tuckey, by then managing director of MEPC, discussed the same merger with his opposite number at Hammerson, Ronald Spinney, but once again the talks came to nothing.)

As far as Benson was concerned, the great advantage of his being required to visit Sydney and other places in Australia, was that he loved the country. Whenever he had some spare time in Sydney he rented a motor yacht and used that for work purposes and leisure — as he was not prepared to go back to rowing to get around. When he and Joe Thorley went out to Australia for the opening of the Stock Exchange Building, they took their wives with them; having some time to relax together, they became close friends. Together they spent one evening in the bush watching large numbers of kangaroos arriving at their watering place; on another they saw thousands of young turtles hurtle towards the sea.

Thorley treated Benson in an avuncular manner and increasingly seemed to regard him as a possible successor. He felt able to advise his younger colleague on different matters, as part of his career development. One piece of advice that Thorley gave and Benson accepted turned out to be disastrous. Thorley told him that if he wanted to get on in the City, he ought to be a name at Lloyds. When Benson expressed some concern about the risks entailed, Thorley assured him that they were minimal, but he still felt a little apprehensive and made inquiries about stop loss insurance policies. He was assured that they were not necessary: nobody ever lost money at Lloyds. Benson unfortunately forgot the old adage that if something looks too good to be true, it usually is. He soon afterwards joined several syndicates, and nearly each one turned out to be disastrous, mainly because of the massive storm damage claims from the United States. He managed to find the money to cover his quota of the loss each time when called upon to do so, but sometimes with considerable difficulty. A failure to comply speedily could have led to a bankruptcy notice. Far from helping him to get on, being a name at Lloyds nearly ended his promising career.

Benson and Thorley shared a sense of humour and were always at ease in each other's presence. When they were returning from a successful opening of one of the developments, The Friary shopping centre in Guildford, Benson said, 'Well, your photo should be appearing in the Press now.' Thorley asked him what he meant and got the reply: 'When things go well there is always a photo of you. When they go wrong, they show me.' Thorley advised him to do what he did: engage a good public relations consultant. On this occasion Benson ignored the advice he was given by his senior.

When Thorley eventually decided to retire in January 1984, he was not immediately replaced by Benson as chairman, but by Robin Adam, who had joined the company as a director just over a year earlier. Benson had served for some time as an advisor on property matters for the trustees of the British Petroleum pension fund and had been very impressed by Adam, who was BP's deputy chairman and a managing director. His vast business experience would prove, as Benson had predicted to his board colleagues, of great value to MEPC. 'His was a very steady hand on the tiller,' Benson has recently stated.

In parenthesis it should be noted that when Benson was first appointed as an advisor to the BP trustees in September 1979, Bruce Kinloch, a shrewd financial journalist, wrote in *Estate Times* that the appointment was 'most interesting and could indicate that the funds are at last waking up to the fact that there are property experts outside the major firms of estate agents.' He added, 'Property experts of the calibre of Mr Benson may well know any particular investment before it is put to the fund manager, and they would certainly know the pitfalls to watch for which lay trustees would not.'

Benson travelled extensively in Australia, looking at actual and potential development sites. In due course MEPC had developments not only in Sydney and Perth, but also in Brisbane and Melbourne. On one visit he flew round the edges of the continent, stopping repeatedly en route to examine properties owned by a company that MEPC Australia wanted to acquire. One memorable stop was at a small place called Wipers — doubtless so named by a veteran of the battle-fields around the Belgian town of Ypres. Benson and his colleague wanted to see the shopping centre that the company had been offered as part of the package. They asked the only taxi driver to take them to the shopping centre, but he corrected them by saying, 'Shop!' On the way Benson made a comment about the beautiful beach being completely empty. The driver gave a credible explanation: 'If the jellies don't get you, the sea-snakes will. If the sea-snakes don't get you, the sharks will. If the sharks don't get you, the crocs will. Nah! Nobody on the beach today.' Much as he usually enjoyed swimming, Benson gave it a miss that day. He also decided that MEPC could get by without the shop.

CHAPTER FOUR

Continued Progress

Benson and Davies, with the help of many colleagues, had in the space of a few years dramatically improved the perilous situation that had arisen earlier, partly as a result of general market conditions and partly as a result of some poor decisions on the part of board members. However, there were to be no recriminations — as long as past mistakes were not repeated. One of Benson's innovations was the introduction of a house magazine, which attracted contributions from various members of the staff, as well as from invited outsiders. Benson wrote in the first number: 'The purpose is communication. I want the house magazine not only to give details of *what* we are doing, but also *who* is involved.' One contributor later wrote that the six stages of a project were as follows:

1. Wild enthusiasm.
2. Disillusionment.
3. Panic.
4. Searching for the guilty.
5. Punishing the innocent.
6. Rewarding the non-involved.

However much he may have chuckled and agreed with the accuracy of the description of the first three or even four stages, Benson certainly never adopted either of the last two.

Interviewed by the magazine *Money Observer* in September 1992, Benson cheerily summed up his early years at MEPC from 1974 by saying:

> That was an interesting time to join any company. I spent quite a bit of time stumping around the world mending fences and building bridges. Eventually, as the cycle changed and the remedies took effect, MEPC restored itself to rude health. Then I became its managing director and lived happily ever after.

By mid-1979 the success of the steps taken by Benson and Davies became apparent not only to their board colleagues but also to outside observers. On 10

July Andrew Taylor reported in the *Financial Times* on the sale of the Munich site, adding:

> MEPC has now recovered from the serious difficulties which followed the collapse of the UK property market in 1973/4 and at the end of last week announced a 42% increase in first half pre-tax profits to £6.3 m. At the same time the group announced a successful £36.3 m rights issue — with around 87 per cent of the new shares taken up — to fund new developments.

On 18 January 1981 Melvyn Marckus wrote in *The Sunday Telegraph*:

> Seated in the elegant offices of MEPC's Brook House headquarters in Park Lane, the company's vice-chairmen, Chris Benson and David Davies, speak with the air of men who have encountered a special sort of property torment from which they have at last been released. It is an understandable impression because, in the mid-seventies, MEPC was on the brink of bankruptcy.

That may have been an overstatement of the company's earlier plight, but it was not miles away from the truth. Marckus continued:

> Now, with 1979–80 results showing a near 50 per cent jump in pre-tax profits to £21 million, its fortunes have turned full circle. The recovery is complete. MEPC is now bulging with cash of £54 million and Benson and Davies are in an expansionary mood. But as Benson stresses, 'It is going to be cautious expansion.'

Eleven months later Patience (now Baroness) Wheatcroft wrote in *The Sunday Times* of 6 December 1981:

> Five years ago MEPC shares stood at an all-time low of 24 p and newly-installed managing director Chris Benson was desperately trying to persuade the world's bankers that there could be a future for his company. Last week he produced the definitive proof with profits of nearly £27 m, assets of more than £1.6 bn and a share price of 250 p. Today it is the bankers who battle to win Benson's business.

Wheatcroft also mentioned a very important practice of the company and Benson:

> In the intervening years many a pundit has prophesied the death of the property investment company, insisting that its future could only be as project manager for the institutions who would own the product, the building. But MEPC and Benson have always taken the opposite line. They like to take the risks involved in property development, from finding the site through funding the building to putting in a tenant, so that when the scheme starts making money, as in Sydney, it goes straight into the company's coffers.

In 1981 Benson's success at MEPC was recognised by his being invited to be President of the British Property Federation for two years. On 26 May 1982 he was invited to a fund raising event for a charity chosen by the Lord Mayor of

London, Sir Ronald Gardner-Thorpe. Benson was introduced to Prince Philip, the Duke of Edinburgh, who asked him, 'And what do you do?' Before Benson could reply, the Lord Mayor said, 'He's a property developer.' 'Oh no!' cried the Duke with a pained expression, 'Not another bloody property developer.' He then moved away hastily.

Benson was a little disturbed by this exchange, as on the following day he was due to chair the annual luncheon of the British Property Federation, which was to be attended by roughly a thousand colleagues of his. The guest of honour and speaker was to be the Duke. He was at a loss to know how to greet his guest, who was bound to recognise him, so he phoned MEPC's public relations consultants. He was put through to a woman he had not met before and put his problem to her. She advised him; 'When His Royal Highness asks you, "Haven't we met recently?" you tell him that you met last evening and that he was bloody rude to you.' Benson replied, as might be expected, 'I can't say that.' She insisted that he must and assured him that his guest would not be offended.

As predicted, when Benson greeted the Duke on his arrival, he was asked, 'Haven't we met recently? Benson, quaking slightly, like a sub-lieutenant addressing an Admiral of the Fleet, answered, 'Yes, sir, yesterday — and you were bloody rude to me.' 'What did I say?' he was asked. 'You said, "Not another bloody property developer," and now you're going to meet a thousand of them.' The Duke roared with laughter, saying, 'Let's get on with it then.' He seemed to enjoy the event despite the occupation of the multitude and the fact that he was expected to make a speech.

The gods, on the other hand, punished Benson for his lese-majesty. When the Duke was about to address the assembly, Benson could not find the cheque that he was first meant to present to him for his Award Scheme. He had a few minutes desperately searching the papers on the table and his pockets. The possibility of using the old, old story, 'The cheque is in the post', flashed through his desperate mind. It was only at the last possible moment that he found it and handed it over. By then the Duke and others were laughing at the situation — and the photographer recorded Benson's discomfiture for the June issue of *The Property Journal*.

The next time that Benson met him, the Duke noticed that he was wearing his Royal Naval Volunteer Reserve tie, which he was entitled to wear because of his commission. That tie had a wavy line on it, to match the wavy line showing an RNVR officer's rank on his jacket sleeve. 'Shouldn't you be wearing a straight tie?' the Duke asked, referring to the Royal Navy tie, which had a straight line on it, like an RN sleeve. Benson replied that he should really be wearing a 'chain gang' tie, but could not find one in the shops. The chain referred to by Benson

The elusive cheque for the Duke's charity

was the effect of two thin intertwined wavy stripes worn on the sleeve of the Royal Naval Reserve. 'Go to Gieves and tell them I sent you,' the Duke told him, referring to the well-known naval and military outfitters. Benson obeyed the Admiral and was sold a tie appropriate for a midshipman (RNR).

After that encounter Benson met the Duke on a number of occasions. One day, he attended a meeting at St James's Palace of the venerable RSA (Royal Society for the Encouragement of Arts, Manufactures and Commerce), of which the Duke was the President. On recognising Benson he asked him what he was doing there. Benson reminded him that he was present as his nominated Vice-President.

The ensuing few years saw further major acquisitions by MEPC, which greatly increased the total holdings of the company. One of best opportunities appeared in 1985. At the end of 1973, Benson's joint venturers in the Port Talbot shopping centre, Star (Great Britain) Holdings (who had left him with a gross sum of ten pounds for his scheme), changed the name of that company to English Property Corporation Ltd.(EPC). EPC managed to get badly into debt and so received a takeover approach from a Dutch property giant in December 1978. Paul Reichmann and his brothers, who owned Olympia & York, a private Canadian company, were particularly interested in EPC's holdings in America and outbid

39

the Dutch bidder. In March 1979 Olympia & York bought EPC, took over its Canadian properties and allowed the rump to continue trading in Europe as Olympia & York Developments (UK) Ltd under Stanley Honeyman, a former director of EPC.

When offered the Olympia & York UK company, together with its subsidiary EPC, at a good price, Benson and his colleagues jumped at the chance. Paul Reichmann initially asked Benson what he would pay for the various properties, including a project in Nice on which a start had been made. Benson knew from David Davies, who had seen the site, that it was little more than a hole in the ground, and so told Reichmann that he was not prepared to buy it on any terms. He met Paul Reichmann several times and liked him very much. After several phone conversations they had little difficulty in arriving at a final figure that turned out to be very favourable to MEPC.

In July 1985 MEPC bought the company, without the Nice hole in the ground, for £28.1m in cash, plus new ordinary shares to the value of £82.5 m. For the total consideration of £110.6 m Benson and his board had acquired property assets in Britain and mainland Europe valued at almost double that sum, £215 m to be precise. Benson and Paul Reichmann were to meet again in connection with Canary Wharf in due course; Honeyman joined the MEPC board but retired a year later to work for Reichmann.

The EPC properties acquired included a development of shops and offices totalling 170,000 square feet on the site of Ponting's store in Kensington High Street; a shopping centre and offices, 220,000 square feet, in Farnborough; and Milton Park, a trading estate near Abingdon, with 2 m square feet already developed and many acres of land crying out to be developed. One of the later developments on that land by a subsidiary of MEPC, was for 225,000 square feet in three buildings for a Dutch chemicals company. The annual rent for that development alone was close to £1.7 m. Another of MEPC's acquisitions was Second Covent Garden Property Company, which EPC had bought in its Star days for £20m, despite its portfolio being worth much more. Second Covent Garden was the freeholder of the Royal Opera House and also — as Benson thought at the time — had the right to occupy the box, originally the perk of the Duke of Bedford. It turned out later that his colleague, Stanley Honeyman, had somehow managed to get the Duke's right transferred to himself and colleagues.

One of the explanations for EPC's financial problems was that they had not been very successful with their lettings — one of MEPC's fortes. Benson instituted a drive to get the newly acquired premises let and the staff responded magnificently. By the end of 1985 he was able to announce that new leases for former EPC premises had added £2.6 m a year to the company's rental income.

The ability of the staff to get premises fully let where previous owners had failed to do so, was to come up trumps after the company's next major purchase, one that included the well-known, or notorious, tower known as Centre Point, designed by Richard Seifert.

Harry Hyams was one of the undoubted geniuses of the property world. In 1960, as a thirty-one-year-old estate agent, he bought Oldham Estate Company for £50,000. In the next ten years he developed numerous office blocks in London and elsewhere. By 1967 his company's properties were valued at about £46m. In 1958 he took his rivals' breath away by an audacious move. The old London County Council was attempting to sort out the traffic knot at St Giles Circus, where Oxford Street crossed the junction of Tottenham Court Road and Charing Cross Road. A flyover or a tunnel were out of the question. Hyams had bought two blocks of Victorian properties in the centre of the knot. Various designs left the council facing the fact that there was not enough money available for any of the alternative schemes. Lord Goodman, the solicitor known as Mr Fixit for his all-round ability to solve insoluble problems, introduced Hyams to the chairman of the council's planning committee, saying, 'He thinks he can help you at St Giles Circus.'

Subsequent discussions led to the first of two historic planning gain agreements, both of which were to benefit MEPC over the next few years. Put very briefly, such an agreement allowed the developer to pile up some of his unused air rights onto an adjoining site, which would otherwise have been restricted to the normal development limits. Hyams was prepared to transfer land to the council for the new roads. In exchange, the council allowed him to build on their land to what was then an unheard of height in the capital, a thirty-two-storey building, 385 feet high. Once it was built, and not before, the council granted Hyams a lease for 150 years at a rental of £18,500 — a small sum, provided the tower was let.

Centre Point, as the tower was named by Hyams, became the central point of many a discussion: technical, aesthetic, social, political. Whatever the merits of the building, one point stood out like a sore thumb: it was left empty, despite complaints about that fact in Parliament and elsewhere. Hyams was unfazed; apart from anything else, the tower's capital value increased steadily.

In 1974 MEPC and Hyams embarked on a joint venture: a new office block in High Holborn, close to the tube station. Benson had some slight disagreement with him over the choice of architect, but that problem was overcome and the building was in due course completed.

In February 1987 the Cooperative Insurance Society (CIS), which had funded a number of Hyams's projects and owned seventy per cent of the Oldham shares, decided to sell them to MEPC. The negotiations for the sale were conducted by the CIS chief executive officer and MEPC's finance director, Jim Beveridge. For some reason CIS decided that Hyams should not be informed of the discussions until an agreement had been finalised. Although there was no obligation on MEPC, as potential buyer, to notify the minority shareholders about the negotiations, Benson did not approve of this secrecy and decided that he would personally inform Hyams as soon as possible.

As it happened, when agreement was reached, Hyams was on holiday in Sri Lanka, but Benson still felt obliged to see him immediately. He flew at once to Paris, where he changed airports, and then overnight on to Colombo. After a long taxi ride he arrived tired and dishevelled at Hyams's hotel — and bumped into him outside his suite, immaculately turned out. Hyams greeted him with the words, 'Ah, I believe you have something to tell me!' Someone had already informed him about the deal, so Benson had wasted his time with his long journey.

Pending the arrival of a valuation, Hyams said, he would make no decision about selling his own shareholding; he was also concerned that the other minority shareholders should be safeguarded. In fact, he kept Benson waiting for some months for an answer. On 23 September Hyams informed him that he would sell and that he would resign from the board of Oldham six days later. Shortly afterwards MEPC held 99.8 per cent of the Oldham shares and acquired some 3.7 m square feet of office space, together with 350 shops and some development sites. As Colin Sheppard (son of the company's legendary Dick Sheppard) pointed out in his account of the transaction in the MEPC house magazine, it was 'the largest United Kingdom property takeover ever!' The scale of the payments required for it was so large that complicated arrangements had to be made for them.

Carole Nicholson had first worked as an accountant with the auditors of MEPC, but had been invited to join the staff in 1981 as an internal auditor, and then to become the group treasurer. She worked particularly hard on the Oldham takeover. Payments for that major transaction had to be arranged by her, so that several banks could make different large payments on the same day in October 1987 on receiving her confirmation over the telephone. On the day before the completion date Nicholson went home to Sussex, leaving her cumbersome early mobile phone in her desk at the Park Lane office.

That night witnessed the hurricane which uprooted thousands of trees and hit Sussex especially hard. Her electricity and phone were cut off. All that day she imagined what would happen if the Oldham payments did not go through because of her inablity to give the final go-ahead to the banks. (What is the accountant's equivalent of falling on one's sword? Surely not the pen.) When the power supply was restored to her house on the Sunday, two days later, Nicholson was rather relieved to hear on the radio that, because of the chaos caused by the storm, all the banks had in fact been unable to transmit any funds.

Hyams had always relied a great deal on agents and consultants, and was content to have a staff of only fifteen to run his large empire. They cooperated fully in the handover, so Benson was soon able to get his much larger staff working on the problem of voids. Hyams had always insisted on letting to a single tenant for the whole of the Centre Point tower; none had come forward so the building remained unlet while in his, or Oldham's ownership. MEPC was quite prepared to let to different tenants at a market rent and so in the space of six months Centre Point was fully let for the first time — and MEPC was able to buy the freehold shortly afterwards. The Confederation of British Industry took several floors — and is still there. Also in that short period, Hyams's large Duke's Court development in Woking, which had been empty for two years, was one-third let.

Hyams had a very substantial number of MEPC shares and attended the company's annual general meetings from time to time, so he could gauge the success or otherwise of various ventures. Sometimes, as he was fully entitled to do, he questioned the wisdom of some of the directors' decisions and asked questions on behalf of the minority shareholders. His large holding of shares resulted in Hyams being entitled to a very large sum in respect of his dividends. The first cheque that he received from MEPC had so many noughts at the end of the amount in figures, that the machine printing it out was overwhelmed by the length and omitted the numbers that should have been immediately after the £ sign. Needless to say, Hyams was not amused and gave MEPC a piece of his mind. In return, the company gave him a fresh cheque for the correct amount.

One joint venture had been entered into shortly before Benson joined MEPC, but he was concerned with further developments. In the 1970s the newspapers started to move out of Fleet Street and its surrounding area, some of them choosing to move a short distance to the east to the former London Docklands, where there was ample room for larger premises at reasonable prices. The most successful supplier of newsprint for the press was Reed International, which had also undertaken printing work and acquired a significant portfolio of properties in London, some of them housing printing presses. In 1972 the two corporations formed a joint company, MEPC-Reed Properties, to redevelop some of those properties. One was the former Odham's Press building in Long Acre, close to the Royal Opera House. The others were in Fleet Street, High Holborn, Farringdon Street, New Bridge Street and Southwark Street.

With Terry Farrell, architect of Alban Gate

MEPC had a fifty-one per cent holding but was able to acquire Reed's forty-nine per cent eight years later by exercising its option to purchase. By then only the largest of their projects remained to be built, on the Long Acre site. That was for nearly 200,000 square feet of offices, financed by Legal & General Assurance on a profit-sharing basis. That development, together with the adjoining local authority development of flats for its tenants, was criticised for its overpowering size and style, but the earlier Odham's Press building, with its basement printing presses, had been on a similar scale.

The other major air rights development was constructed by MEPC on one of the sites acquired with the takeover of the English Property Company. One of the office blocks included was Lee House, on London Wall in the City, which was to be demolished and replaced by a suitable modern building. Terry Farrell was appointed as its architect by MEPC and, with Ove Arup & Partners as engineers, drew up a breathtaking scheme for a seventeen-storey building strad-dling the roadway. The massive amount of steelwork needed to span the road was designed bearing in mind the lessons learned from the construction of deep-sea oil platforms. In exchange for permission to use the airspace above the public road, the City planners agreed to accept open spaces and less building on adjoining sites. The result, built by Mowlem, was named Alban Gate and provided 400,000 square feet of office accommodation. In addition, the scheme made provision for some residential property and an improved Monkwell Square. Roger Squire, as MEPC's development director, played a major part in this massive project, but Benson made sure that, in accordance with his usual practice, that he was continuously kept in the loop.

The development of Alban Gate had revealed some disagreements. There were often reservations about the future and arguments about whether there were too few or too many office developments in the pipeline. One of Benson's colleagues, who felt that the project was both too large and untimely, was Lord Boardman, whose views were entitled to respect, as he had served for a time as Minister for Industry and as Chief Secretary to the Treasury. As it happened, bad luck intervened and almost made his views come true.

If there had been no major problems and the building had been completed on time, letting would have proceeded as well as it usually did. Unfortunately, the start of building was late and completion was delayed by fifteen months for various reasons. As the construction was largely taking place over a major road in the City, London Wall, the planning authorities had insisted on such work being carried out during the weekend, when the City had little traffic and that road could be closed. The steel workers had an industrial dispute and decided to have a go-slow. They had the clever idea of banning work on Saturdays and Sundays; as a result work came to a stop for some time. There were in addition some technical problems that caused minor delays. For example, as the building was a glorified bridge, it had more movement in it than the conventional office block. The differences in tolerances were minor only but required time-consuming attention.

The loss of fifteen months turned out to cause a threefold financial loss. Extra construction time inevitably caused extra building costs. The delay meant that rent only started to come in later than planned. What was most unfortunate was that the property market saw a downturn in the same period. That had a double adverse effect: tenants were harder to find and the rents that they could be asked to pay had to be reduced. Fortunately, some floors had been pre-let and in due course Alban Gate was fully occupied, but some of the gilt had certainly been taken off the gingerbread.

MEPC had various regional offices in England; one of them, with John Addelsee as its director, covered the square mile of the City of London, the traditional financial heart of the capital. Once Alban Gate had been let, the capital value of the MEPC properties managed by the City region staff alone, totalling 1,865,000 square feet, was some £500m, with an annual rental income of £40m.

In that region a further 730,000 square feet were under construction, with a value on completion of £300 m and an anticipated rental income of £30 m. The impressive combined total was some 2.6 m square feet of prime properties, worth £800m and producing £70 m annually. Not only could the income be used partly for paying off previous loans, and partly for new developments, but those sort of figures made it easier for MEPC to obtain funding for new schemes, from banks and insurance companies, both in the United Kingdom and abroad, once the property market had returned to its previous position.

When asked by the writer about the amount of his own input in the various schemes, Benson made it plain that he concerned himself in every project during his twelve years as managing director, though slightly less so in his five years as chairman, when he gave James Tuckey space to act as managing director. Every development had a small team of in-house experts allocated to it, although the architects and engineers were as a general rule outsiders appointed at the appropriate time. Each team had a leader, but Benson always participated in the discussions. He instituted the practice of having a meeting of all the leading staff members every Monday afternoon, to discuss outstanding matters, although his trips round the globe interfered with his attendance on numerous occasions.

In 2004–05 Benson was Master of The Company of Watermen and Lightermen of the River Thames and was invited as such to dine with different City Livery companies. One evening he was invited to dinner by the Barbers' Company at the Barber-Surgeons' Hall in Monkwell Square. That was the square that had been rebuilt by MEPC as part of the Alban Gate development. MEPC had paid a considerable sum to the Barbers for a piece of land, plus compensation for loss of light and for disturbance. Benson was asked to reply after dinner to the toast to the guests. During the meal he admired the interior of the hall and noticed some large metal objects hanging from the ceiling. He was told that they were representations of the fleams, the razor like instruments used in the past for bleeding patients. In his speech he could not resist the temptation to remind his hosts of the large sums they had received before work could be started on their new surroundings. 'You bled us white,' he said, rather rudely. One of his hosts enthusiastically shouted out, 'Bloody right we did!' — so honours were even.

Mention has been made of the fact that during these years Benson usually returned from Australia via Hawaii and the mainland United States. Some of the American schemes proved very profitable for MEPC, and were not without interest for various reasons. He experienced unpleasantness on some of his visits to the United States, but nothing so serious as the incident involving James Tuckey, who was a keen runner. He left his hotel in Dallas one morning in running kit. He was stopped by an armed man who demanded his credit cards, which Tuckey speedily surrendered. Despite that cooperation, the man shot him in the stomach. Fortunately, thanks to speedy surgery, delayed only because several householders declined to open their door to a man who said he had been shot, Tuckey survived to act as managing director after Benson became chairman.

During his time in America, Tuckey had very successfully launched a number of projects, some of them when working under Peter Anker. In Minnesota alone there were three good developments, two in Minneapolis and a third in Rochester, which involved a major expansion of an existing shopping centre. In Texas there were projects in Dallas and in Houston.

The development in Las Vegas, Nevada, proved interesting for Benson on a couple of occasions. MEPC had earlier bought the Boulevard Mall there but then enlarged it substantially with a £28 m expansion and renovation project that included a 200,000 square feet department store. He was standing outside the newly built part when he was approached by two men who seemed to belong to the local mafia. They asked the Englishmen whether he owned the place and were told that his company did. They asked who was going to be supplying the machines for the premises. When he asked what they were talking about they said, 'Gambling machines.' He assured him that there would be none. When they expressed doubts about his answer and required an assurance that there would be none at all, he told them that the only new machines to be installed would be toy cars for the younger customers. That seemed to satisfy them for the time being. 'IF that IS the case, you won't be hearing from us again.'

The second incident in Las Vegas occurred when Benson was staying in the Sands Hotel and expecting an important phone call at 4 am. He was tired from his travels and did not dare go to sleep either on his bed or in a chair, as he knew he was unlikely to wake up in time. He decided the only safeguard was to stay on his feet, so he walked round the large hotel, taking in the awful sights, such as old ladies shovelling their life savings into slot machines, and men willingly handing over their, or someone else's, money at the gaming tables. Suddenly, when he was near a roulette table, he found himself lifted off his feet by two security men, who carried him to the side of the large room and demanded to know what he was up to. He explained the reason for his perambulation. They were not convinced and told him that he had twice crossed the croupier's 'wire' and so intimidated the poor man. The croupier had a rope around his location so as to keep everyone at bay. Benson was not conscious of having walked over anything on the floor and said so. He was given the benefit of the doubt, plus a warning not to do it again. Still concerned about the incoming call, Benson sat on the stairs for the next two hours.

47

Benson, when chairman of the board, had a less serious and more amusing incident when in Honolulu for a meeting at MEPC's Hawaiian local office. Having flown from Australia the night before, he relaxed in a deckchair in the sun and fell asleep. He woke up to find his face burning and went into the washroom to cool it down with cold water. He saw in the mirror that he had gone as red as a beetroot. The company's local janitor saw him there and asked, 'Are you drunk?' Benson assured him that he was not. The man added, 'Your face is red. Mine goes like that when I'm drunk.' Benson was tickled by this exchange and mentioned it to a colleague shortly afterwards. The story spread quickly and the poor janitor was told by colleagues that he was bound to get the chop, as the red face belonged to the big boss from London, England. He was relieved to find that the chairman was not offended but amused, and that his job was secure.

On one flight from the US west coast to Chicago, Benson had a pleasant surprise. Soon after take off the pilot announced that he had received instructions that he would have to 'loiter' over the Chicago area for some 20 minutes before landing at O'Hare, because of heavy traffic. He asked whether the passengers would prefer to spend that 20 minutes having a look at the Grand Canyon. They agreed enthusiastically, so the pilot made two banking runs over the canyon, giving the passengers on each side an equal chance of the wonderful view.

Benson's greatest flying experience as a passenger, as opposed to the more exciting times as a pilot, was when he returned to London from Singapore on one of the few Concorde flights from there. The aircraft was tried out on the Europe-Australia run, but it proved impracticable and was discontinued. He was invited during the flight into the cockpit and to sit in the jump seat behind the pilots. He introduced himself to a man sitting next to him, who gave his name and said he was an accident investigator. Benson flippantly asked, 'Before or after?' but the man continued to speak to him. He turned out to be the father of a young farmer getting work experience on Benson's farm.

For nearly all of Benson's years with the company its headquarters were in Brook House, Park Lane, which had been built in the 1930s as a luxury block of flats, the top floors being occupied until the outbreak of war by Earl and Countess Mountbatten, as they became. After the war, in view of the shortage caused by bombing, Westminster Council permitted the premises to be used temporarily for office purposes. The company found the Park Lane address very convenient and one where guests could be entertained and impressed. One of MEPC's most important staff members was the excellent cook, Mrs Dixon. Every member of the head office was saddened when she retired, so Benson thought he had better try and get a good chef to replace her.

The Roux brothers had their Gavroche restaurant close by and tendered for the contract. Their terms were very reasonable so they were signed up and regularly produced food up to their high standards. Albert Roux once commented to Benson that he never came to the restaurant for a meal, pointing out that their lunch prices were very reasonable. Benson arranged to have lunch there and was joined by Roux for the meal. Afterwards Roux would not let Benson pay, but he insisted successfully. The Roux brothers were later to figure in the Docklands and Canary Wharf story in a strange way.

In due course Westminster Council insisted on the Park Lane building site being returned to residential use, so MEPC arranged to move elsewhere and for a new development of luxury flats to replace the pre-war building. The new headquarters were to be in two adjoining listed buildings by Robert Adam and Thomas Cubitt at nos 11 and 12 St James's Square, which needed very careful refurbishment before they could be occupied. They were also to be linked by an atrium to the office block MEPC was to build for its own use behind the two houses, in Ormond Yard. Tuckey and Benson were appalled by the interior condition of the Cubitt building. False ceilings had been inserted, which hid the glorious plasterwork of the tall rooms; beautiful doors had been covered with plywood; floors had been covered with modern materials and light fittings were basic. Despite that, the appropriate authorities were insisting that those 'incremental alterations' be retained. Benson and Tuckey protested until common sense prevailed. MEPC was then able to restore the building to its former glory.

When the work was completed four specially commissioned statues of Greek muses were placed on the parapet of the classical frontage designed by Adam. He had intended to have four such figures there but they had never been provided. Although the company is no longer there, anyone able to identify Melpomene, Euterpe, Polymnia and Clio from the ground, and from left to right, may be shocked to find that the first letters of their names add up to MEPC. It is an even more outrageous breach of good town planning than the OXO tower on the Thames, but Benson disclaims responsibility. The move to St James's Square took place in the summer of 1991. In July of the following year Benson announced his decision to retire from the company at the end of July 1993, eleven days after his sixtieth birthday, which was on 20 July. In the interim he made a point of making a quick trip to say goodbye to his MEPC friends in Europe, Australia and the United States. In his final chairman's statement in the annual report for 1992, Benson pointed out that since he had become a director, the company had 'successfully ridden out three major economic hurricanes.' He made an interesting statement of the duties of a chairman. He said that they included the duty 'to shape the board and with them, to find his own successor.' Lord Blakenham, the chairman of the Pearson Group, had been a non-executive director of the MEPC board since 1990 and would take the chair from 1st August.

Benson's retirement at the age of sixty came as a surprise to some people — not least to him, as he had tentatively thought he might stay on for another five years. His plan was aborted at a meeting of the full board in July 1992, attended by Sir Patrick Meaney, a non-executive member since 1986, who was chairman of the Rank Organisation and a deputy chairman of the Midland Bank. Meaney stated that the company was not complying with the recently published recommendations of the Cadbury Report on the Financial Aspects of Corporate Governance, as Benson was chairman of three companies. If he wanted to remain chairman of MEPC, Meaney suggested, he would have to give up the chair at Boots and Sun Alliance. Benson was not prepared to be cajoled into giving up those two posts or either of them. He thought that Meaney was a very ambitious man and was keen to take his job.

As Benson had obtained the approval of his fellow directors on both occasions before accepting the two other part-time chairmanships, he disputed Meaney's contention. The only relevant recommendation in the Cadbury Report was that all non-executive directors should be independent of management and 'free from any business or other relationship which could materially interfere with the exercise of their independent judgment.' There was nothing to suggest that it was wrong to be the part-time non-executive chairman of three companies whose interests did not clash at any point. Nobody had ever suggested that Benson had been involved in a conflict of interest situation. No other non-executive director expressed any opinion, while the executive directors, as is usual, kept out of the discussion of the chairmanship. Feeling isolated and badly let down, Benson then announced that he would retire a year later and shortly afterwards asked Lord Blakenham to succeed him.

A few days after that meeting Meaney collapsed and died at the age of sixty-seven. Ian Watters, one of the executive directors, after expressing his regret at Meaney's sad end, said to Benson: 'So it's OK: you can stay?' He was mistaken as the die was cast: Benson had appointed his successor.

Benson had spent nearly twenty years with MEPC, during which he also oversaw the completion of numerous other successful schemes that have not been mentioned. Throughout that time he had firmly believed in quality: quality of design and quality of service for tenants. The quality of design was achieved, of course, by some of the leading architects in the country. Many of the developments received awards for excellence. Towards the end of his time there a correspondent of The Times wrote of him: 'As chairman of MEPC, he is arguably the most senior establishment figure in the British property industry. His achievements are a testimony to his tenacity.' That unofficial ranking was confirmed to some extent as, unusually for a director of a property company, Benson was a member of the Panel on Takeovers and Mergers for nine years, and also a member of the Asset Valuation Standards Committee of his professional body, the Royal Institution of Chartered Surveyors. A correspondent in The *Estates Gazette* made the very pertinent comment: 'If the property industry were to have a goodwill ambassador, it would be MEPC's outgoing chairman.'

Roger Squire, who had started as Benson's European manager and had then been the development director for some years, gave the writer his recollections of his former boss. In his early days with MEPC he was told by Benson: 'Only bring me recommendations, not questions. If you bring me three to which I say No, you're out.' Squire added, 'Despite that he was tolerant and let you get on with things. He was an astute, likeable person; a good people person and a good leader.'

Benson had once mentioned in the office that he had missed having a sixteenth birthday party as he had been completing his time in *HMS Worcester* on the Thames then. The staff decided to give him a belated — and surprise — sixteenth celebration when he was leaving the company. On 10 July 1993, ten days before his sixtieth birthday, he was attending a cocktail party at the office of British Design Partners (BDP), one of the leading firms of architects. His wife Jo arrived in a taxi and dragged him away, giving a ridiculous explanation. The taxi took them to HMS *Belfast*, permanently moored in the Thames opposite the Tower of London — a very suitable venue for the ex-sailor and LDDC chairman. He was led into a large cabin and found all his closest colleagues there. He was very touched — and many of them were equally moved.

The progress of the company during the twelve years he acted as managing director and the five as chairman, can be gauged to some extent (for compliments are customary at that stage) from the remarks made on his retirement by his successor as managing director. James Tuckey pointed out that during Benson's twelve years managing the company, 'Shareholders' funds had risen tenfold from £243 m to £2341 m and during this period earnings per share grew at thirty per cent per annum compound. Some record. Well, how does he achieve this? Hard work, encouragement for others, approachable breezy style. An ability to get on with people at all levels, to make them feel in touch with what was going on. A ready sense of humour and an unfailing ability to recapture a hilarious or serious moment for years afterwards. At the Board he has always been a most considerate and patient leader, never forcing his views on the Board but encouraging a consensus to emerge through discussion and debate.'

Lord Blakenham, in his first chairman's statement in the 1993 annual report, paid the traditional compliments to his predecessor, but added : 'He has ensured that he leaves behind a Cadbury-friendly board.' It might have helped, Benson thought bitterly when he read those words, had its non-executive members, and especially Meaney, read the Cadbury report carefully, and earlier.

More revealing are the comments made long after the farewell party by one of the few senior women in the property world, who had worked for Benson for twelve years. Carole Nicholson, still the group treasurer and a director of a subsidiary company at the time of his departure, agreed to meet the writer to give him her views on her former boss. She had so many good things to say about him that she had made a list of some of them before their meeting — but still added more compliments to Benson when they met. Among Nicholson's comments were the following

> He made everyone in the company feel there was a common purpose. He was an inspired and inspirational leader who believed in you, the person, and brought out the best in people. He had the knack of being able to get people to work harder for him because they really wanted to help him. He was a father figure and mentor. He had a guiding principle of core values and a core purpose beyond just making money. He instilled a culture of self-worth. He created a climate of mutual trust and understanding.

Nicholson added one expression that had earlier been used by Roger Squire, the director, and which could be said to sum up his chief qualities; 'He was a good people person.' She also told the writer that when Benson told members of the staff, 'My door is always open,' he meant it. He deliberately used an office in the passageway leading to the staff canteen, and kept the door open unless privacy was essential. Even the most junior members of the staff, she added, would drop in on Benson if they had a problem. He made a point of knowing the names of their spouses and of inquiring about their children by name. Nicholson also paid tribute to Jo Benson for her contribution to the happy family atmosphere at MEPC: she always attended functions and played a full part as Benson's partner, taking an interest in everyone she met. It is perhaps not surprising Nicholson felt the place was never the same after Benson's departure. However, MEPC's loss was to be other companies' gain.

CHAPTER FIVE

Rescue Archaeology and Heritage

One of Benson's great concerns as a developer was to ensure that the history of any site being worked on should be properly recorded. Apart from the interest of members of the public in knowing the details of their forefathers' dwellings and mode of life, he also felt strongly that a new or altered building was entitled to have its history recorded as much as possible.

As digs for the foundations of large buildings in cities and towns got deeper and deeper, the danger of the extensive and unrecorded destruction, or covering over of the remains of an earlier civilisation intensified. Archaeologists and historians were aware of the danger and increasingly advocated rescue digs for sites, particular in places like the City of London, where there was always a possibility of Roman and Saxon remains being disturbed, damaged or lost. Benson encouraged MEPC to make contributions to such investigations. Over the years there were a large number of investigations and many contributions, particularly in London.

The first report of a rescue dig appeared as early as October 1974 in the second issue of the company newsletter, at that stage comprised of four pages only. One of the projects that had been started was the building of The Friary shopping centre in Guildford. Humphrey Woods, an Oxford archaeologist, was in charge of the team of diggers, whose investigation was funded by contributions from the Department of the Environment, Guildford Museum and MEPC. The locations of the earlier friary cloister, priory, nave and south aisle of a fourteenth-century church were all found. In what had been the floor of the chapter house the team discovered tiles with patterns that bore a striking resemblance to those in Westminster Abbey, which might have been deliberately copied. Two skeletons were found buried, one male and the other female, one each side of the altar. They were probably those of two generous benefactors of the church, who had requested such a burial. The archaeologists reached the conclusion that the site had been used for a number of different purposes in the past, apart from as a priory, as there were also traces of a royal hunting lodge, a barracks, a brewery and a private mansion.

The same article referred to a company development in Northampton, which had exposed the remains of six medieval houses, showing both stone and clay floors, together with ovens. Fragments of earlier buildings were found beneath those remains. Tannery clay pits and malt roast ovens were found and dated as being from the fifteenth century. What was particularly interesting at that site was the finding of what was thought to be the remains of a Saxon concrete mixer, with a wattle-work lining. The article included an artist's impression based on information from the team. It showed two men at opposites ends of a horizontal beam, which had a vertical axle housed in the centre of a circular mixing tub. They were shown walking round it, pushing the beam with mixing paddles fixed underneath it. The director of the excavation commented, 'It is rare enough to be able to excavate a single complete medieval house. To find a whole environment preserved virtually intact is quite incredible and very significant.'

The issue of the house magazine that appeared in August 1980 carried an article by Harvey Sheldon, the Greater London Archaeology Officer at the Museum of London, situated most appropriately on London Wall. It had the swinging title, 'Archaeology; Do You Dig It?' and contained a great deal of interesting information about his work, particularly in Southwark, the important suburb of Roman London where the first bridge landed — and later the site of the Surrey Docks. Sheldon made a very good point when he stated:

> The increased number and size of the potential sites will pose a considerable problem for the archaeologists, especially if, as seems likely, the level of public funding remains no more than static. Consequently, if the redevelopments are not to be accompanied by unrecorded destruction, the developers will need to be persuaded that at least part of the cost of the archaeology should be borne by them.

Benson agreed heartily with those sentiments and saw to it that MEPC responded appropriately.

One of the most interesting sites was in Throgmorton Avenue at its junction with Austin Friars, close to the Bank of England in the City, where MEPC was in effect rebuilding an office building completed in 1890 and known as The Garden House. The garden referred to was that of the ancient Drapers' Company, which had built Throgmorton Avenue partly on it. The excavation finds on the site were so fascinating that MEPC commissioned the historian of the Drapers' Company to write a very attractive book on the subject entitled *The Garden House* (1987). In his foreword Benson made the valid point,

> This text, prepared by Dr Penelope Hunting, tells the story of the site and the activities that have occurred on and around the property over the last 2000 years. It is a testament to the dynamic nature of the City of London and reminds us that commercial city centre redevelopment is nothing new.

The site turned out on examination to be partly over the line of the eastern branch of the former Walbrook stream, which had joined the nearby Thames. In the second century the stream had silted up and the land had reverted to marshland. Fortunately the wet conditions were good for the preservation of leather and other items used by the earlier Roman settlers.

The rescue archaeologists from the Museum of London found the remains of timbers that had been part of a wooden track alongside the stream, together with a square timber-framed structure lined with chalk cobbles, which was possibly part of a water supply system. The water of the stream had clearly attracted leather workers to the site and a range of footwear remains were found, including parts of shoes, sandals and slippers, as well as part of a goatskin saddle bag. A number of wooden and metal objects had also been preserved by the damp conditions.

The most exciting find was that of two writing tablets from the early second century, made up of two equal wooden parts, like covers of a book, tied together. The writing would normally have been done on a coat of beeswax but that was no longer present on either inner surface. However, as luck would have it, the writer on one of the surfaces had pressed so hard with the tip of his stylus, that he had not only written in the beeswax but had pressed through to the wood under it. The writing in the wooden surface showed that the document was dated March 118 AD and apparently well written in Latin by an educated man. It appeared to be a legal document relating to a property dispute. Part of a Roman seal box was found nearby; it had probably housed a large seal fastening the two surfaces together. A number of styli were dug up, as well as bone needles and pins.

Roman pottery was found that could be dated from the year 70 to 140; some of it showed burn marks that could have come from a great fire in the early second century. The pots were from different parts of the Roman Empire, including Cologne, Gaul, Spain and Palestine.

Dr Hunting also gave an account of the arrival of the Augustinian Friars in 1253. The site of their priory ran westwards from Old Broad Street and included the location of the archaeological dig and the later Garden House. Some 300 years later the friars leased a plot of land to a man they later had reason to fear, Thomas Cromwell, Earl of Essex (nowadays better known, thanks to Hilary Mantel's biography). In 1532 he leased a substantial plot of building land and gardens but soon afterwards extended his holding by pushing some of his neighbours off portions of their land. In the dissolution of the monasteries by Henry VIII the remaining friars were expelled in 1538. Their lessee Cromwell followed them off the site two years later. Although he was the King's chief minister, he had fallen out with him over what might be called a matrimonial dispute, was charged with treason and convicted without a trial. He was beheaded on one of the King's many wedding days. His property was forfeited to the Crown and later acquired by the Drapers' Company.

The building that MEPC built in the years 1986–88 took in 11–19 Throgmorton Avenue, together with an adjoining building in a small road that reminds us of the Augustinian Brethren, though their name has been shortened by the Londoners. That house had the address of 21 Austin Friars. Whenever MEPC was replacing the stone facade of a listed or otherwise interesting building, Benson insisted on the architect using the modern technique that ensured the building looked 'right' when completed. The original carved stone blocks rested on one another. The replacement facade stones could look identical even though made much thinner. Unlike their predecessors they could not be built one on top of the other, as they were not thick enough, so they had to be built up as separate structures, floor by floor, resting on the floor itself'. This method of replacing earlier stonework was used by the company not only for the Garden House, but for a number of replacement facades in London squares and other sensitive sites. For example, a building in Ecclestone Square was rebuilt so as to accord with Cubitt's original style, and to match the other houses there.

On a more modern note, the Garden House had another point of interest. It was occupied for the whole of its life, from 1890 to 1981, by a firm of solicitors, Ashurst Morris Crisp, which will soon be celebrating its bicentenary, as it was founded by William Ashurst in 1821. In 1879 the later partners were all present at the laying of the corner-stone, when a time capsule in a glass jar was buried. When the building was demolished by MEPC's builders, the glass jar was discovered intact. The firm was to figure twice in Benson's later career. The legal adviser to the London Docklands Development Corporation throughout Benson's chairmanship of it — and indeed for the whole of the lifetime of the Corporation — was the senior property partner of those solicitors, Laurence Rutman. Among other achievements, he was to draft the great Canary Wharf contract. When Benson was later invited to be non-executive deputy chairman of the Thorn Lighting Group, at a time when it was it was seeking a Stock Exchange listing, the solicitors for the group were Ashurst Morris Crisp, now Ashurst.

There were several other sites disturbed by MEPC's developments in the City of London that yielded information about the Roman and Saxon inhabitants. At 62–63 Queen Victoria Street, where in conjunction with London Underground the company was building offices over a reconstructed Mansion House station, the archaeologists were given the opportunity to find evidence of a Roman quarry and Roman remains from the late 1st century. The company on that occasion also provided six small bursaries for students from the Department of Ceramics and Mural Studies at Hammersmith College of Art and Design, so that they could design and make a sixty foot long historical mural for the exterior of the new building, overlooking Hudson's Bay Gardens, which were landscaped as part of the development. During a dig at a nearby site, close to the Thames in Queen Street, several canon balls were unearthed by the Museum of London. They had probably been fired into the marshy ground during practice shoots centuries earlier — as no hostile navy had ever made it that far.

Apropos the bursaries for students, one young artist Benson was able to encourage was Stephen Wiltshire, the remarkable autistic boy with an amazing gift for making architectural drawings, largely from memory. He was given access to MEPC sites and drew a considerable number of the new constructions. The company's annual report for 1989 included six of his sketches, including one showing the large office block bridging London Wall, during construction.

Carter Lane is a small street running to the east of the main road up Ludgate Hill leading to St Paul's Cathedral. In earlier centuries it was used as the beginning of the principal route to bypass the cathedral on its south side. When MEPC paused to let the archaeologists onto the site at 69 Carter Lane, they were able to find traces of yet another monastery, namely that of the Dominican Order of the Blackfriars. One of the most interesting finds was that of a large window of the fourteenth century, which was in due course advantageously incorporated in the new building. A good selection of vessels in turquoise, green and clear glass, was found, together with two wine glasses and other evidence of earlier occupation. MEPC also supported the cost of other rescue digs in the City; in 1989 alone the company gave grants totalling £500,000. As far as Benson is aware, there was never any complaint from a shareholder that his money was being frittered away on a lot of time-wasting digging.

Henry VIII certainly made plenty of land available for redevelopment when he abolished the monasteries, but sometimes many years passed before such land was built on again. Benson's and MEPC's experience at Reading demonstrated that point. After the dissolution of the monasteries, Reading Abbey, like many another ecclesiastical building, was treated as a free takeaway site for building materials until little remained above ground. As the site had yielded stone, timber and metal for many local builders, some of them decided to dig for gravel on the site as well.

In 1844 Reading prison (known for holding a very unhappy Oscar Wilde — and only recently closed down) was built in the east end of the abbey grounds, partly overlapping the site of the abbey itself. However, the waste land to the west of the prison remained unused. Some excavations were carried out by local archaeologists but a major spur to further investigation was the grant of planning permission in 1981 to MEPC for three office blocks, totalling 300,000 square feet, on the south side of the abbey grounds. They were sympathetically designed by the architects T. P. Bennett Partnership and well built in due course by Sir Robert McAlpine & Sons Ltd, but a rescue dig was clearly called for — and supported by Benson and his company.

That dig revealed more of the hidden parts of the abbey, including the cloisters. Of greater interest were the findings relating to the River Kennet. The abbey had been founded by Henry I and built by Cluniac monks in the twelfth century. Much of the stone probably came from Normandy, via the port of Caen, to the Thames and the Kennet, then possibly into the Holy Brook, which may have been specially dug to provide a landing area for deliveries. Thereafter supplies for the abbey and its large community will also have been delivered by water. The investigations in the water and on its banks showed that there had been many changes made over the centuries, with timbers that had been recycled from time to time.

In 1983 the *Reading Chronicle* published ten articles on the Abbey site and the digs, written by Leslie Cram, the Keeper of Archaeology and Social History at the Reading Museum and Art Gallery. Those articles formed the basis of the booklet which was written by him and published by the Museum in 1988. Benson again arranged for MEPC to fund the publication.

Benson regularly encouraged members of the company to support various good causes. In 1982 and 1983 MEPC and The Grosvenor Estate jointly sponsored the Civic Trust awards. This was the first occasion on which the property industry had produced sponsors for this excellent cause. One of the innovations that the two companies introduced was the sponsorship of a new award for the best example of a central area regeneration. They stated that they were sponsoring the prize 'because it is particularly appropriate to highlight the work being produced by the building and development professions in inner cities.'

Benson gave a great deal of time to the Trust during those two years. Somewhat unusually for a developer, he was invited to become chairman of the Trust in 1985 and served as such for the next five years. He welcomed the opportunity to give more of his time to that worthy body, which had been set up in 1957 by Lord Duncan-Sandys, as an independent charity to encourage and protect the environment. A considerable proportion of that time was taken up by his visits to all the buildings shortlisted for an award. Nearly a thousand local societies, with a total membership of over 250,000, were registered with the Trust, which also worked closely with another charity, the Architectural Heritage Fund.

During one meeting Benson was a little peeved when a man suggested that it was incongruous that the chairman of the London Docklands Development Corporation should be chairing the Civic Trust. He seems to have thought that Benson spent his time knocking buildings down, whereas he consistently worked hard to conserve suitable buildings of all kinds. Support for that assertion is to be found in an attractive book published by the Corporation during his chairmanship in 1987: *Docklands Heritage — Conservation and Regeneration in London Docklands*, edited by Carole Lyders and Averil Harrison.

During his chairmanship Benson asked Prince Charles whether he would consider becoming the Royal Patron of the Trust. The Prince, always interested in conservation and architecture, accepted and soon agreed to speak at the Trust's annual exhibition, held most appropriately that year in the Grade II listed Royal Agricultural Hall in Islington. He gave what Benson thought to be an excellent and very constructive talk. It did not contain a single attack on any particular modern 'carbuncle'.

In 1985 Benson together with the MEPC chairman, Robin Adam, was able to host a worthwhile event at the company's offices in Brook House, Park Lane. It was the launch of the new Lutyens Trust, formed as an educational charity to provide information and guidance on all aspects of the restoration, care and maintenance of the buildings, gardens and other designs of Sir Edwin Landseer Lutyens (1869–1944). Lutyens was best known for his design of the Whitehall Cenotaph and many war cemeteries, as well as the Viceroy's House in New Delhi and the British Embassy in Washington. Several of Lutyens's grandchildren were present, including Nicholas Ridley MP, who was to be one of the Secretaries of State of the Environment when Benson was chairing the London Docklands Development Board. The choice of the MEPC offices for the launch was entirely appropriate as Lutyens had designed the outside of the building. MEPC at the time also owned a building at 36 Smith Square, Westminster, which Lutyens had designed shortly before the 1914–18 war.

Sir John Soane's Museum in Lincoln's Inn Fields has for years acted as a wonderful reminder of Soane, the architect of the Bank of England and of the Dulwich Art Gallery. By 1988 water was penetrating the roof and endangering both the fabric of the building and its priceless collections. As a result of a survey, the trustees of the museum launched a campaign to raise £2.5 m to cover a five-year programme of fabric restoration, estimated to cost £1.6 m, together with comprehensive conservation work on both the interior and the contents. Benson visited the museum one rainy day and saw the water coming through the ceiling. He felt strongly that MEPC should contribute generously to the appeal and hoped that he would be able to persuade his colleagues to give £100,000. He was pleasantly surprised when his board of directors immediately responded enthusiastically and unanimously approved of a contribution of £1m, to be paid by five equal annual instalments.

Benson asked himself how that donation might be enhanced and so phoned Sir Robin Butler, the Cabinet Secretary and a friend, for an appointment, and was invited to come at once. Butler was immediately enthusiastic about the idea of helping the museum and made a call to a colleague. He then asked Benson if he had a few minutes and was told he had. 'Then pop round to the Department for Arts in Horseguards, where Charles Henderson will be waiting for you.' Henderson met him on his arrival and asked, 'Are you the chap who is giving a million to the Soane?' Benson confirmed that his company was intending to do so. Seconds later he was shown in to Richard Luce, the Minister for the Arts, who readily agreed to try and match MEPC's gift. After telling the writer about that speedy Civil Service and Ministerial response, Benson sighed: 'Would that such things could happen today!'

James Tuckey, by then the managing director of MEPC, was asked by Benson to attend and represent the company at the press conference at the museum on 23 November 1989, where he announced the company's decision to help. Richard Luce followed that with the good news that the government intended to match the sum promised by MEPC. With those two promises four-fifths of the sum needed had been raised.

Peter Thornton, curator of the museum, said: 'MEPC's generous offer, and the Minister's imaginative decision to match it, means that our deep concern, wondering where on earth we would find the money to mend the roof and attend to all the other troubles besetting the fabric of this marvellous little building, now suddenly seems to be at an end. I am immensely thankful. I think Sir John Soane would have been delighted to see big business combining with the Government in order to rescue his beloved foundation.'

James Tuckey was appointed as a member of a small steering committee of the museum, so that the company was able to see that its donation was being well used. The first stage of the work, planned by the architect Julian Harrap, dealt with the urgently needed roof repairs, which were executed in 1990 and 1991. They were followed in 1992 with the restoration of the facade of 13 Lincoln's Inn Fields and the replacement of some of the plain glass windows, inserted after wartime bomb damage, by appropriate stained glass. In 1993 the ground floor of the adjoining house at number 12 was restored and a link passage was opened to the ante-room in number 13. Most of the balance of the exterior and interior work was executed in 1994. Emulating the best practices of the MEPC, the rescue team completed the whole five-year programme on time and on budget in April 1995. A worthy cause if ever there was one.

Susan Palmer, the museum's archivist, who was there at the time of the appeal, has described the gift in the following terms:

> It was an absolutely ground-breaking donation at the time — the first of any great size in the museum's history. And the work that it enabled us to carry out has been the solid foundation of all the building and restoration work we have carried out since.

One other, albeit minor, contribution to London's heritage that Benson made was one that gave him great pleasure. The Temple Bar archway, originally sited outside the Middle Temple at the junction of Fleet Street and the Strand, was erected in 1672, having probably been designed by Christopher Wren. (It is strange that there is no certainty about the matter, but the original drawings were in the possession of his son, who was both a member of the Middle Temple and an architect, so the probability is a high one.) It remained there until the Strand was widened in 1878. Fortunately, it was carefully taken down and each stone was numbered. Sir Henry Meux, the brewer, bought them all, and re-erected the arch at his estate near Enfield.

In 1976, on the initiative of Sir Hugh Wontner, a former Lord Mayor, the Temple Bar Trust was established with a view to returning the Bar to the City of London, its rightful home. The Trustees were a combination of City worthies and others concerned with the country's architectual heritage. Benson became one of them. Different sites were considered over the years, as replacement on the original one was ruled out by traffic. Eventually, a place was found for the archway, close to the north side of Wren's masterpiece, St Paul's Cathedral. The Trust purchased it and it was erected once more by modern masons, with only 5% of the original stonework needing replacement. The gateway was reopened as a pedestrian entrance to Paternoster Square, by Robert Finch, the Lord Mayor, in November 2004. Benson was one of the approving citizens present.

CHAPTER SIX

The London Docklands

By 1970 the combined London docks had ceased to be one of the world's great ports. Their size and location had made them unable to cope with the new reality of large ships carrying great numbers of containers. As so often happens with early success stories, later modernisation brings them to an end. London had lost its vast trade to more modern ports able to cope with the new commercial facts, such as large container ships, too large for the Thames above Tilbury docks. Some of the docks, especially in Southwark, had already been filled in with the rubble of their former warehouses.

The most unfortunate consequence was that thousands of dockers living in the East End of London had lost their jobs, and that many of them had neither retrained nor obtained alternative employment. Both banks of the Thames below the Norman Tower of London and the Victorian Tower Bridge were depressed, and depressing areas. Bob Mellish, a moderate former Labour Chief Whip in the House of Commons, who had represented one of the local constituencies for many years, described them as follows: 'Eight and a half square miles of absolute dereliction and desolation. A story of disaster. No other word can describe it.' Few businessmen were willing to invest in them by setting up there and few builders were prepared to build houses in areas where buyers were scarce. Something drastic had to be done. The closure of the huge Beckton gasworks made the local employment situation worse, but provided a possible site for redevelopment, subject to the problem of the polluted land being detoxified. The Docklands Joint Committee, formed by the Greater London Authority, together with five local boroughs, suggested new housing and industry for Beckton. Drainage of the marshy land was commenced and so was building, but little progress had been made by the end of the 'seventies.

In 1979 Michael Heseltine, the newly appointed Conservative Secretary of State for the Environment, who had become aware of the major problems while a shadow minister, decided that a new public body should be set up, with sufficient backing and powers to find solutions. The money would come from the Treasury but some of the powers would have to come by way of transfer from the local authorities. Any new scheme might well get nowhere if, say, the three chosen local borough councils remained in control of all planning decisions. Margaret Thatcher, the Prime Minister, approved of Heseltine's ideas; Parliament responded by passing the appropriate legislation and so the London Docklands Development Corporation (LDDC) was born. Public funding followed in different tranches over the years, but one of the main presents given to the new infant was by Geoffrey Howe, as Chancellor of the Exchequer, who made a large part of the Isle of Dogs an Enterprise Zone, with even greater incentives for investors, in the form of tax benefits, than the rest of the area had been given.

The LDDC came into existence legally on 2 July 1981, but the previous year had seen some significant activity. Heseltine had appointed Nigel Broackes, a very successful developer, as the first chairman, with Bob Mellish as his deputy. Together they had chosen Reg Ward as the first chief executive. That turned out to be an inspired choice, as Ward, who had earlier been the chief officer of both a London borough and a county council, proved to be a combination of wizard and dynamo, who got things done.

Benson had kept an eye on the progress of Heseltine's ideas through their Parliamentary stages and would have liked to be the first chairman of the new Corporation. He felt that his experience in the years before he joined MEPC, coupled with that acquired or honed during his time with that company, was a highly relevant qualification. He had presided over the development of many town centre projects, mainly commercial, but some with a residential element also. Some of those developments had been taken on only after a request from the city or town council concerned. Fred Roche, the architect who had acted as the chief executive of the Milton Keynes Development Corporation and later participated in the reconstruction of Docklands, was once asked whether his experience with the new town, now city, was comparable with his Thames-side work. He replied:

> Oh yes. Because I actually think that development almost anywhere you do it in the world, has many similar characteristics, whether it is in a rural or in an urban environment. There are different constraints and different opportunities but many of the problems are the same.

Benson, who had been an advisor to the Department of the Environment on New Towns, had come to a similar conclusion.

When Nigel Broackes was named as the first chairman, Benson was disappointed but approved strongly of the minister's choice. He knew Broackes well as a fellow developer and was an admirer of his skills, which unusually included those of a first-class silversmith. When Broackes was approaching the end of his three years as chairman, Benson was asked whether he would care to succeed him. He responded enthusiastically and was appointed to the chair as from 2 July 1984. So as to give him an opportunity of shadowing Broackes, he was appointed as an ordinary member of the Corporation for the preceding two months as well. He greatly valued that opportunity and soon learned how much had been achieved by Broackes and Mellish — and particularly by Ward, of whom he later said he could not speak too highly, adding, 'Without Reg Ward nothing would have happened.' When Ward died in January 2011 at the age of eighty-three, the *Daily Telegraph* obituary called him 'the irrepressible mastermind' behind the major projects of the LDDC.

When Benson first met him, Ward was working very hard and regularly sleeping in his office — not that such a habit always produces efficiency. Benson's appointment to the Docklands Board was on the basis of two days' work a week. In practice he found it was more like six or seven busy half days, with a similar amount of time devoted to MEPC matters. He managed to work long hours partly because he could manage with five hours of sleep a night, but mainly because the work was both important and stimulating. Incidentally, like Broackes before him, Benson had to agree as a condition of appointment, that his property company would not seek to obtain any contract in the area covered by the Board.

When asked by the writer to explain how, even with little sleep, he could possibly fit in all the work entailed in simultaneously heading two of the country's major enterprises, Benson replied that he was very lucky with his support staff: a brilliant aide in his Park Lane office, Nicola Westcombe, and good drivers, especially Tom Hodges. In the car from Waterloo to Docklands, Benson would deal with the morning's MEPC mail with the help of a mobile phone. His aide had always opened and arranged his letters in advance and he could then dictate replies. After a morning's work for the LDDC he would usually arrive at his Park Lane office by lunchtime, sign his letters and then deal with MEPC business for the rest of the afternoon and evening. That routine was altered, of course, for foreign and domestic visits and meetings. When Benson became chairman of MEPC, Nicola Westcombe chose to stay on as aide to the new managing director, James Tuckey, and was succeeded by Lisa Fuller. She eventually followed Benson to Albright & Wilson and to Costain, as did Tom Hodges, now a family friend.

One of Ward's earliest achievements, with the support of Mellish, who had been given responsibility for housing, proved to be a ground-breaking one, as it greatly helped to open up the Docklands for the business of producing affordable accommodation for local residents. Ward found a site in Beckton, in the north-east corner of Docklands, that was suitable for housing. Beckton was on the edge of the development area in the borough of Newham and close to existing transport links. Ward suggested to some leading house builders that they should build some good affordable houses on the site that could be made available to them. Four of them, Barratt, Wimpey, Comben and Broseley, were prepared to run the minor risks involved and each agreed to build 150 family homes for sale. Those 600 houses were, despite some gloomy doubts, sold very quickly. Partly because of that success, it was not long before Beckton had 4000 new homes. The other areas followed suit.

The Corporation adopted the strategy of giving priority to those local tenants who could prove the genuineness of their claim by producing a local authority rent book. The proportion of local residents able to buy turned out to be relatively small, as few had sufficient savings or income. Later some more expensive homes were built as well, as the policy was to have a mixed population, made up partly of locals and partly of people filling some of the many new jobs that were were being created, reinforced by some buyers who merely wanted to live in an exciting new area close to the City of London.

The Corporation had one great advantage over the local authorities. Its officers were able to bear in mind the needs of London as a whole, whereas local councillors were rightly concerned with their own borough only. The Corporation was anxious to improve Docklands as a part of London, restoring them in due course to their local authorities, reinvigorated and able to play their full part in their home city. Mixed housing would bring the balance of public/private housing down from a 90/10 split to one more in line with the rest of the city.

The local authorities had sometimes refused a change of use from industrial use to housing because they hoped, in vain, to attract ship-related or other industry back to the empty warehouses. A good example of that wishful thinking and its consequences was given by Elizabeth Williamson, the author of the Pevsner *London Docklands* Architectural Guide, 1998. 'Conversion from industrial use to residential property was frustrated by zoning policies which sought to retain industrial areas in industrial use. For instance, another 1970s scheme, the remodelling of a row of warehouses in Narrow Street, Limehouse, by the designer Rae Hoffenberg, was delayed for years. It was not until the LDDC took planning control in 1981 that changes of use became generally acceptable, facilitating the mixed developments described above and, latterly, a plethora of flats.'

Bob Mellish remained as Benson's deputy for a matter of months only, as he was promoted to the House of Lords. Benson liked him as a man and as his deputy, and was sorry to lose him. Mellish told him that he had informed Harold Wilson, the former Labour Prime Minister, that he would not take the Labour whip in the Lords as he intended to sit as an independent on the cross-benches. Wilson, who knew that Mellish had resigned from the Labour Party earlier, had given the statesmanlike reply, 'In the Lords, Bob, it doesn't matter a bugger where you sit.'

It took some of the Labour councillors in control of the three local authorities, Southwark, Tower Hamlets and Newham, a long time to accept that the Corporation was actually going to benefit their constituents. They repeatedly complained that only outsiders would benefit from the new developments and that there would be no new jobs or houses for the residents. They also obstinately refused to serve on the Corporation for some time: they clearly did not want to be accused of being accomplices in an imagined Tory plot to benefit only incoming businessmen and their cronies.

Mellish described the problem as follows:

> We had terrible trouble with local authorities, in particular with Southwark. Southwark refused to cooperate. Southwark Council refused to answer letters; they gave instructions to their officers that they were not allowed to talk to ours.

Laurence Rutman, the very experienced property solicitor and partner in Ashurst Morris Crisp, who served as the LDDC's legal adviser throughout its existence (though not as an employee), remembers arranging to meet the officers of Southwark or Tower Hamlets on different occasions. They had been given strict instructions by their councils not to be in the same room as Corporation representatives. He accordingly had to arrange to have them sit in two separate rooms and then shuttle between them. Newham, he recalled, was not quite as uncooperative as the other two boroughs.

Such behaviour on the part of the leaders of the local communities was doubtless partly responsible for some of the protests and the occasional attempt to sabotage meetings arranged by the Corporation. On one occasion Benson witnessed a lorry driver deliberately unloading a number of sheep and several beehives, no doubt taken from one of the community farms, among those attending an open air public meeting, including some parents with their children. The speaker was Robin Leigh-Pemberton, later Governor of the Bank of England, who immediately announced; 'I am a bee-keeper. Sit still. Don't swot the bees and they will settle.' Everyone took his advice and the bees caused no trouble — nor did the sheep. Each of the three boroughs already had a community farm; Benson was keen to introduce more of the children of the area to animals, but this was not what he had in mind.

Instead, he encouraged the setting up of a farm at Mudchute on the Isle of Dogs, which was greatly appreciated until the land was needed for building. In the Surrey quays a small spoil tip was converted into a small ecological park — one of a significant number. When Benson arrived to attend its informal opening, he noticed three ducks flying overhead. Immediately afterwards two skylarks took off from the top of the mound and burst into song. The Corporation not only encouraged bird life with an increased number of open expanses of water and thousands of newly planted trees, but also with nesting boxes throughout Docklands. On another occasion he asked the children in Silvertown what they wanted most. They asked for a cycle track. In view of the amount of past vandalism he asked them whether they would look after it. They agreed to do so and in due course treated the track, lined with lime trees, with respect. These various ecological initiatives, like other steps taken by the LDDC, are being copied in many countries.

Benson is always keen to stress that the local community played its part in creating a better environment with better facilities; they were by no means all provided by the Corporation. One programme that he visited regularly gave him great pleasure: the Riding for the Disabled Scheme, which was mainly for children, some of whom had learning difficulties as well as severe medical problems. On one occasion when he visited the home of the scheme, by old railways arches, he could not see a single child. Puzzled, he looked inside one of the arches and saw that the children were giving their mothers introductory riding lessons. He was moved to tears.

By the time that Benson took over from Broackes a great deal had already been achieved, with obvious benefits for the local communities; despite that the leader of the Southwark Council refused to discuss anything with Benson on the phone, save to give him his somewhat startling reasons. He told Benson that he was speaking to the leader of the People's Republic of Southwark; as far as they were concerned the LDDC did not exist and so Benson could not be its chairman. Benson retorted that if the leader did not meet him, he could not know at whom to throw the rotten eggs. After a while the local politician grudgingly agreed to meet him, stating his non-negotiable terms bluntly: 'Back door of the Town Hall, Monday morning at 8.'

On a cold Monday morning Benson, who lived in Wiltshire, got up very early and arrived at the back door as commanded. There was no sign of the leader, so he waited in the freezing cold. After some considerable time had elapsed he decided to phone the MEPC office (he was still the managing director) to see whether there had been a phone message about the appointment. His receptionist said, 'No, but there's a gentleman here who says he has an appointment with you.' Benson asked her to put him on the line. The leader complained that he had been waiting for ages for Benson, who replied that he had been told to be at the back door of the Town Hall. Both broke the ice by laughing about the fiasco and met shortly afterwards at the Town Hall. From then on they always got on well enough, although the leader would have preferred not to deal with the LDDC at all. Fortunately, Benson could never be regarded by anyone as formal or unapproachable; as a result he always found it easy to get on with strangers. As several people later said to the writer, he was 'a good people person'.

In an interview in 1987, Benson made it clear that he had greater confidence in the local population than some of its leaders appeared to have. He said:

> I have more hope than most of the Docklands critics for the local population of East Enders, because I believe very firmly that these people have not only great natural resilience, which they have shown time and time again, but also great intelligence. I find it somewhat offensive when I am told by our local newspapers that we are not providing jobs for local people. All the local people have got to do is respond to the initiatives and train themselves, as everybody else will have to do, for the jobs. And the jobs will be there for them. And I have absolutely every certainty in my mind that the East Ender will take those, will be prepared to do them and will want to do them.

In response to a question he added, 'If you go into the Futures Exchange, you will find they are all East Enders. They have responded.'

Criticisms came in all shapes and sizes and Benson tried to deal with them wherever possible. He was surprised one day when Colin Amery, the architectural correspondent of the *Financial Times*, supported by the famous artist, David Gentleman, accused him of 'ignoring the natural contours of the area.' Benson invited them to come and point out those contours, as apart from man-made tips, Docklands was at river level and all flat. Gentleman conceded defeat and kindly gave him a drawing of the notional contours, now framed and on Benson's wall.

Benson could win over one or other of the opposition leaders by personal contact, and others by showing them the many new homes and facilities for the local population, but he could never please everyone. A large number of books and pamphlets about Docklands appeared during the life of the LDDC. One of the most informative was a publication in 1986 with the singular title *Dockland*, by the North East London Polytechnic in conjunction with the Greater London County Council. It contained interesting articles about the past, including several covering the work of the various professions and trades in the earlier docks. However, the Cassandra who provided the foreword included the following passage:

> The remedy imposed on London — the creation of a democratically unaccountable authority — was the beginning of a process which we are now seeing driven to a bitter conclusion, with the capital city itself plunged back into its mid-nineteenth century condition, fragmented, controlled not by unified elected government but by a muddle of quangoes and joint boards.' He went on to identify the principal villain: 'By one of

those ironies only history can provide, ten years after sailing from KGV [dock] I was elected to represent a riverside ward on Southwark Council and later in 1981, to represent Bermondsey on the GLC. As the chairman of the GLC's planning committee I became custodian of the baton handed on from Abercrombie's time only to find myself locked in battle with another ex-seaman, the present incumbent of the Chair of the LDDC.

Benson cannot recollect being locked in any heroic battles, but he does remember this particular opponent of the LDDC and all its works, who for a while was regularly offensive to him personally. Then they met socially at the Company of Watermen and Lightermen, where someone referred to Benson's time on *HMS Worcester*. The other ex-seaman asked him whether he had ever been in a swimming competition against the *Arethusa* lads of the Medway. When he confirmed that he had, his opponent said, 'We must have been competing in the same pool then.' Thereafter, though his opposition to Benson's work persisted, at least he stopped being offensive to him.

The absence of adequate transport links presented the LDDC with major problems, which were still pressing when Benson took over. Docklands generally, and the Isle of Dogs in particular, had a very limited number of roads and construction traffic often blocked those. A new Thames road bridge had been planned for the eastern edge of the Docklands area, but that idea was abandoned by the government. Speedy progress with road building was virtually ruled out by the clutter of the giant building site. There were inevitably only a limited number of bus routes in the area for the residents and anyone coming in to work. River buses could only satisfy a limited number of travellers.

If thousands of residents and commuters going to work were to be transported efficiently, an extension of the London Underground, most people agreed, would have to come into Docklands. An extension to the Bakerloo line was one possible answer, as its southern terminal was at Elephant and Castle, south of the river and near the Surrey Docks. Such an extension was considered more than once, including by the Canadian developers, Olympia & York, but it was ruled out on technical grounds. (In 2014 the Mayor of London had some good news for the really patient Londoner: the Bakerloo line may be extended from the Elephant to Hayes via Lewisham by 2040!) When the Queen's Silver Jubilee was celebrated in 1977, the Stanmore branch of the Bakerloo line was duly renamed as the Jubilee line in Her Majesty's honour. It also changed its colour on the Underground map from brown to silver.

The plan was for that line to continue south under the Thames to Waterloo, on to the Surrey docks and the Isle of Dogs, finishing north of the river at Stratford, where it would connect with the eastern part of the Central line. The trouble was finding the money for the extension, the absence of which cast considerable doubt on the viability of large developments requiring transport facilities for thousands of employees. In the Summer of 1980 the idea of an extension into Docklands was abandoned by the government and the Greater London Council on the grounds of cost. The much-needed extension to Stratford was not built until after Benson's years as chairman were over.

To many developers the idea of building in the east was ruled out by the absence of the tube. Oddly enough, one man was grateful for the abandonment of the extension in 1980, the newly appointed Reg Ward, who later wrote: 'I, for one, was overjoyed because I had been given the task of regenerating this area in a short period of time, and the promise of a railway in the year 2000, which blighted every development location it went through, really wasn't a help.' At that time, of course, he had little idea that there would soon be a massive growth of office blocks on Canary Wharf.

The large construction company, Mowlem, planned to open a small airport in the Royal Docks to the east of the Isle of Dogs, with a runway long enough to take short take-off and landing (STOL) planes of the quieter type. This idea greatly interested Benson, who flew both a fixed wing plane and a helicopter. As always happens with airports, there were objections about the danger of pollution, noise and the danger of aircraft crashing near them. A great deal had happened in the history of the airport before Benson's arrival, but some of it is worth relating here.

At the end of 1981, Ward had the idea that it might be possible to have an airport in the Royal Docks, on the quay between the Royal Albert and the King George V docks. He discussed it with Philip Beck, the chairman of Mowlem and together they consulted Bill Bryce, the chairman of Brymon Airways, the only operator then flying the Canadian de Havilland Dash 7 in Britain. Though powered by four engines, that aircraft was quiet and had short take off and landing capabilities.

Once the idea became a proposal and public knowledge, there were inevitably objections from some residents. In the summer of 1982, Ward was invited by Bryce to bring some local people on a flight by a Dash 7 from Heathrow to Plymouth, his base. One of the party Ward had selected was Patricia Holland, a feisty resident of Newham, who lived near the proposed airport site. Both her husband Patrick and his father had been stevedores. She asked if she could bring her husband along, as she had never flown before and was nervous about flying, and Ward agreed. She told the writer that she was in favour of the airport in principle, as 'we had nothing in Beckton, and that would shine a light on us.' She enjoyed the flight to Plymouth. During a buffet lunch there, Ward said that he wished more of the residents of Docklands could see the plane in action. Patricia Holland advised him in a few carefully chosen words: 'Bring the bloody thing in.'

In the following week Ward phoned her and announced, 'I'm bringing the bloody thing in.' He explained that Heron Quays, next to Canary Wharf on the Isle of Dogs, had been sufficiently levelled and that he had obtained permission for a demonstration landing and take off. He hoped that she and all her neighbours would come to see the Dash 7 there. Patricia Holland reminded Ward that transport was almost non-existent, so he agreed to provide a number of coaches, as he had done for the trip to and from Heathrow. After that demonstration, the majority of the local residents were in favour of the airport but a small number still objected and managed to delay progress. The Secretary of State ordered an inquiry which took seventeen weeks. During that time the Inspector and his technical adviser, Air Vice-Marshal Brian Young (a Battle of Britain pilot), asked for a demonstration flight, so the Dash 7 landed at Heron Quays again and then flew them around. The deliberations by the Inspector and consideration of his report by the minister took another 19 weeks, by which time Benson had arrived.

Benson's contribution to the airport was limited. He obviously encouraged the construction of the runway and terminal building, designed by Richard Seifert's practice, and very happily participated in a further demonstration to the Dash 7. With a number of others, including Docklands residents still concerned about the airport, and a senior City common councilman, Benson went to the former de Havilland factory runway at Hatfield to have a demonstration of the aircraft's performance. He had arranged that with Professor Roland Smith, the chairman of British Aerospace. During three short flights with a simulated full load, the pilot, with Benson in the co-pilot's seat, demonstrated its quietness, as well as its short take-off and landing capabilities. It also had a range that could take it to most west European capitals. Once the airport got the go ahead after the lengthy planning proceedings, it was completed very quickly by Mowlem. The proximity of the airport to central London, coupled with speedy check-in facilities, was soon found by businessmen and tourists alike to be a great boon. The runway was later lengthened and other types of aircraft were permitted to use it as well.

Mowlem's other venture, the Docklands Light Railway or DLR, did not go quite as smoothly: the trains were plagued by numerous teething problems in the early days, partly caused by a shortage of funding. Not long after his arrival Benson, accompanied by Ward, Keith Bright, the chairman and chief executive of London Regional Transport and Dr Ridley, the CEO of London Underground Ltd, attended a meeting in Whitehall. The Department of the Environment, the

Ministry of Transport and the Treasury were all represented, and Benson thought that he was going to receive a cheque for £74 m as the first tranche of the cost of the DLR. Patrick Jenkin, the Secretary of State for the Environment (who had appointed Benson), came in late and obviously harassed, followed by a very relaxed Nicholas Ridley, the Secretary of State for Transport.

Jenkin turned on Benson and demanded: 'How dare you come here without a 20-year profit plan?' Benson had never heard of the need for that and said so. He passed a note to the all-knowing Ward, asking, 'What have we done wrong?' The answer was brief, '——— if I know!' Neither of his other colleagues knew, though expressing their ignorance in slightly more formal language. A cheque for a smaller sum than expected arrived shortly after this strange meeting, largely as a result of the efforts of the junior minister, Lynda Chalker. However, this cut in funding inevitably resulted in 'designing down' to a lower budget, which brought problems of its own.

Work started on the first sections of the new railway in December 1984 and was completed in 1987. One of the major shortcomings of the DLR was that it was a sensitive driverless system. Unlike other such systems, its trains were required to cross other lines and to use points. Computers controlled all move-ment and stopped trains if there was the slightest hint of a problem. Benson soon discovered another problem: in order to keep the costs down, the trains had rigid tram axles. When the train went round a curve in the track, the contact with the electric current supply was repeatedly cut off. The Queen came to open the DLR in July 1987 and her train refused to move until the engineers had fixed some computer problems. During her journey the train made unscheduled stops, which according to a much embarrassed Benson, Her Majesty was kindly pleased to treat as being for her benefit so that she might see the sights.

Benson had the pleasure of meeting several members of the Royal Family while chairman and found them all very enthusiastic about the rebuilding of Docklands, none more so than Queen Elizabeth The Queen Mother, who recalled her visits to the East End during the bombing of 1940 and 1941 with her husband, King George VI. He discovered that she had an amazing memory and that she missed little. The Queen Mother was invited to the North Woolwich railway station, which had been turned into a small — and, as it happened, shortlived - railway museum. Much to Benson's surprise, when The Queen Mother looked out of a first floor window she remarked that a family, whose name she men-tioned, had lived in the house on the opposite corner during the Blitz. After the visit was over Benson went across to the house and asked the young woman who opened the door whether members of that family still lived there. He was told that they did not, but that they had done so until a few years earlier.

The Queen Mother is welcomed back

On The Queen Mother's next visit Benson was invited to join her in her car close to London Bridge station in Tooley Street. As the car went along the street The Queen Mother remarked that some of the houses had an unusually large number of air-bricks at their bases. Benson, who had never noticed that, despite his professional interest in buildings, saw that the observation was correct. When asked for an explanation he suggested that reason must be that the houses had

73

been built on polluted land — a great problem in Docklands — and that the builders had been obliged to include an exceptionally large amount of sub-floor ventilation. On checking later he found that he had guessed correctly, the site had been polluted, but he was still amazed by The Queen Mother's powers of observation.

Later in the same visit The Queen Mother was greeted like an old friend by some of the elderly residents, and even now one can see why. The King and Queen had been greatly admired by East Enders during the war for sticking it out in London and sharing the dangers of the bombing with them, rather than running for cover in the country or in one of the Dominions. After the King and Queen had been bombed while in Buckingham Palace, Her Majesty famously said that she could 'now look the East End in the face.'

Benson saw ample signs of the popularity of The Queen Mother when he accompanied her during her visit. At one point the Royal car was stopped outside a pub by a crowd of friendly elderly locals, some of whom called out, 'Hello, darling!' and 'Hello, Liz!' The Queen Mother was clearly pleased. When one of the older men asked, 'Are you coming in for a drink, luv?' she was out of the car like a shot. By the time Benson and the alarmed Royal protection officer had got out, she was already in the pub with the door shut behind her. They went in to find The Queen Mother with a small pony glass of beer in her hand, enjoying the company of some of her wartime fellow-sufferers.

When The Queen Mother came out of the building she was shown a small wartime memorial display that had been prepared for her visit, fronted by a wall of sandbags, with balloons flying over it. When the balloons were released an enlarged photograph was revealed, showing the King, in Royal Air Force uniform, and the Queen during one of their famous visits to the bombed docklands. The Queen Mother was visibly moved by this momento.

Much as Benson enjoyed the visits by members of the Royal Family, who were all enthusiastic about the various developments they saw, he was much more concerned to meet local people and get their views. Soon after his arrival in 1984 he had told Ward of that wish. Ward at once phoned Patricia Holland and asked whether they might come and see her. She protested that she had just moved into her newly-built house and that everything was still being unpacked. 'You've got a kettle and cups, haven't you?' the typical male replied. She agreed she had, so he immediately took Benson round to her house to meet her.

Benson learned that his hostess had a record as a concerned local citizen. She had earlier tried, without success, to get the Newham Council to do something about the construction traffic that was a persistent nuisance in the road she had just moved from — and which had included a lorry knocking down her garden

Wartime memories

wall and driving on. Patricia Holland's complaints about the dangerous roads and the lack of facilities for children, was backed up by many of her neighbours. As a result she had succeeded in getting some land from the Port of London Authority and £250,000 from the Docklands Joint Committee for a new park, named the King George V park when opened, and an urban city farm. After all that effort she found the park too dangerous for children to use, as it was used as a racetrack by local roughnecks for their trotting horses. Her efforts to stop them were met with threats to her, including one of them driving a car at her, and with her husband's car having paint stripper poured on it. The stevedore's union let it be known that their conduct was not acceptable. The troublemakers and their horses fortunately trotted off.

Benson told Patricia Holland that he was very anxious to get her views and those of her neighbours. He asked her for advice and she suggested that he attend meetings in local churches and community centres. He assured her that he would do so. She also implored him to be honest with people: to tell them if their house was in danger of being knocked down, if that was the case. He assured her that

75

there would be no trouble on that score. Benson was later able to report: 'During my first year as chairman I attended 74 meetings with community groups; and the community liaison officer and his team held a further 1,000 meetings.'

Patricia Holland later worked as a tour guide for the Corporation, showing around parties of journalists and others, and then went into that business as a freelance. She regularly gave her opinion when asked by Benson or Ward. Although opposition to the airport and to the LDDC dwindled, there were unpleasant reminders from time to time of how ruthless protesters could be. A number of disturbing phone calls were made to Benson's home in Salisbury, some threatening and others merely offensive. As Benson was out of the house most of the time, his wife Jo was the one who answered the phone. After a while Patricia Holland inquired whether Benson had received any threatening calls. She asked because she and her neighbours had all had leaflets through their door giving Benson's home phone number, so that he could be badgered there. Asked by the writer to sum up what she thought of him, she described him as 'genuine' and as 'a compassionate man who charmed people.'

To round off her story, in 1998 Patricia Holland became a Newham councillor. She felt that dockers like her husband and his father deserved to have some memorial in the former docks and spent eight years collecting for one from different sources. The sums ranged from the widow's mite to £30,000 from the developers of the Ramada hotel on a quayside, as a planning gain, and a matching sum from Newham Council. The total raised was £250,000 once more and that paid for a wonderful bronze sculpture of two stevedores and a tally clerk (posed for by her husband Patrick). It was by the Australian sculptor Les Johnson, who also made the statue of the Battle of Britain 11 Group Commander, the New Zealander, Air Vice-Marshal Keith Park, now in Waterloo Place. The statue of the three dockers is opposite Canning Town station, hard by the Royal Victoria dock and the ExCel Centre.

There was a danger of hostility on another occasion when Benson was due to speak at a public meeting. He was advised to enter the building by the back door, as there were a number of protesters at the front, waiting to greet him with a shower of eggs and rotten tomatoes — for the benefit of a waiting television camera crew. He sent them a message that he would be arriving at the front door, so the camera could film the protesters being stupid. While he would merely need to get his suit cleaned, they would have proved, on camera, how ridiculous their conduct was. The protesters clearly regarded him as a spoil sport — and had all gone by the time he arrived at the front door.

One of Benson's greatest satisfactions was seeing the new homes going up in their hundreds. Some were new houses or flats in newly erected blocks, while

The dockers remembered

others were in converted warehouses that were worth keeping. Some rundown council blocks of flats were renovated, others were sold to developers for renewal and sale of the flats to private buyers. When new buildings were put up close to an old warehouse, the architects were required by the Corporation to have regard for the old style of building, without being asked to copy it. All homes were to be modern in every respect and to provide for a mixed-generation population. Wherever possible private or public gardens were to be provided, as well as adequate and discreet parking. Large numbers of trees were planted wherever possible. Shortly after taking over from Broackes, Benson praised him and his team for their commitment generally, adding, 'And finally, because of the old bad image of Docklands as London's "backyard", they'd decided that design standards of building and architecture had to be higher than anywhere else in London.' He was more than content to continue with those same higher standards.

It should be added that while some of the new architecture has been praised by professional journals, rather more of it has been given the thumbs down. Bill Jack, the chairman of British Design Partnership, who chaired the Corporation's planning committee from 1991 to 1998, explained it to the writer in the following way. At first, when the Corporation was desperate to get developers and builders to start building in Docklands, it was not too fussy about what it accepted: it was anxious to get the ball rolling. Once the area had caught on and one developer after another was anxious to participate in the great adventure, the Corporation could, and did insist on higher standards of design. The message soon got through that a good design would be approved more readily than a poor or mediocre one.

Benson played his part in one architectural gain. He was sitting next to Lord Blakenham, chairman of the Pearson publishing group, at a conference, and pointed out to him that the design for the group's proposed printworks for the *Daily Telegraph* in Docklands was disappointing. Benson said he thought it a pity that Pearsons were going to put up something resembling a huge shed. Lord Blakenham accepted the offer of a helicopter ride to see the area. Shortly afterwards the idea of a monstrous shed was abandoned and Nicholas Grimshaw, a leading architect, was instructed to design the attractive printworks which can now be seen in Blackwall.

New housing reinforced the need for new shops, especially supermarkets. Asda built one on the Isle of Dogs and then a second in Beckton. One of the developments near the second Asda interested Benson for a number of reasons. It was built by Barratts on land provided by the Development Corporation and financed by the Housing Corporation. Work started soon after his arrival and was completed in June 1985. The development comprised twenty-four flats and six bungalows for the East London Housing Association, which were all allocated to elderly local residents.

One of the large-scale riverside conversions that greatly impressed Benson had been completed shortly before he joined the LDDC: the Thames Tunnel Mills, converted very skilfully for the London and Quadrant Housing Association. The old mill, which had been empty for ten years, was converted into seventy flats for single people, to the design of the architects Hunt Thompson. Priority was given to residents and former residents of Rotherhithe. In 1985 that development was given an award by the Civic Trust.

When he was later chairman of the Housing Corporation, one of Benson's welcome tasks was to assist housing associations with funds made available by the Department of the Environment. He soon realised that they were quite often hamstrung by being unable to produce satisfactory accounts when applying for commercial funding. He proposed that in future they should keep proper accounts that more closely followed normal commercial practice. With such accounts they could prove that they had a stable financial background. The Minister duly approved the suggestion and the proposed change was implemented without the need for any legislation.

One of the most attractive features of the rebuilt Docklands is the use made by the planners and architects of water. Before the Corporation was established, some of the old docks had already been filled in, prompting Benson to comment at one meeting:

> Would you believe it, we are digging a canal system in the 140-acre infilled Surrey docks, at a cost of £7 m, to provide a water orientated environment. Here it was that warehouses, that would today be listed buildings, were crashed into the water to make more land!

The Corporation made a point of saving as many stretches of water as possible and reopening others, so that a large proportion of homes could have a water frontage or a view of water nearby. The luckiest residents, obviously, were the ones who had a new home on the river. The planners and architects used their ingenuity in different ways.

In The Lakes project in Rotherhithe the plan was for 174 new homes, but by 1970 the original dock on the site had been filled in. A new shallow lake was incorporated in the new development. In several other schemes new small canals were constructed. One commentator wrote: 'The LDDC has already transformed the Surrey Quays infrastructure by providing linked canals and walkways, giving it a delightful Amsterdam-type atmosphere.' Incidentally, Dutch and Danish developers and their architects produced some of the most attractive contributions. The Royal Victoria Dock Partnership not only built new housing on specially built piers jutting out into the old dock waters, but also cut small inlets into the existing quays so as to maximise the number of waterside sites. Benson, with his interest in sailing and other water sports, was keen to encourage such ideas. He was sorry that the first plan for a 2000 m rowing course had to be abandoned as the only site then available proved just too short. Waters for sailing fortunately were readily available.

Benson, with his love for, and experience of the sea, was always anxious to preserve the maritime and dock heritage of the area. He encouraged the preservation of cranes and other reminders of the past; Ward had fortunately earlier saved the cranes from being sent for scrap. Benson was particularly keen to ensure that some ships, old and new, should find a berth in Docklands. There was one classic ship that he was anxious to see preserved there: the last remaining cable-layer, one of those amazing British ships that had laid most of the original undersea cables around the globe. He was a director of the charity, The Historic Cable Ship *John W Mackay* Trust, but unfortunately the estimated costs proved so high that the restoration plan had to be abandoned. Benson regarded the loss as disastrous not only for Docklands but also for the country and its maritime heritage.

A less ambitious private project proved more viable. The *Tereza Joanne* was a double-hulled crane barge from Gdansk, which had lost her crane (and possibly her way) and was first employed as a Thames landing stage for water buses. She was then taken to the King George V dock and used for a time as a water sports centre. She is still there, but has been promoted to entertainment use, including licenced weddings — if you can call those entertainments.

Benson received a compliment that went well with his love of water. Edward Erdman, a well known estate agent, had been one of the experts he had consulted as a young man when considering setting up on his own. Erdman had asked him one question only, when asked for his advice: 'How well do you know Brixton?' Benson, then still a provincial, admitted that he did not know it at all and was told, 'Well, lad, when you've learned your London, you can come back to me.' Years later, when Benson was chairman of the LDDC, Erdman was the chairman of a housing association that had built flats close to the Thames in Wapping. Erdman asked him whether he might name one of the association's quays after him. Very flattered, he agreed at once. His ego was somewhat deflated on his next visit to Wapping when he saw that 'Benson Quay' was, in his carefully measured words, 'about a metre long.'

There were two further occasions when Benson thought he was being complimented for his work in docklands. He was in the Strand one day when a woman came up to him. 'I think you are marvellous for all you are doing over there,' she said, waving vaguely towards the east. Two days later, in the same place, another woman said, 'It's wonderful what you are doing for London.' Benson felt encouraged until she spoilt it by adding, 'The Globe is going to add marvellously to the theatre scene.' He had twice been mistaken for Sam Wanamaker, the American actor and director responsible for the rebuilding of Shakespeare's Bankside theatre, who was fourteen years older than him — but both of them had friendly, well-worn faces, so there was some similarity.

A few days later Benson saw Wanamaker on a Thames ferry and told him about the two encounters; he roared with laughter.

CHAPTER SEVEN

Canary Wharf

The most famous commercial development in the London Docklands was undoubtedly the one built on Canary Wharf on the Isle of Dogs. It had an extraordinary beginning. The restaurateur Roux Brothers were looking for a 5000 square feet site to develop for their business and consulted their banker, Michael von Clemm, the chairman of the Credit Suisse First Boston (CSFB). He was invited to lunch by the Corporation. As chance would have it, the lunch was arranged on an old barge, moored alongside the large open door of a warehouse on Canary Wharf. The banker looked into it and said to Reg Ward, 'I don't know why we don't take a warehouse like that and convert it into a 200,000 square feet back-up office.' As Ward commented later: 'Many more visits to Docklands followed and the back-up office concept changed to consideration of a front office development. The rest is history.'

The first reason that foreign bankers and other financial institutions became increasingly interested in moving into large new buildings in Docklands, was that in October 1986 the so-called Big Bang had opened up the sale of stocks and shares to all comers. A second reason was that the City of London was unable to provide sufficient office space with large areas suitable for trading floors. In America these were known as 'large open area floors' or LOAF. The third was the generous financial inducement offered by the Government tax concessions, especially in the Enterprise Zone in much of the Isle of Dogs. That made building in Docklands much cheaper than in the rest of London.

Von Clemm consulted G. Ware Travelstead, First Boston's property adviser, who in due course arranged for the setting up of a new company with the name Canary Wharf Development Co. Ltd. CSFB had a thirty per cent interest in it, as did Morgan Stanley, while First Boston on its own took the remaining forty per cent. Travelstead got the Chicago architects Skidmore, Owings & Merrill to draw up plans for Canary Wharf, showing twenty-two buildings with a total of 10 m square feet. The estimated cost of building was £2.5 bn. Benson, who had experience of what had been considered as large developments on three continents, remembered, 'I think we all blinked four times when we actually had the drawings uncovered for us. It was a shock because it was so huge, exciting because it was so new and it really could transform the whole of the East End.'

After careful consideration of the proposal, Benson and the Corporation agreed in principle to provide Travelstead's consortium with a 200-year lease of seventy-one acres for the planned buildings, at an annual rent of £400,000 per acre; all subject to a contribution of £68 m to provide for the necessary extension of the Docklands Light Railway to Bank tube station from the existing Tower Gateway terminal. Unfortunately, Benson was unable to promise the early arrival of the Jubilee Line.

Travelstead was told by the consortium that they would only proceed once he had managed to pre-let 2 m square feet of the first buildings — a fifth of the total planned area. He was unable to comply — partly because English financiers were reluctant to move away from the traditional City financial district — and so two of the companies pulled out as backers, leaving First Boston on its own. The Department of the Environment was getting concerned about the delays and also worried that Ward was possibly allowing Travelstead too much leeway. Sir Terry Heiser, the Permanent Secretary, called a number of meetings of the central characters involved. To bring matters to a head, Benson told Travelstead that he would have to sign the master agreement with the LDDC by midnight on 17 July 1987 or the whole deal would have to be called off. Travelstead realised that without sufficient backers in place, he could not sign and so dropped out of the running. Benson's firmness on this occasion certainly saved the development of Canary Wharf from a long period of drift — and possible abandonment.

Paul Reichmann of the Canadian Olympia & York private company, learned of the opportunity and grasped it with both hands. He felt confident about London's future as a European and world leading financial city and hurried there. Anthony Bianco in his comprehensive biography, *The Reichmanns*, quotes him as saying: 'The importance of London as a worldwide center of financial services industry has been reaffirmed. There is and will continue to be a demand for prime office space in London which, for various reasons, the traditional business districts cannot begin to satisfy.' He had added the firm prophecy, 'For the next decade, we expect London to be the strongest commercial real estate market.'

Olympia & York were made the same offer of advantageous terms for the Canary Wharf site as had been offered to Travelstead. The only additional welcome term, was that they would also pay £2.5 m for job training for local residents. Reichmann was confident, in view of their current substantial rental receipts, that he and his family could finance the whole first stage of the project, without the assistance of any bank.

With Sir Terry Heiser

Late on Friday 17 July 1987, Michael Dennis, a Christian representative of the Canadian Olympia & York, signed the agreement with the Corporation at the offices of Clifford Chance, the solicitors for one of the parties. The drafting of the contract had proved a considerable challenge for Laurence Rutman, the Corporation's legal adviser, as there had never been a transaction quite like this in the UK. Fortunately, Rutman, after studying law in England, had gone to Yale Law School as a Fulbright scholar, and had made a number of friends there. Through his contacts he was able to obtain copies of the contracts that had been used for Reichmann's massive Manhattan project, as well as for the Baltimore regeneration scheme. They proved invaluable as precedents, despite the need for many variations.

Reichmann himself was unable to be at the signing as he was an observant orthodox Jew: by that time his Sabbath was about to begin. He missed a great occasion. After both parties had executed the agreement, the staff of the solicitors brought in champagne and a large cake they had made in the shape of a canary, enjoyed by all those able to attend, including a gratified Benson and a disappointed Travelstead.

Unfortunately for Olympia & York, the crash which came as soon as 19 October, wiped $1 bn off their stockholding. Paul Reichmann nevertheless proposed putting up twenty-four buildings instead of the previously planned twenty-two with an extra 2 m square feet of offices. The first stage was to comprise eight towers. He took on Stanley Honeyman, the former director of both EPC and MEPC, to assist with the project. Like Travelstead, Reichmann also failed to obtain sufficient tenants in advance. He could have obtained more but for one stubborn decision of his. He was determined not to let any of the new development at a lower rent than £27 to £30 per square foot, even though he was prepared to grant generous fitting out allowances and other financial inducements.

Despite the financial problems, in November 1987 Lord Young, Mrs Thatcher's Secretary of State for Trade and Industry, drove the first pile into the mud at Canary Wharf. For good measure, Mrs Thatcher came over in May 1988 and managed to drive the first pile again. A photograph shows the Prime Minister sitting in the operator's seat of the powerful machine used, with Benson leaning into the cab. Quite why he thought he could instruct her in the operation of a machine he had never operated, clearly puzzled the two bystanders, Paul Reichmannn and Reg Ward. After that, everyone adjourned to Inigo Jones's Whitehall Banqueting Hall for what Benson called a Love-in, with the Prime Minister and Paul Reichmann praising one another. Benson was quite content, as the whole project needed not only ministerial approval at all levels but also publicity for Canary Wharf.

Benson next met Reichmann when on a business trip to Canada, as he wanted to give him some friendly financial advice. He asked him for fifteen minutes of his time, but instead they spent a pleasant two hours together. Benson told him that he thought he was foolish to keep on helping out failing Canadian corporations when they had financial difficulties: he was merely creating more for himself. Reichmann revealed a love for Canada with a passion, and made it clear that he was happy to run some risks to help out a struggling Canadian enterprise.

Some time after Benson had given up the chairmanship of the LDDC at the end of October 1988, Olympia & York went into liquidation, but Reichmann managed to get a fresh consortium together, which eventually got the master plan built, with most impressive results. Shortly after the formation of the rescue organisation, Reichmann asked Benson to come and see him in New York. Benson, who was no longer at the LDDC, flew over at his own expense and was gratified to hear Reichmann say that he was his choice as the man to get the Canary Wharf plans implemented. Benson flew back to London full of hope, but heard no more about that wonderful job. Years later an embarrassed Reichmann told him that one of the principal members of his consortium had vetoed his appointment, but he gave no explanation for his failure to notify him of that at the time.

Michael Heseltine felt guilty about the initial collapse of Reichmann and his company. In his autobiography he wrote that Paul Reichmann had been made welcome,

> and as part of the deal the government agreed to extend the London public transport system — ultimately by way of the Jubilee Line and in the interim by the Docklands Light Railway — out to this part of East London. For Paul the two projects went hand in hand; Canary Wharf without effective lines of communication would, as a concept, be dead in the water.

That was a very apt metaphor. The former Cabinet Minister added frankly: 'I had great sympathy. Canary Wharf was now going into receivership. I believed that to a large extent this was the government's fault. How could one let office space in buildings, however prestigious, if people couldn't get there?'

While the water almost surrounding and cutting up the Isle of Dogs was one of the reasons that adequate transport links had to built above and below ground, at least the construction on Canary Wharf was facilitated by it. At Benson's insistence, no less than eighty per cent of the materials were brought in by barge, most of them having been trans-shipped at Tilbury, a few miles down river.

Reichmann once proudly showed Benson around one of his large buildings when it was nearing completion. Suddenly he pointed to a line of large granite floor tiles that ran straight along the ground for some way. 'Look at those!' he said with disgust. 'That line between them isn't straight.' Benson could see nothing wrong with the work and was interested to learn later that it had been relaid, regardless of expense. Reichmann was intensely proud of his oversize baby and clearly could not bear to see any blemish on it. Roger Squire, a former MEPC development director, who was with the LDDC for its last seven years as assistant, and then joint chief executive, also commented to the writer on the high quality insisted on by Reichmann for his buildings and their setting.

The man who had dumped bees and sheep to wreck one of Benson's meetings was a local opponent of the Corporation, Peter Wade, who never became a supporter of its work. However, he was prepared to work for the Canary Wharf development, as he correctly realised he could get something out of it for the benefit of the local community. He was offered a job as a community relations officer, which he accepted. As a result of his efforts he managed to obtain significant sums for various community projects. As well as those, the local

With Jo at the Palace

residents increasingly appreciated the benefits that the rebuilding of Docklands could bring for them and their children. However, many local councillors could never get over the 'non-democratic' deprivation, by a democratic and sovereign Parliament, of their planning controls and their transfer to the Corporation for some years. During the lifetime of the Corporation, incidentally, their powers were restored to them piecemeal, as and when the work on the infrastructure and amenities of various areas were sufficiently completed.

The success of Canary Wharf, aided by the eventual arrival of the extended Jubilee Line, paid for in part by the developers, led to increased interest on the part of others, who became increasingly aware of the opportunities for enterprise. Some years later the start of work on the new railway line crossing the capital, basically from west to east but taking in Docklands, named Crossrail, proved an additional attraction. The first chairman of Crossrail appointed by the Labour Mayor of London, Ken Livingstone, was Christopher Benson.

Benson had been appointed as chairman of the LDDC for three years but was reappointed for an additional sixteen months, to the end of October 1988. He enjoyed his job very much and appreciated the opportunity to contribute to the rebuilding of the Docklands. His public services had been recognised by his being appointed a Knight Bachelor in the New Year Honours list in 1988. Although reconstruction was not completed, the Corporation was finally wound up on 31 March 1998. The final report showed what had been achieved in the preceding seventeen years. Even the sternest critics of the idea of the government-aided scheme must have been pleased to see some of the figures, especially those relating to housing and employment. 24,000 new homes had been built for a population of 83,000, made up of local people and outsiders attracted into the area. 85,000 people had jobs there, many of them in the newly built 25 m square feet of commercial or industrial space. Today there are well over 100,000 people working at Canary Wharf alone.

It was unfortunate that Reg Ward could not stay on at least until Benson's term of office came to an end in 1988. Ward had left thirteen months earlier, in September 1987. There was no doubt about the fact that Ward was a wonderful man, who thanks to his genius and hard work, had achieved more than most people could ever have done. He had numerous good ideas, such as his proposal that commercial undertakings should be encouraged to come to Docklands. Unfortunately, as well as refusing to answer a Minister's phone call, because he did not want to hear an unacceptable message, he often bent or ignored the rules, despite warnings from civil servants about the need to comply with the basic rules applying to publicly funded bodies.

Laurence Rutman, the legal adviser from the start, also regularly had to caution him, 'Reg, you can't do that. It isn't permitted.' Ward's response to Rutman was quite often a petulant one, such as: 'Oh, you people! You're always trying to stop me doing something.' He also made a number of promises that could not possibly be kept. Roger Squire, for one, had the unpleasant task of trying to deal with some of them in later years. In all the circumstances, Benson had felt obliged to make the regrettable decision to let Ward go. After his death the obituaries in the Press were rightly complimentary about his achievements, but *The Times* may have been justified in adding, 'The corns he has stepped on would have filled more shoes than even Imelda Marcos possessed.'

A retired general was appointed as Ward's replacement. He was a former member of the Royal Engineers, a Corps with a distinguished record of building major projects, including docks and railway systems — not to mention super-vising the building, in Docklands, of massive parts for the 1944 Normandy invasion Mulberry harbours. He came to see Rutman to obtain an outline of the work of the LDDC, including the legal provisions governing its actions. The lawyer gave him a detailed briefing that lasted for more than an hour, and noted

With Michael Heseltine and Michael Honey, Ward's successor

with some surprise that the general did not take a single note. Next morning he resigned his new post. His successor was Michael Honey, of whom Benson wrote shortly afterwards: 'I am happy that the new chief executive has declared from the beginning of his tenure that he is concerned about local people and their needs.'

During his years with the Corporation Benson met not only many opponents of the LDDC but also many supporters. He met a large number of people and made a number of friendships. An early contact seemed to get off to a bad start but ended well. Benson was introduced to Jim Thompson, the Bishop of Stepney (later of Bath and Wells), at an evening event. He kicked himself later for his choice of words, as he used the expression 'market forces' in the course of making some remarks. Next morning he heard the bishop as the speaker on the BBC radio daily programme, 'Thought for the Day'. The bishop expressed his dismay at having heard the expression 'market forces' used, and added that he feared that the Docklands logo of toucans might be replaced by that of vultures. Despite that Benson and the bishop cooperated on different local issues and became friends.

When Benson had finished his four-and-a half years with the LDDC, he was especially gratified to have his interest in, and efforts for the community acknowledged. At the last meeting of the Corporation board that he attended, a long-standing member, Lewis Moss, expressed his admiration and appreciation for the way in which he had carried out his work — and particularly his work within the community. That was capped by the arrival at the meeting of the chairman and vice-chairman of the Association of Island [of Dogs] Communities, who presented him with an early painting of Docklands to thank him for all the 'marvellous work' he had done on behalf of Docklands residents.

He also received a number of warm letters. By then Nicholas Ridley was the Secretary of State for the Environment. After expressing his 'thanks and warm appreciation for your invaluable contribution to the development of Docklands,' he added: 'Under your leadership for the past four years, the Corporation has secured the future of Docklands as a major growth area after many years of decline and decay. You helped the Corporation move into the second phase of its life, securing private sector investment to follow the initial infrastructure and reclamation work. You were responsible for securing the Canary Wharf development, following difficult and delicate negotiations. I know that you have been personally and closely involved in a number of other major deals which have helped ensure the successful regeneration of Docklands.'

Benson had always got on extremely well with the Department's Permanent Secretary, Sir Terry Heiser, whose farewell letter included the passage, cited earlier: 'But I want to say that I have no doubt that what is happening now in Docklands will figure in histories of the metropolis which will be written in the years to come. So will you.'

Local Labour politicians, whether in Parliament or one of the three councils, regularly made a point of saying that they disagreed with the idea of Parliament transferring any of the powers of local authorities to an unelected quango. Accordingly, one letter that was particularly welcome came from Peter Shore (later Lord Shore of Stepney), the left-wing Labour MP for Stepney and Poplar, and Heseltine's predecessor as Secretary of State for the Environment. He wrote to Benson: 'I am most grateful to you for the help that you have given to myself and my colleagues over these past four years and on so many questions affecting the development of the Docklands and the interests of our constituents.'

There may still be some residents of Docklands who regret that outsiders took over some of their local councillors' powers, and then created chaos for years with contractors' traffic, building not only housing but also offices, shops, schools and transport links. They must be comparatively small in number by now, and are probably not conscious of the fact that they resemble some of the characters in the famous Monty Python film, 'Life of Brian', in which the question was repeatedly put: 'What did the Romans ever do for us?' followed by the reluctant concession, 'Well apart from ...'

Let us be bold enough to ask the question: 'What did the LDDC do for us?' For the three London boroughs of Tower Hamlets, Southwark and Newham it paved the way for regeneration in place of dereliction. It made provision for well designed and soundly built housing for thousands, together with many facilities for the local residents of all ages. For London as a whole it helped to bring the Docklands back into the mainstream of London life, as a living part of a great city.

The North American buildings on Canary Wharf, with its landmark 800 foot tall stainless steel tower at 1 Canada Square, would never have been built without the LDDC and the favourable terms it could offer as incentives to developers. That tower, incidentally, was designed by Cesar Pelli to be 850 foot tall, but had to be reduced in height by fifty feet because of the glidepath of aircraft landing at the new airport in the Royal Docks. Without those rival buildings spurring it into activity, the City of London might well have continued to rest content with its pre-existing inadequate stock of office accommodation, despite the urging of the chairman of its Planning and Communications Committee, Michael Cassidy. The City would then have struggled to be considered one of the main financial centres of Europe and the world. (Ward had been so cross with the Lord Mayor and his colleagues at one point, that he thought of threatening to call, that which he regarded as his patch, Eastminster.)

To be fair to the City, as Benson has pointed out, it was difficult to know what was needed once Canary Wharf had provided a large amount of new office space. When the City chief planner, Peter Rees, retired after twenty-nine years as such in 2014, he told the *Evening Standard*:

> We asked banks what they needed over the next ten years. Sedgwick's chairman said: 'Good God, I'm not sure what we need in the next 18 months.' We asked two agents to estimate what was needed to cope with Big Bang. One said: '20 million feet.' The other said: 'Zero, Canary Wharf will suck up the space.' We took the average — 10 million feet. That turned out about right.

The people of London, including the East Enders, had during the bombing of the 1939–45 war defiantly stated, 'We can take it.' The architects, surveyors, engineers and builders of the new Docklands, together with its transport links, had shown the world, 'We can make it.' When one recalls how close Paris came to being awarded the 2012 Olympics, it is safe to say that without the LDDC and all those who were bold enough to take advantage of the opportunities it offered, London would not have been chosen as the venue for a third time. The gods on Mount Olympus were no doubt placated when they saw that the efforts of Olympia & York had contributed significantly to the successful bid for the Olympics Games.

Shortly after his retirement from the LDDC, Benson said: 'Apart from mixed feelings of intense pride and growing humility, it gives me great pleasure to hear Australians, Americans, Germans, French, Japanese and Chinese in their own countries citing London's Docklands as the greatest example of urban regeneration in the world — an example they wish to emulate.'

Since then Benson has watched with interest the continued growth of developments and job opportunities in Docklands, thanks in part to the improvement of the transport links. The Docklands Light Railway has been extended since his time there, with one of the additional spurs serving the airport in the Royal docks, and with lengthened trains. Two new tunnels under the river now take the line to Greenwich and Woolwich. The Jubilee Line has tied the area into the London Underground network, so that the commuter arriving at, say, Waterloo station by train, need only catch one tube train to get to Canary Wharf. The Brunels' twin-track pedestrian tunnel under the Thames is now used by the Overground trains, which link Southwark with Wapping and, between them, circle London. Finally, Benson has had the great joy, having been its first chairman, of seeing construction work started on the Crossrail railway line. Light railway, Underground and Crossrail will all have a station at Canary Wharf. A businessman arriving at Heathrow airport will soon be able to go directly from there by Crossrail to his appointment at Canary Wharf without changing trains — a distinct improvement on the earlier obstacle course requiring half a dozen different vehicles.

CHAPTER EIGHT

The Royal Opera House

In the summer of 1982 Sir Claus Moser, the chairman of the Royal Opera House, who knew Benson as a regular attender as an opera and ballet lover, invited him to join as a director and to chair its development board. He made it clear that he wanted him for his development skills and that he was not expecting him to raise money for improvements. Benson was thrilled to be asked and accepted the offer at once. The truth was that the landmark building in Covent Garden was in trouble for a number of reasons. Built by Edward Barry and opened in 1858, it was old and showing its age. It was too small and expected to do too much, as it put on performances by both the leading opera and ballet companies. A few improvements had been made in 1964, when the two upper seating areas, the gallery and amphitheatre, had been combined and modernised. However, the building remained inefficient and a fire risk, and did not warrant inclusion in the list of the world's top opera venues.

In 1974 the removal of the Covent Garden fruit and vegetable market to a large new site at Nine Elms, south of the Thames, had made it possible to think about the enlargement of the Opera House site and the improvement of its facilities. The government then purchased just over three acres on its south side, facing Russell Street and shortly afterwards, some properties in Floral Street and Long Acre to the north. They were vested in a Development Land Trust for the purposes of the improvement and enlargement of the main building; the Opera House and the Arts Council were appointed co-trustees and beneficiaries. The mention of enlargement made it clear that some of that land was likely to be needed for that purpose, but the possibility of using the rest of the government gift for commercial and residential purposes was not ruled out. Any profits arising from a redevelopment of those 'leftover' sites could properly be used to part-fund any new work on the Opera House.

Early in 1979 Prince Charles launched an appeal for £10 m, which was quickly raised and applied to the building of an extension on the west side of the House, and behind the stage, facing James Street. That limited work was completed in

1982 and provided some urgently needed rehearsal and dressing rooms. Possibly the most welcome additions were the two ballet studios, but of great value also were the additional rehearsal rooms for the opera and the chorus. The extension was designed so that it could be linked with any future additions and improvements. However, many more fundamental changes were needed all round — and not just for the House, but also for its surroundings. That was where Moser's need to send for Benson in 1982 arose.

Benson's development board met regularly in the second half of 1982 and throughout 1983. On 6 February 1984 Benson wrote to Robin Adam, the new chairman of MEPC, about his various commitments, as he had been offered the chairmanship of the LDDC, and wanted the approval of his board colleagues before accepting it. The letter included the following information about Covent Garden:

> As a member of the Development Board of the ROH I have a spasmodic, not very demanding supervisory role. However for the past eighteen months I have devoted a great deal of my time to the task of Advisor to the House in determining the route it should take in its next major development proposals. This is now largely established but even more time is demanded during the next few weeks in selecting the architect to carry through this major undertaking.

The use of the word 'architect' in the singular was significant, as will be seen shortly.

The route referred to divided into two separate but interlinked streams. The main purpose of the redevelopment was to make the House fit for use by both the opera and the ballet companies. Benson was not alone in being appalled by the backstage conditions in which the artists and others were expected to work. The men's dressing rooms and washing facilities were primitive and the accommodation for the ballet was not much better. Scenery cloths were kept under the stage and orchestra pit, constituting a fire hazard. Scenery painting was carried out in a fly tower that was not tall enough, out of date and potentially dangerous. There was also an urgent need to make improvements in the working conditions of both the orchestra and the chorus; and to improve the facilities for the audience, including air conditioning. That entailed, among many other considerations, making sure that the ballet could be provided with adequate accommodation on site, as opposed to being based, as was the case, miles away at Baron's Court.

The secondary purpose was to make the most of the opportunities afforded by the properties given by the government. Improving them so as to increase the rental income would be one benefit. A good rental would also increase any sale price. It was becoming clear that the government was not going to fund any major works, and that it was up to the Royal Opera House to raise enough money for improvements, by a combination of sound property deals and appeals to the public. Benson's board decided that it would not rely on an outside developer, who would want to make a profit on his work, but to keep the development in-house. One of the ideas for increasing the income of the whole site, was by building a large office block on Russell Street. That idea was eventually abandoned in favour of further facilities there for the Opera House.

In August 1983 Moser wrote to the Minister of Arts asking for leave to put in a planning application. He enclosed the appraisal prepared by the development board. Approval was given — but not until June of the following year. The government then gave the necessary leave but made it abundantly clear that there would be no more contributions from central funds: the Opera House had to make sure that it did not embark on anything for which it could not pay.

The selection of the architect was probably going to be the most important decision for the development board. It was obvious that his task was going to be an extremely complicated one. He was going to have to keep Edward Barry's Opera House of 1858 substantially intact, while equipping it with all the necessary modern adjuncts of a stage suitable in every important respect for both opera and ballet performances. He would not be free to work on a separate island site: he would have to tie the new works in with neighbouring buildings of different types and ages, including listed ones. Whatever method he adopted, the result had to be a satisfactory building containing adequate space for the many people working in it, plus all their props, from a selection of scenery to costumes and ballet shoes. The scenery was going to need a much larger fly tower than the existing one; at the same time the existing sight lines for the audience should be improved. The audiences were also entitled to expect better facilities. The project would inevitably be high profile, and very much under media scrutiny at every stage. The architect would have to include in his plans provision for all the sur-roundings buildings that were available. He was going to need the skills of a juggler with the almost impossible task of keeping a dozen balls in the air.

Having regard to those and other talents required, Benson's board made a rather unusual stipulation when inviting architects to declare their interest in entering a competition and being appointed. Recognising that they were going to have to find a genius, they insisted in the first instance, at Benson's suggestion, on the applicants all being single architects, rather than established partnerships. One of the very experienced architects reading that requirement with some puzzlement was Bill Jack, a senior partner and subsequently chairman of Building Design Partnership (BDP), the largest British group, with some 1200 staff, roughly half of them architects. The second requirement that Benson and his colleagues had included was also unusual. They did not want finished designs at that stage, but submissions indicating an understanding of the major problems, and asking for the applicant's proposed solutions. Having obtained the application documents, Jack had to fly at once to Chicago on business, and read the brief carefully on the plane.

On arrival, Jack told the writer, he had a long bath and considered the qualities and particular skills he thought were essential for an architect to compete. He thought of 16 points, which included: experience of listed buildings; adding new to old; the ability to deal with a highly political scheme; the ability to deal with a very large job; experience of theatre construction. He had personally dealt with numerous large-scale projects and had designed the Haymarket Theatre for Leicester. He reckoned that he satisfied eight or nine of the sixteen necessary requirements. His major lack was of experience of listed and historical sites; his work had all been modern, with no need to tie in old buildings with his new ones. The Royal Opera House was retaining its nineteenth-century auditorium and other features, so new build would have to be linked sympathetically and in a manner that satisfied bodies such as English Heritage.

Jack wondered whether, given the scale of the problems, two architects might be acceptable. He thought of Jeremy Dixon (now Sir Jeremy), who was in practice with his wife, and who had earlier asked Jack to join him in a large project at Cambridge, which needed his muscle and know-how. He liked Dixon and thought highly of his abilities, so he asked him whether he would care to join him. Dixon jumped at the chance and soon demonstrated that he had the missing attributes, such as a deep knowledge of London and its history, and his experience of old buildings, not only in the UK but also in Italy. Dixon had an analytical approach to the problem of linking old and new, a matter that required many small decisions. Jack told the writer, 'He had a very rare talent.' He had historical references, which proved very useful in their discussions. Dixon cannot get over his good luck in having been chosen by Jack. He told the writer that Jack had little direct experience of his talents, as he had spent most of his time teaching at the Architectural Association and practised only from a bedroom in his home.

Dixon correctly identified the explanation for the fairly novel approach used by Benson and his colleagues for the contest, namely, that traditional architectural competititons were falling out of favour. What had happened was that projects had been submitted for competitions, largely judged by other architects, only to be rejected by the client. As a result a new form of competition was becoming favoured, one in which the client, such as the Opera House board, formed the jurors, who encouraged the architects to show outline designs. The

Royal Opera House was intent, he thought, on pursuing the novel idea of 'choosing an architect rather than a building'.

Jack had his registration as sole architect 'of BDP' changed, and Dixon and he put in their submission in joint names. Benson, who knew of Jack and his work, thought they made a strong pair and so raised no objection. When the two men attended as part of a shortlist, nobody raised the fact that they were not solo, but someone expressed concern that they might not be able to work together until the end of a very long project. Jack pointed out that he had worked with many other colleagues and could act as lead architect. Also, BDP were going to insure their work. Jack had, of course, agreed essentials with his partners.

Dixon fortunately knew the Opera House site well as he had used it for a student project that he was supervising at the Architectural Association. Because he had that advantage, Jack entrusted him with the slide presentation to the board once the shortlist was down to twenty-two candidates. After that the list was down to twelve. Among the problems that had to be solved at some stage, was how to provide two arcades at right angles to one another, fronting the old Covent Garden market square, and leading to a new entrance to the House at their junction. That arose when the architects on the short list were asked to prepare sketch schemes based on a full length brief, but with little time to do a detailed design, so that they only had the opportunity to express ideas at that stage. Dixon told Jack how Livorno (Leghorn) had found a solution for a similar problem in the late seventeenth century. The architect called upon to improve a piazza there had designed a six-metre wide colonnaded building to act as a skin to cover the differing old buildings. They could use a similar scheme for Covent Garden, respecting the existing colonnades but not aping them, and including discreet shops. Jack had experience of designing shops and knew that binding provisions in leases could ensure their attractive fronts were kept as designed and built, and free from modern clutter.

The short list went down to four, the other three being Richard Rogers, Edward Cullinan and Jack Diamond of Toronto. In a second interview Jack and Dixon were asked many more questions by the board about the way they were going to tackle specific problems. They gave satisfactory answers and the short list went down to two: Jack and Dixon plus Rogers. They were shortly afterwards informed that they had won the competition. (Cullinan also impressed Benson, who engaged him later to design the Chilworth Science Park, a development partnership between MEPC, Southampton University and Romsey Council.) At the last stage of the competition Sir John Sainsbury, the chairman of the main board, took over the chair from Benson. He also, fortunately, had a great deal of experience of development and building, and chaired the last two interviews with a new jury panel and advisors.

When the scheme got under way the two architects had strong support from the board. Benson was particularly important, Jack told the writer, in view of his extensive experience in the building world. He was an 'anchor man' in getting the work going, 'anchoring the project in reality when others were getting carried away.' Some of his colleagues, Jack felt, were more concerned about their own constituency. Others were very concerned to exploit the commercial potential of the site, considering the income from let premises to be highly desirable. Benson urged caution, as the opera, ballet and orchestra needed the limited extra space available. Jack described Benson as a 'well-rounded man', who appreciated the cultural comments of his colleagues. There had to be a balancing act of the cultural and practical considerations. It was like a company, but more like a village. Jack added that he and Dixon had to arbitrate between the departments when, for example, the costume head asked for more than could reasonably be made available, at the expense of colleagues' interests. Dixon told the writer that he agreed with Jack's summary of Benson's contributions.

Jeremy Isaacs, the general director of the Royal Opera House from 1988 to 1997, when the House closed down for the major rebuilding, described in his interesting and delightful book, *Never Mind the Moon*, just where the development committee fitted into the hierarchy.

> In theory the main board was the client; in practice, I was. The architects saw me as such, reporting through me, to the development board. This had a major task to perform, and a clear supervisory role and purpose: securing planning permission for a scheme to redevelop that would meet the House's need; and putting in place the managerial systems and controls that would see the job safely through to completion. Under Christopher Benson, Martin Jacomb, Kit McMahon, Angus Stirling and now, Stuart Lipton, this has been accomplished.

Isaacs in his book also gave excellent accounts of the multitude of problems encountered by the redevelopment, including the hostile activity of the local action group and the various financial crises. For example, even once a Lottery Fund grant had been approved, the instalments were paid over at the last possible minute — and almost too late.

Jack stated:

> Benson was very practical: he had common sense, and I depended on him. He had a very easy manner to relate to; he didn't waste words but was a plain speaker. He had a very quick mind; you did not have to explain too much. It was a very complicated project; having an individual with a clear incisive mind made it very easy to put points over.

Although the design brief originally called for its complete replacement, once appointed the two architects decided to incorporate some of the original Floral Hall adjoining the Opera House and also designed by Barry. A fire had virtually destroyed it and it was being used for scenery storage and car parking. They specified that six bays of the hall should be rebuilt as a foyer for the public in performance intervals, with bars and eating facilities for use then and at other times. Alan Baxter, a leading structural engineer with experience of historic buildings, had been appointed immediately after the architectural competititon. He knew where some of the original pieces of wrought iron were to be found. They eventually traced the original ironworks, which still had the moulds used in the 19th century. Benson was particularly pleased when the finished wrought iron skeleton was laid out for checking in Docklands.

Because of his heavy commitments as BDP's chairman, Jack found he was only able to get to the office in nearby Percy Street, that he and Dixon had opened for the Opera project, in the afternoon. He could then work on into the evening, but he was rarely available in the morning. When Dixon asked him whether he could spare more time, he had to say he could not. They discussed who could be brought in to help them and agreed on Edward Jones, a close friend of Dixon's then in Toronto. They phoned his office in Canada but were told by his secretary that he was on the phone. When they hung up their phone rang immediately. It was Jones, who did not know they had just tried to get him. He had called to ask whether there was any chance of his joining them. Jones came almost at once and formed a separate partnership with Dixon. He proved a very useful and talented addition to the team's leadership.

In July 1988, when Benson was still a member of the Opera House board, he persuaded MEPC and its Australian subsidiary company, to sponsor a Gala performance there by the visiting Australian Ballet in the presence of the Queen. It was the Silver Jubilee of the Ballet and the bicentenary of the arrival of the First Fleet in New South Wales, under the command of Captain Arthur Phillip RN. The proceeds of the event were to be split between the Opera House Development Appeal and the Australian Ballet Development Fund. The glossy programme included a revealing — and almost pathetic — note about the Opera's Development Appeal. It pointed out that since the £10 m raised for the extension which was opened in July 1982 — exactly six years earlier — the appeal had raised a further £1 m.

Fortunately, it was clear to Sir John (later Lord) Sainsbury, who had replaced Moser in the year before, that collections, even with the help of the Monarch, were not going to get the place rebuilt. He agreed to provide an initial gift of £25m, as did Vivienne Duffield. The new National Lottery, introduced by John

Major's government, provided a substantial amount that could not have been foreseen at the outset of the scrabble for funds, so the need for parsimony went. There was no longer such a pressing need to think about significant income from rentals or the sale of rented properties. The work proceeded slowly but steadily. Jack appointed a BDP architect, Charles Broughton, to act as the site director. Broughton was skilled in directing architectural operations during construction on large projects, and he brought this skill to the team's leadership. The in-house chief executive in charge of development from 1988 was Dick Ensor, who was replaced for the main building stage by John Fairclough.

Dixon has emphasized how there were other strokes of luck. When John Major escorted his opera-loving wife, Norma, to the Opera House, he mentioned that National Lottery funds should be available within a year. As a result of that, the Opera was the first in the queue and succeeded in obtaining a grant. Had it been further down the queue it might have received nothing. There was some indignation on the part of the public when the Lottery paid a large sum for Sir Winston Churchill's papers, and a distaste for the idea of public funding for 'posh' projects.

The Covent Garden Residents' Association had a great success a few years earlier in opposing the plan for a road to be driven straight through the centre of the market area. The Association, led by an enthusiastic architect, also opposed the Opera House development, on the grounds that the local community would suffer from any major building project. Dixon pointed out to the writer that the fact that shortage of money and other factors had stretched out the design period over many years, was a blessing in disguise. The architects were able to deal with different areas in small parcels and to change their minds as and when necessary. The height of the fly tower was one of the major concerns for the planning authority, so the architects had to be careful to ensure that the Opera House did not loom over the area like a bully, and that the local residents had nothing to fear.

The protests of the residents, particularly those of their architect leader, put the building programme back some two years. As it turned out, thanks to that delay, the Opera House had avoided starting work on a potentially disastrous version of the project and was thus able to take advantage of the National Lottery. It gave Dixon, later, some satisfaction to be able to thank the leader of this opposition for his 'indispensable help' — without which the redevelopment might have come to a premature end.

The work was completed in 1999. Dixon received a knighthood in the following year for his wonderful contribution. Jack has never received any official recognition for his.

Three footnotes. The first relates to a further collaboration between Jack (as BDP once more) and Dixon during the time they were working on the Royal Opera House and while Benson was still chairman of the London Docklands Development Board. Together they designed a housing development at Dudgeon's Wharf, now Compass Point, on the Isle of Dogs and on the river. Dixon's knowledge and love of London architecture was evident in the carefully designed houses. However, there was more to it than that: the houses facing the river had stepped gables. *Building Design* stated:

> The riverside terrace is taller than the remainder and less obviously London in inspiration. The references are Dutch, though as much in the Dutch Pont Street style of Norman Shaw and Ernest George as the real thing.

The builders were the Costain Group, of which Benson was to be chairman. Bill Jack was later appointed a non-executive director of the Docklands Development Corporation and served as the chairman of its planning committee in the years 1991–98, that is, some time after Benson's had completed his four-and-a-half years as chairman of the board.

The second point is that Benson's flying experience turned out to be of great benefit to Dixon. He mentioned to Benson one day that he was dreading an impending flight to Canada, as he had a fear of flying. Benson assured him that most people have that fear merely because they hate being in an enclosed space with no opportunity of looking the way they are travelling. He invited Dixon to come and sit in his own aircraft and arranged for a carefully briefed instructor to be available. With Benson in a back seat, the instructor let Dixon taxi the aircraft, which he did very happily, and then invited him to open the throttle and take off. Dixon flew around for a few minutes and the instructor then landed. Dixon's fear of flying had flown.

Finally, years later, when Benson was chairman of the Salisbury Cathedral Magna Carta project, Dixon was appointed as master planner to design new housing for the Cathedral's priceless original charter, in time for the 800th anniversary of the signing in 1215. That was to be on a site adjacent to the ancient cloisters that was formerly the Bishop's garden. Benson describes Dixon's proposal as brilliant, but unfortunately there were insufficient funds for it to be implemented. That grand idea had, accordingly, to be abandoned.

CHAPTER NINE

Harrods? No Thanks!

Benson's first steps outside the property world were as a director of House of Fraser plc, from 1982 to 1986, while he was still the managing director of MEPC. House of Fraser was the leading stores group with a good reputation and included in its holdings were many of the country's leading stores. The Fraser chain included Harrods, which had been acquired in 1959. That store alone was so successful that it produced about half of the total profit for the group, which had some 27,000 employees. There was one major problem that was concerning its board of directors: it was under attack from one of its own members, a businessman with a well-deserved unsavoury reputation, who was determined to take the group over for its financial attractions. He was so obsessed with winning his takeover attempts, that his obsession could almost be said to amount to monomania. As it happened, he was to meet his match, as Benson was to witness.

Before accepting the offer of a non-executive directorship, which came from the group's chairman, Professor Roland Smith, Benson checked with his MEPC chairman and colleagues to find out whether they had any objection to his taking on an additional directorship, but with one notable exception, they had none. On the contrary, since MEPC was the freeholder of several Fraser stores, and they could see no risk of any conflict of interest, they were in favour of the idea.

The exception was The Hon. Angus Ogilvy, the longest serving non-executive director of MEPC. He knew one of the directors of House of Fraser well and had years earlier, as a merchant banker, recommended him to Lonrho, a company with extensive interests in Africa. The director in question was Roland or Tiny Rowland, by then chairman of Lonrho, and it was he who was trying to take over House of Fraser, so that its income could help out his own financially strapped company. Ogilvy had changed his mind about Rowland and begged Benson not to get involved with him. Benson listened but since he did not feel threatened or put off in any way, he thanked Ogilvy for his advice and joined the Fraser board. He knew some of the recent history and was soon put in the picture more fully.

In 1980 Sir Hugh Fraser was the chairman. He deserved the credit for the enlargement of his father's comparatively small stores empire; unfortunately he was ruining his life with gambling to such an extent that it affected the company. In 1976 he was fined under the Companies Act for offences committed when he sold Fraser shares to pay off gambling debts. The company's bankers later insisted on Professor Roland Smith, a distinguished first professor of marketing at Manchester University of Science and Technology, being appointed as his deputy.

Rowland succeeded in buying from the heavily indebted Hugh Fraser some of his shares in Scottish and Universal Investments Ltd, the Fraser family holding company, which owned 10% of House of Fraser. When Rowland attempted to buy more shares the government referred his bid to the Monopolies and Mergers Commission. When asked whether he was going to bid for House of Fraser he replied, 'We are not considering a bid at the moment.' His limited bid was approved and he immediately revealed his true intention by increasing his holding in House of Fraser to 29.9%.

In January 1981, the year before Benson joined the board, Rowland told his Fraser fellow directors that Lonrho intended to take over House of Fraser. He foolishly could not resist adding a touch of blackmail: he might be obliged to reveal the fact that Hugh Fraser's gambling debts had gone up to £10m, so that he would have to resign. Professor Smith, then still deputy chairman, and his colleagues decided that Fraser would have to go anyway and that Lonrho's approaches should be rejected. Smith became chairman of the Fraser board. Rowland's new bid was referred to the Monopolies and Mergers Commission and that time, in January 1982, he was turned down.

Smith, who had made a shrewd assessment of Rowland's character, understandably saw it as one of his principal concerns to fend off his renewed takeover approaches, and to minimise his wrecking tactics. He later told Benson that he had asked him to join the board as he regarded him as 'a street fighter', who could back him up against Rowland. Quite why Smith thought of him in those terms was something of a mystery, but he certainly knew of Benson's considerable experience and could, of course, rely on him to know the difference between right and wrong, both as far as company law and procedure was concerned, and when it came to questions of probity — and to stand up firmly for the right answer. Smith knew a great deal about the business world and had clearly decided that Benson was not a man to give in to the bullying approach favoured by Rowland. Benson liked Smith, who once claimed that he only survived his various conflicts because of his Mancunian roots, which combined arrogance with humility. (Getting the proportions right for different occasions cannot have been easy.)

Benson only encountered Rowland on a few occasions at board meetings and then found him menacing — but polite to him personally. Rowland normally sent one of his alternate directors to such meetings to be critical and obstructive, but when not plugging his line they proved highly intelligent and capable of making useful contributions. However, for public meetings Rowland and his entourage would attend but his spokesman then was usually the mellifluous Edward du Cann MP, who was also a member of the Lonrho board. Benson was soon a witness to the battle between Smith and Rowland and was present at the meeting in November 1982 at which the professor said to his adversary: 'If this is your idea of a game, please play it somewhere else in future. Get your tanks off my lawn.'

In May 1983 Rowland nearly succeeded in getting sufficient shareholder support for his takeover. He had apparently managed to persuade a large number of people that as he had been able to make a great deal of money in Africa and elsewhere, he could and would increase their Fraser dividends substantially. Some of them must have forgotten that if something looks too good to be true, it probably is. Greatly encouraged, Rowland thought he might at last get a majority at the annual general meeting in the following December. He probably decided that he would improve his chances if he were to divest himself of his existing tranche of shares for a while.

Rowland had done business with Mohamed Fayed some years earlier and had invited him to join the Lonrho board. Fayed served on it for a short while only before resigning. In 1983 the two men met again and were on reasonable terms. Rowland in October of the following year made the crucial decision to sell his Fraser stake to Fayed. There was later a dispute between them as to whether it was a legitimate sale without strings, or one with a promise to sell them back. Rowland proved his unsuitability for any office by claiming that he had only warehoused those shares with Fayed, so as to deceive the government and the take-over authorities as to the extent of his holding for a time, after which he was entitled to buy them back. Fayed maintained that it was a straightforward sale. There was no written contract to resolve the dispute: the agreement had indisputably been on a cash against documents basis, the cash being the not inconsiderable sum of £138 m, for forty-six million House of Fraser shares at Rowland's price of £3 per share. Rowland may well have felt that there was no danger of Fayed making his own bid for Fraser: he had not indicated any such desire and Rowland was sure he did not have enough money of his own.

Once Fayed had Rowland's shares, he immediately decided to make a bid for House of Fraser. Rowland was livid when he found out and managed to buy 6.3% of the shares, though it is hard to see what he hoped to do with them if he did not get his larger tranche back from Fayed. When Fayed offered to pay £4 for each of the remaining seventy per cent of shares, Smith advised the Fraser shareholders to accept the offer; but for one director, the board agreed with him immediately. The odd man out was Benson, who urged his colleagues not to accept the price offered by Fayed without having their own independent valuation. His colleagues agreed that they should obtain one. In the event, it turned out that Fayed's banking advisers had pitched their offer at the right price, and so the takeover was completed, subject to the government not blocking it. Even Rowland had sold his new 6.3% holding to Fayed.

There had been a number of discussions at board meetings and in Whitehall about the ability of Fayed, even with his brothers, to find first £138 m and then another £435 m, unless someone else was backing him. There were at least two reactions. The first was, What does it matter, as long as the price is paid in full? The other, certainly in the mind of Smith and some of his board, was, Anyone is better than Rowland: at least he will disappear. In March 1985 the government decided to let Fayed's bid go through. (For anyone wishing to read more about the heavyweight title fight of Rowland versus Fayed, Tom Bower has written a biography of Fayed, which the writer has drawn on, and a separate one of Rowland.)

Like the other stores in the group, Harrods had its separate legal identity and its own board of directors. Fayed phoned Benson and said he would like to discuss the possibility of his taking on the job of chairman of the Harrods board. Intrigued by the offer, Benson agreed to meet him and was invited to lunch at Fayed's Park Lane office, a short way down from the MEPC headquarters. Benson strolled down and was made welcome by Fayed. Benson asked why he was making his proposal, since Professor Smith was already the chairman. The response was that Smith was to be elevated to Al Fayed Trusteeship.

Drinks and lunch were served by pleasant young women dressed in the short skirts of the time. During the meal Fayed asked Benson whether he had noticed the girls. He admitted he had. 'No knickers,' his host announced. 'I beg your pardon,' the guest replied. 'No knickers — take your pick.' Benson was still sitting at the table, stunned into silence, when the next course was brought in by one of the girls.

'Do you know what this is?' his host asked. Benson enjoyed his food but failed to identify it. 'It's a truffle; I have one flown in every day from Italy. Try it: you'll find that you can — all night.' Benson said, 'I think I'm in the wrong place,' and left. He was sure that the young women were perfectly respectable, and that Fayed was only being crude because that was his way. The chairmanship of Harrods was no great loss, Benson decided: had he taken the job on, he would not have lasted long in the post. It was a moot point which of them would have been the first to end the relationship.

Despite the unpleasantness of the boardroom conflicts, Benson enjoyed most of his four years on the board of House of Fraser. He liked visiting various stores and found the retail world most interesting. Alec Craddock, the managing director of Harrods, who was a fellow board member, told him that he would enjoy 'the theatre of retail' — and indeed he did.

In 1986 Benson complained to Smith that he was not calling any Fraser board meetings. The chairman replied that they were not necessary as Fraser was by then wholly owned by Fayed and his brothers. Benson said he would have to leave if he could not act as a director, complying fully with his legal duties. He resigned and was puzzled why Smith felt able to stay on. Whether it was Benson's good example or whether for some other reason, Smith also resigned shortly afterwards.

The second opportunity to see something outside the property world presented itself in 1989, partly because of the fragmentation of one of the giants of the newspaper and printing world. Reed International had come into existence in 1970 as a result of the merger of the Reed Group, one of the principal suppliers of newsprint, with News International, the newspaper and magazines publishers. As mentioned in chapter 4, in 1972 a joint company, MEPC-Reed, was set up to redevelop some of the former Reed printing works, such as those in the Fleet Street area and in Long Acre, Covent Garden. Initially MEPC had fifty-one per cent of the shares and Reed the balance. In 1980, when Benson was managing director, MEPC exercised its option to buy the remaining forty-nine per cent from Reed. During the latter years of the joint company, as a result of their joint ventures, Benson had regular contact with some of the Reed directors, who obviously had an opportunity to gauge his skills.

In 1985 Reed International decided to concentrate on publishing and to sell its other interests. Paper and packaging was sold off in what was in effect a management buy out on the part of some of the directors. The new company was named Reedpack, and Benson was invited to consider becoming chairman of the board. He was interviewed by the existing directors, who asked him a number of questions, the final two being: 'What do you see as being the ultimate role of a chairman?' 'To sack the managing director if necessary,' Benson replied without hesitation, as that was his consistent view. 'And other directors, too?' 'Yes,' was his answer. He felt that his questioners were uneasy about those answers, but they nevertheless asked him to take on the job of chairman. He learned later that a former Cabinet minister had been their first choice, but his financial demands had been too great.

The unspoken corollary to Benson's statement of the chairman's role, was that the ultimate role of the non-executive directors of a board was to make the position of the chairman untenable. That precept was to affect him personally in a painful way in two later incidents that were too close in time for comfort.

Benson always enjoyed learning something new and appreciated the opportunity to learn something about manufacturing. One of the facts that impressed him greatly was that twenty-six per cent of the workforce were shareholders. He accepted the offer and served as chairman of the new company in 1989 and in 1990, when it was sold for a good price.

Under the leadership of its managing director, Peter Williams, Reedpack was a dynamic broadly based paper making, packaging, paper reclamation, plastic bottle blowing company, which also owned Spicers stationery business and a Dutch reclamation and paper maker. Benson later described his time with that business as 'fascinating and full of value'. He added, 'I was amazed at the number of PhDs we had working alongside accountants, other graduates and less qualified people. All highly motivated and proud of the goods they were producing *together*.'

Benson enjoyed seeing manufacturing plants in action both in England and in the Netherlands. Visiting the high quality design and manufacturing boxmaker in Blackburn in Lancashire gave him great pleasure, as his father had sometimes played the organ in the Cathedral there and his mother had been the matron of the local fever hospital.

Reedpack had become a very attractive target for other similar, but larger companies and was bought by one of them in 1990. Benson was pleased that the worker-shareholders did well out of the takeover and were all kept on by the new owners. Curiously, many of the component parts of the company were later sold back to their individual managements, which also did well, especially those of RPC and Spicers. Benson's participation had been curtailed by the takeover, but he had both enjoyed and learned from his time with Reedpack.

———————

As mentioned earlier, when Benson set up on his own in 1969, he was given valuable help for most of his private development schemes by Sun Alliance, mostly in the person of Michael Dew. When he was with MEPC he often dealt with that insurer on much larger projects. A number of them involved new buildings in Mayfair, where the freeholder was The Grosvenor Estates, the Duke of Westminster's property vehicle, which like MEPC, used Sun Alliance as its lead insurer. In 1978 Sun Alliance invited Benson to become a local director of their West End branch in St James's Street. This was in the nature of a compliment to him and to MEPC and a sinecure rather than as a job where a great deal of work was expected of him. However, the nature of his involvement with the insurance giant changed drastically in 1988.

It was preceded by an invitation from a former Cabinet minister to join the board of a different and smaller insurance company. Benson had some misgivings about the offer and sought the advice of one of his insurance friends at Sun Alliance, who could be trusted to give him a frank answer. He was Geoffrey Bowler, then a director but earlier the chief general manager of the company. His response to the request was brief: 'Give me 72 hours.' In that time he must have consulted his chairman and other colleagues, for he called back and invited Benson to join the main board of Sun Alliance, rather than the other insurance company.

Benson accepted the invitation and served as a non-executive director from 1988 until 1991, when he was appointed vice-chairman. In the following year he was made deputy chairman and in May 1993 he took on the onerous role — as it turned out to be — of chairman. After five years on the board he felt ready for the task. Apart from his extensive knowledge of finance and business, he had by then learned a significant amount about insurance. He had been helped by the presence in Sun Alliance of a highly skilled staff, anxious to explain their work to a newcomer. Also, non-executive directors were expected to work by taking it in turns to chair a different divisional committee for a year at a time. In his first year Benson's responsibility was for life insurance, about which he learned a great deal. In his second year he was asked to take on marine insurance, a subject about which he knew the basics but was interested to learn more. As vice and deputy chairman he was no longer expected to undertake any one of these divisional tasks.

As the insurance company's assets were mainly in property, Benson was given the chairmanship of the investment committee. Arthur Hayes, who ran the company's investment side for a time, then worked closely with him. The full board meeting was on the first Wednesday of every month. Hayes reported to the investment committee at ten o'clock on those mornings, while the main board, which he attended even before he became a director, met an hour later. Hayes was always impressed by the way in which Benson was then able to summarise the property issues on which he had just briefed him, and to make appropriate recommendations. 'He was sharp as a knife,' he told the writer.

Hayes always found Benson affable and mentioned that the company benefited from his charm as a host at receptions, and 'the way he worked the room', whether at the Royal Opera House or elsewhere.

One of the crosses that Benson had to bear as chairman was the regular attendance at annual and extraordinary general meetings of Nigel Watts, a shareholder, who regularly complained in intemperate language about the iniquities of Sun Alliance. His principal point initially was that the company had refused to make a payment to his sister, when her husband had died, not long after taking out a life policy. The company had refused on the grounds of the material non-disclosure of a fatal illness on the part of the deceased, but time and again Watts publicly complained about that decision. Benson always regarded the company as scrupulously fair with policy holders. Interestingly enough, in his first annual statement, published in the report and accounts for 1993, he had mentioned some support for that opinion.

He had stated:

> Whilst it is necessary to scrutinise claims, policyholders are entitled to be treated fairly, and in this respect our experience with the Insurance Ombudsman Bureau speaks for itself. The Group pays more than a million claims each year in the UK; in only a tiny proportion of cases does this give rise to a complaint unresolved by management action and referred to the Ombudsman. In 1993 the Ombudsman found for complainants in less that 14% (49 out of 368) of the Sun Alliance cases referred to him, compared with an industry average of 33%.

Watts was not persuaded and continued his barracking not only at meetings of Sun Alliance, but also at similar ones chaired by Benson as chairman of the Boots Company and later, of Costain, the civil engineers. Puzzled and increasingly angry shareholders of those companies, including directors, were regularly obliged to listen to complaints about Sun Alliance. While the right of free speech for a shareholder is important, even if he owns only one specially bought share, the majority of those attending are also entitled to hear what the chairman has to say, and may reasonably expect their fellow shareholders not to filibuster or to attempt to wreck the meeting. On one occasion when Benson implored Watts, who had already had plenty to say, to let him speak, he shouted back that he would not allow him to do so. Benson had no alternative but to adjourn the meeting, saying that he would resume once the heckler had gone. The police were called and decided to remove him, a matter that led to a successful claim for damages against them. To date nobody has found a satisfactory way to prevent the continual interruption of meetings by really determined pests. Dew thought that Benson handled the hecklers at Sun Alliance meetings very well.

The background of that particular meeting was that on the previous day Benson had been in Lancashire on a business visit. He was intending to catch an evening train from Preston to London, so that he would have no difficulty in getting to the morning meeting he was to chair. Unfortunately, that train had technical problems further north and was cancelled. Benson got onto the next train but it also broke down, shortly after leaving the station. The passengers were stuck on it all night. Next morning the engineers got it going but Benson realised that he was bound to be thirty minutes or so late for the meeting. He called the company secretary to explain, asking that the senior director present should tell the shareholders that he was delayed briefly by train problems, and should chair the meeting for him until his arrival. As soon as he arrived he took over the chair and apologised. Despite that Watts at once was on his feet, shouting and rebuking Benson for his gross neglect in arriving late and demanding an apology, presumably, a better one.

It is just possible that at some stage Watts realised that his point about his late brother-in-law was not appealing to others as much as it appealed to him. He apparently decided that he might have more success if he were to support and adopt a complaint made by another shareholder of Sun Alliance, the author Count Nikolai Tolstoy. Tolstoy had earlier written two books accusing the chairman of the company from 1971 to 1985, Lord Aldington, of having been guilty of serious crimes in 1945. As a brigadier in the Eighth Army in Italy and Austria, Toby Low, as he then was, had handed over Cossacks and other Soviet citizens, many of whom had reluctantly supported the German army, to Stalin's and Tito's soldiers, who had shot them. Aldington maintained that he had been carrying out orders that were founded on the terms of the Allies' Yalta agreement, which required such a return. Stalin at that time held large numbers of allied troops, former prisoners of war, as bargaining counters or hostages.

Aldington took no action after the publication of either book. Watts decided to write a vehement leaflet based on some of Tolstoy's work. In it he attacked Aldington strongly. Tolstoy read the draft of the leaflet and made some alterations. Watts had 10,000 copies printed and distributed them to anyone who might know Aldington, as well as to thousands who did not. Aldington felt that he had to sue for libel and commenced proceedings. Tolstoy, possibly basing himself on the well-known Imperial Russian saying, *noblesse oblige*, asked to be joined as a defendant, a request that was granted.

The Sun Alliance board decided that as Aldington was being attacked in a way that affected the company, they should lend him some £20,000 for litigation purposes. That decision was later repeatedly questioned by Tolstoy and Watts

— and they may have had a valid point. However, it was not a reason to prevent meetings being conducted in an orderly fashion.

The outcome of the libel case is relevant only because it led to the eventual withdrawal from the field of Watts. The jury awarded Aldington £1.5 m in damages; he was also awarded £500,000 costs. The European Court of Human Rights, in a decision that was welcomed by many lawyers, later held that the damages were so excessive as to violate the right of freedom of expression. Watts, who had been made the subject of an injunction or had given an undertaking to the court not to repeat the libel, in due course published another leaflet accusing the former brigadier of being a war criminal. He was sentenced to a term of imprisonment for contempt of court, but was released by the judge four days later, after purging his contempt. The message at last got through to him; he left Aldington alone and he troubled Benson no more at any of the meetings of his various companies. (The disturbance Watts caused at a Boots annual general meeting, described in the next chapter, occurred before his imprisonment for contempt.)

Benson travelled extensively on behalf of Sun Alliance, including to two of his favourite countries, Australia and New Zealand. In 1994 he was invited to join a trade mission led by the Prime Minister, John Major, to the Middle East and South Africa. Benson found the visit to Riyadh in Saudi Arabia horrifying. On the way from the airport to his hotel he noticed that all the sides roads were blocked off, not by traffic cones or police officers, but by armoured vehicles, to speed John Major on his way. It was not long before Benson's section of the motorcade was halted in order to let a river of people cross the road. When he asked for an explanation he was told that as it was Thursday, it was execution day. The great attraction that day was that a wife found guilty of adultery was going to be stoned to death, not by the primitive method of throwing stones at her, but by the 'modern' method of burying her up to the neck and having a tipper lorry dump its load of stones on her head.

Sun Alliance had continued its business in South Africa during apartheid, but under the trade name of Protea, that of the national flower. Benson was in the country with John Major when he addressed the legislature and also on the next day when he met President Mandela. Benson was near the end of the line of those waiting to be introduced to the great man, but when he got to him and shook his hand the President kept asking, 'Where is Sir Colin Cowdrey?' He wanted most of all to meet one of his own cricketing heroes. He was happy to learn that Cowdrey had not attended as he was busy giving cricket lessons to the youngsters of one of the townships.

In 1995 Benson went on another visit to South Africa for Sun Alliance. As a former rugby player he knew that the world cup final was to be played at the Ellis

Park stadium in Johannesburg on 24 June, a day when, 'by a strange coincidence', he was going to be in that city with a ticket for the match burning a hole in his pocket. South Africa had only been admitted to the competition with the ending of apartheid, and the President was making great efforts to turn the game from one of interest only, or mainly, to the white population, to one of universal appeal.

Benson had been allocated a seat near the President's, but as he had a tight schedule to catch his flight home, he swapped it for one nearer the exit. He found himself the only Brit in a mixed race section of the stadium. Far from being tense, the crowd was very relaxed, with universal support by all South Africans for their team. Biltong was shared all round. Benson remembers the opening ceremony as the most impressive event he has ever seen. South African servicemen abseiled onto the pitch from helicopters, while bearing the flags of the sixteen nations in the finals of the competition.

The final itself was between the host nation and New Zealand (almost a match between all whites and All Blacks) so the atmosphere was electric. South Africa won in the last moments of extra time with a drop goal from Joel Stransky. The 65,000 capacity crowd erupted with almost universal joy. The writer asked Benson whether he had been able to join in any of the celebrations that followed. His answer was that, as shown in the excellent film made about the match (*Invictus*, with Matt Damon as the national captain, François Pienaar), a South African Airways jet flew over the stadium at the winning moment. 'That was my ride home,' he explained, 'so I had to leave at once and missed the party.' However, when President Mandela visited England in the following July, Benson had the honour and pleasure of being present both at the Prime Minister's lunch for the President at 10 Downing Street and on the following day at a similar event hosted by the Governor of the Bank of England.

Sun Alliance had a number of offices in London. The main one was in Bartholomew Lane, opposite the Bank of England, and on a large triangular site that included the Stock Exchange building. Sun Alliance was the freeholder of the whole triangle. Not long after he had become a director, Benson met Paul Reichmann, on one of his many visits to London from Canada. Reichmann suggested that the whole triangle could possibly be redeveloped jointly by Sun Alliance and Olympia & York. Benson discussed the idea with one or two colleagues but the suggestion came to nothing. In any event, it was not long before the Canadian company failed spectacularly.

One thing that impressed Benson greatly when he first saw it in the City office, was a wall covered with dozens of firemarks (identifying shields) of insurance companies which had been acquired over the years by Sun Alliance. The company, like many others, was always on the lookout for suitable targets to acquire or join. One name that came up in discussions was Royal Insurance, with which Sun Alliance had had some minor joint ventures. On previous occasions when the Royal name had come up, the Sun Alliance executives had been concerned about the Royal's exposure to claims in the United States, based on damage caused by extreme weather (like that unfortunate Lloyds name, Christopher Benson). On this occasion, however, they seemed to have overcome their concern and so discussions commenced, first between their two chief executives, Roger Taylor and Richard Gamble, and later between committees of non-executive directors of both companies. Benson personally was not that keen on a merger with the Royal, as he thought there were better prospects for a merger with two other insurers.

While on holiday Benson received a phone call from the chairman of Royal Insurance, who said that the discussions were going well, and that in the event of a merger the Royal would like Benson to be the chairman of the new enlarged company. Nothing was said at that stage about who should be the new chief executive, but the Sun Alliance team, having initiated the discussions, believed that it was a foregone conclusion that their man, Taylor, would be chosen. However, the Royal Insurance board believed that their chief executive, Gamble, was the better candidate, though they did not say so. Concerned that Sun Alliance had earlier worried about Royal's US exposure, but being repeatedly told that their manager, Bob Mendelsohn, was a class act, Benson decided to see for himself. He flew to Charlotte, North Carolina, especially to meet him by prior arrangement, but was kept waiting for a day before Mendelsohn turned up. Benson found him friendly and knowledgeable about the American insurance world, but thought he knew rather less about Europe.

Negotiations between the two companies proceeded very quickly, rather faster than Benson thought desirable. Apart from anything else, there had still been no agreement about the choice of chief executive. Each side seems to have assumed their nominee would get the post. It was only after all other important matters had been settled that the misunderstanding became apparent. The Royal representatives then said that if Roger Taylor of Sun Alliance was to be the chief executive officer of the new merged company, then one of their men should be chairman. That point was not acceptable to the Sun Alliance negotiators.

Eventually, to break the deadlock Benson agreed that he would act as interim chairman of the new company until a fresh outsider could be chosen. Patrick Gillam was appointed chairman in May 1996 and asked Benson to stay on as deputy chairman. He had originally decided to leave as soon as the new chairman was found, but against his better judgment he allowed himself to be persuaded to stay on. However, at the end of that year he left. The two chief executives, Taylor and Gamble, could not or would not work together, so Gillam thanked them for their services and bade them farewell. The new chief executive officer was not a Sun Alliance man, as originally expected, but Mendelsohn, who according to Hayes, made a good job of it. Michael Dew, another director of Sun Alliance, was not so charitable towards the new chief executive and thought the merger a disaster. He could not understand, he has said, why his experienced old friend, Benson, had allowed the merger to go through. Benson's explanation is that the director-negotiators for Sun Alliance were Henry Keswick, chairman of Jardine Matheson and John Kemp-Welch, previously chairman of Cazenove and chairman of the Stock Exchange, who were both in favour of the merger, as were others, including Robert Ayling, the CEO of British Airways. Benson had been the only director left with misgivings about the merger.

Like MEPC, Sun Alliance sponsored various charitable and sporting ventures. On one occasion Benson and Hayes, together with Eddie George, the Governor of the Bank of England, dispatched the Vintage Car Club's beautiful old cars on their trip to the Le Mans pre-rally breakfast and four-wheel beauty show. On 8 May 1997 Benson's last task as deputy chairman of the merged company was a particularly pleasant one for the former seaman. Tracy Edwards, the very successful ocean sailor, was about to set off with an all-woman crew to circumnavigate the globe non-stop, with Royal Sun Alliance as the sponsors. On the quayside at Southampton, Benson said:

> We are here today to meet the boat — all of it, and they don't come much bigger, 92 feet overall, a beam of 42 feet and a mast of 102 feet — to rename it *Royal & Sun Alliance*, and to wish the venture all speed and a safe berth.

Apart from the disruption of meetings, Benson had enjoyed his years with Sun Alliance and had appreciated the opportunity he had been given to broaden his knowledge and experience of the business world. However, while glad to have news of successful progress, say, in Scandinavia and about increased business in various areas, it was not quite as thrilling as finding sites for redevelopment, arranging for architects to draw up proposals, choosing the builders, and of seeing a completed new town centre or major office development at the end.

Not long after the merger with the Royal, but after Benson's departure, the premises in Bartholomew Lane were vacated and the head office was moved to Berkeley Square. The board decided that it would sell the contents of the old premises rather than move them to the new location. Among the discarded objects were the portraits of the former chairmen of the company, or 'The Rogues' Gallery'. Benson, when chairman, had his portrait painted at his colleagues' request and at the company's considerable expense, by Michael Noakes, the well-known portrait painter — who became and remains a good friend. Christies conducted the sale of the contents. Benson thought he might bid for his own portrait if the price did not go too high. He was both pleased and slightly offended when he was able to acquire that Noakes masterpiece for a mere £150.

Mention has been made of the fact that Benson owned, or part owned an aircraft and a helicopter at different times, which he used mainly for business but also for pleasure during his limited free time. This is perhaps an appropriate place to mention one of his personal insurance experiences. At a time when he and a friend had half shares in a helicopter worth about £200,000, it was always properly insured. As was customary with aircraft, when it was kept in a commercial hangar with many other aircraft, the rental paid by them for the storage included a sum for the insurance cover obtained by the hangar owner to cover the aircraft in his care. One night several fires broke out in the hangar and all the aircraft in it were destroyed. The owner settled with his insurer and left the scene but he paid nothing over to Benson or his partner. Litigation was clearly not worth while so the two owners of the pile of cinders had to face the loss personally. A later incident involving his aircraft proved less expensive but also very annoying.

Benson had earlier decided to set up a separate company for his own plane and helicopter, with a separate set of accounts. Whenever he used one of them he paid that company its usual rental charges, without any personal discount. On one occasion when a compulsory maintenance check was due, the aircraft was flown a short distance to the engineering base by a professional pilot. After the end of that tax year Benson received a telephone call from HM Inspector of Taxes in the Midlands, who said that there was a discrepancy in his personal tax return. The man added that he would see Benson in London on the following Friday at two thirty. When Benson said that he was very busy that day and would prefer another date, he was warned about the Revenue's rights of entry and search and told that he would have to be available then — or else.

As he was always scrupulously honest with his tax affairs, Benson was very concerned about the implied threat of drastic action. On the Friday afternoon the tax man told him that the discrepancy had arisen from that flight to the maintenance base, as Benson had charged the cost of the fuel to the company owning the aircraft. Benson explained that he always paid for his personal use, but that this flight had been for the compulsory routine check required by his company's aircraft, and so properly charged to its accounts. The tax man showed him chapter and verse in the relevant Finance Act and persuaded him that the liability for that short flight was his own. Slightly puzzled, Benson asked him how much was involved, so that he could pay at once. The answer was: '£16 — but we'll call it £8.'

Benson was dumbfounded but, before he could express his indignation and amazement at this waste of time and public money, the truth came out from his caller, who cheerfully announced: 'Thanks very much, it's 3 o'clock now, so we can conclude this interview.' He explained that if he was on an official call in London until three on a Friday, he was entitled to stay for the weekend and charge his hotel bill to his office. He had brought his wife and son down and was off to meet them. The honest payer of the £8 was left fuming at this outrageous waste of taxpayers' money.

CHAPTER TEN

The Boots Company

It is more often girls than boys who like to spend time in Boots the Chemists shops. Young Benson was different from most young males — but it was his father's fault. His father, as mentioned earlier, was for many years a dentist practising in the centre of Worcester. It is unlikely that people steered clear of him because of his profession, but the fact was that he had very few friends. One man with whom he was friendly was Mr Harries, the manager of the Boots shop that was just down the street from his surgery. He used to drop in on him for a chat and a coffee and sometimes took his young son with him, after school or on a Saturday. After young Benson went off at the age of thirteen to train for the sea in *HMS Worcester* in the Thames, he used to come home on leave in uniform and sometimes accompanied his father to Boots. As he got older he noticed the girls working there and some of them noticed him.

Over the years Benson felt an affection for Boots, which he knew not only as a customer, but because several of his town centre developments included new premises for them; sometimes an existing High Street shop would be expanded into a new shopping mall. When he had developed the Poole shopping centre, he not only persuaded Boots to take a large shop in it, but also to dispense with any glass separating it from the Mall during opening hours. He was always impressed by the efficiency of the company and the helpfulness of their staff, and so was happy to become a non-executive director of The Boots Company in April 1989.

He then made a point of visiting as many branches as possible. One day when he was in the shop in Droitwich near Worcester, a female supervisor, who must have been in her sixties, said: 'Oh! It *is* you!' She had presumably wondered whether the new director was the same Chris Benson she had known in Worcester. He confirmed his identity. 'I remember you when you were a little boy — you used to come into the Worcester store a lot.' A female colleague of hers added: 'We all remember you coming into the shop in your naval uniform. We all fell in love with you.' That was clearly untrue, he complained later, as his teenage efforts to date some of the girls had all failed miserably.

Benson had been asked to join the board mainly because of his expertise in the property field, but he soon found that it was scarcely resorted to, despite the size of the company's estate. Boots Properties, which had just been set up as a separate company to deal both with developments and investments, had a staff of seventy, mainly professionally qualified. Boots was by far the largest corporate body he had been asked to join. It had some 70,000 employees worldwide and a group turnover in the preceding year exceeding £2.7 bn, producing profits before tax over £300 m. In the UK the company had over a thousand stores as Boots the Chemists, though none trading under that name overseas.

During his early days with the company Benson tried to see as much of its different interests as possible. He had considerable knowledge of the fabric of some of the retail shops but not of the retail side of the business, which he found most interesting. He also saw something of the research and production side in the company's laboratories and factories — some of which were on the same large site at Beeston in Nottingham. They had been built over the course of many years and several of them were in listed buildings. Not long after his arrival Benson opened a new headquarters building on the same campus.

During that time he got to know and like both the chairman, Robert Gunn, and the chief executive and fellow board member, Sir James (later Lord) Blyth. Benson was greatly impressed by the competence of the chief executive, who had been with the company only since 1987. He had wide experience of industry and had been knighted for his services as Head of Defence Sales at the Ministry of Defence. In Benson's opinion Blyth had been an excellent choice, who had succeeded in revitalising the company. In his view, 'He was an inspirational leader.'

Benson learned more about the history of the company, a bit at a time, during his five years with it, but especially from an excellent piece of research that he commissioned from Stanley Chapman, the Professor of Business History at the University of Nottingham. Chapman had earlier written *Jesse Boot of Boots the Chemists*, which was published in 1974 and covered the history up to about 1960. Benson asked him to update his work and he did so with an excellent supplement with the working title 'Boots — The Evolution of a Modern Business', 1994. Sadly, that has not been published, either as part of a second edition or as a stand-alone publication. However, it has proved helpful for the present book, first, as a memory jogger for Benson and, secondly, as useful background for the present writer. Benson greatly regretted the fact that Chapman's second part was never published, as his board colleagues would not agree to publication. Their reason for that, in Benson's opinion, was that his executive board colleagues felt that their respective contributions had not been sufficiently acknowledged in it.

Boots had a great tradition and a large number of souvenirs of days gone by. On the Beeston site there was a kind of museum, which was more like a store-room of interesting items from the past. Benson learned that the premises of Jesse Boot's very first shop, located in the Lace Market in Nottingham, was being used as a restaurant. He suggested to his colleagues that the company should try to buy it, restore it to its original state, and place a number of the earliest containers and products in it, but at the same time to equip it to operate as a modern store. Despite their long association with the company that Boot had built up, his colleagues turned the idea down.

After Benson had been with Boots for a year, Robert Gunn announced that he intended giving up the chair in July 1990, after the annual general meeting. He asked Benson to provide him with a short list of possible successors and he duly gave him the names of three outsiders with suitable qualifications. Benson heard no more about his suggestions, until one day Gunn told him: 'We'd like you to become chairman of the company.' Benson had not expected this, as the company had never had a chairman who was an outsider to the company. Outsiders were regularly made non-executive directors but never chairman. He accepted the job with — to use a word only appearing at moments like this — alacrity. He was so surprised and flattered that, hardened businessman though he was, he shed a tear. Although he had not been required to use his technical skills from the property world, he had apparently satisfied his colleagues that his experience of the City, as well as in a number of different areas at home and abroad, was a highly relevant and useful qualification. The appointment was initially for three years.

Boots had its own company newspaper and soon published an interview with the new chairman. Among other things he said, because he felt strongly about it:

> I believe the company's real strength lies in its people. In recent months I have visited a number of centres at home and overseas and I have been deeply impressed by the calibre of staff at all levels. They obviously have a tremendous pride and interest in their jobs and it is very encouraging to see that for its part, the company is developing those people to their fullest potential.

After a reference to the fact that the threat of a hostile bid for Boots was often mentioned in the financial press, Benson made a comment of general application: 'Anyone who thinks size alone is a protection must be in cloud cuckoo land. Boots has got to be a potential target for a predator and we should never be complacent. But my answer is simple and it applies to everything I do — if we don't manage our affairs well enough to deter predators, we don't deserve to succeed.' In view of the fact that Boots was later taken over, it is perhaps a pity that Benson's words were not noted more carefully by later members of the company's board.

His reference to size was interesting, as Boots had a short while earlier taken over the large Ward White Group plc, which included a mixed bag of do-it-yourself and cycle shops: A. G. Stanley and Fads, Halfords and Payless. Benson had joined the board shortly before the takeover was concluded, but had obviously seen the relevant documents, including the offer document addressed by Boots to the shareholders of Ward White. As is not unusual, that had included examples of Ward White's shortcomings together with a brief explanation of how Boots could remedy them. Benson knew something about the other group, but at his first board meeting felt that the usual reticence — and silence — of the new boy was appropriate. However, when the chairman asked whether anyone knew anyone at the top of Ward White and nobody responded, he felt obliged to say that he did. When asked for his assessment of the man concerned, he merely suggested that his colleagues should meet him. The general response was that there was no need for that at the last minute, as the company had undertaken due diligence inquiries for some two years. The takeover went through despite the disapproval of one major shareholder, Carol Galley on behalf of Mercury Asset Management, who felt so strongly that she had called for an extraordinary general meeting. Boots lived to regret the deal, ultimately disposing of the companies acquired.

Benson was interested to learn that the company had not long before considered branching out into larger stores, which would sell the usual Boots ranges but also clothing and other items. One of the suggestions then made was that possibly a link with House of Fraser might achieve that goal. As he had been a director of that stores group he was able to guess that any approach by Boots would almost certainly have been rejected. In any event, the idea was dropped on further consideration.

When Benson's first annual statement as chairman appeared in 1991, he was able to announce that despite the harsh economic climate, profit before tax was up slightly on the previous year, at £358.4m. Blyth reported that Boots Pharmaceuticals had achieved another year of steady growth with profits of £115m, despite a higher expenditure on research and development. He also announced that applications for registration of Manoplax, their new drug for the treatment of congestive heart failure, had been lodged in key markets, notably in the UK, the US and the major European countries.

Two-thirds of the way through the first annual general meeting of the company that he attended at the Grosvenor House Hotel in Park Lane, Benson was amazed to notice that there was a large-scale scuffle in the gallery, followed by a mass exit of shareholders there. It turned out that the rush was caused by the keenness of those shareholders not to miss out on what they clearly regarded as an important part of this annual event. Boots had for some time provided goody bags containing cosmetics and other products as a gift for those shareholders taking the trouble to attend the meeting. The new chairman put a stop to that disruptive piece of generosity.

Unfortunately, Manoplax turned out to have some serious problems and was ultimately withdrawn in July 1993. That was a blow as the company had been relying on it to be great success, on the lines of some of its earlier products, such as Ibuprofen and Prothiaden. Blyth said at the time: 'The withdrawal of Manoplax, the heart drug launched in the UK and US, was obviously a conside-rable disappointment. Some £100 m had been invested in developing the drug but, despite regulatory approvals, we felt the evidence of its possibly adverse effects could not be ignored.'

Soon afterwards the Director of Research, Dr Ian Hunneyball, described the consequences of that failure: the cardio-vascular research programme was closed down with the loss of fifty jobs. The decision had been taken to focus the research and development programme on three therapeutic areas: rheumatism, inflam-mation and immunology; mental illness; and endocrine and metabolic diseases.

The laboratories of the company were obliged to test all their new products in accordance with strict government regulations. Testing some products on ani-mals was essential, as they could not be tested on humans. Animal rights protesters became increasingly vociferous and then some resorted to violence and threats, going way beyond the democratic right to protest. Boots had stopped using primates for experimental purposes, but still used beagles and rats. On one night some protesters broke into a laboratory and released all the beagles. Next morning all of them (dogs, not protesters) turned up for their breakfast. As they had all been kept in solitary confinement, a necessary scientific expedient, they had at any rate been able to enjoy mingling during their few hours of freedom.

The increasing cost of research preceding the manufacture of any drug became more and more of a burden to the pharmaceutical part of the company. It had to compete with large British and foreign pharmaceutical companies that concentrated on the manufacture and sale of such products and could afford to spend many millions on research. After Benson had left the company, Boots sold this branch of its research and manufacturing to the German industrial giant, Bayer, and thereafter confined itself to the very large-scale production of its other products. The decision had been taken because of the economics of the industry and not because of the actions of the animal rights protesters, more of which will be discussed shortly. Benson was envious of his successors: the closure of the research facilities saw an end of the animal rights protesters at Boots meetings — though he was to encounter some of them once they had switched their protests to meetings of Costain, as builders of the Newbury bypass.

Benson's travels to Boots facilities abroad took in places as close as Spain and as far as India and Puerto Rico. In England he could travel in style, as the company insisted that the chairman should always be seen in a Rolls-Royce with a chauffeur. Benson's protest that he had a car and chauffeur already from MEPC was brushed aside. In practice, when he travelled from his London flat to Nottingham he usually went by train, and the company's London office was within walking distance of his flat. One abuse that Benson always abhorred was the padding of expense claims — whether made by a director or a junior employee, but especially when made by a director. He was always scrupulous about his expenses. As he could not persuade Boots to let him travel in a car other than their Rolls, he arranged to share its use and cost with MEPC. Whenever he flew abroad for Boots he tried to arrange some business there on behalf of MEPC and/or Sun Alliance at the same time. He then again arranged for an appropriate splitting of the costs. Rather unusually for a senior executive, Benson insisted on flying standard class for any flight less than six hours.

One of the longer flights took him to Pakistan. On landing at Karachi he was taken at once in a limousine with curtained windows to the old colonial terminal, where he was treated royally and then whisked off to the house of the local Boots manager. Steel gates were opened for the car and speedily shut once it was in the courtyard, by one of the armed guards there. Benson enquired about the need for the weaponry and was told that some people objected to a Muslim manager working for an English company, and might get violent. Because of that danger the manager changed both his car and his route to work regularly. Benson was provided with an armed guard throughout his stay. When he left via the same terminal building he was shown the local paper for the day of his arrival, which announced: 'Assassination attempt on prominent British businessman arriving in Karachi today.' He was glad the Press had got the story wrong, feeling rather like Mark Twain when he commented: 'The report of my death was an exaggeration.'

Boots manufactured pancreatic insulin in New Delhi and also had a manu-facturing plant in Pune in India, which was being expanded. Together with Blyth and other colleagues, Benson attended the opening of the new facility there. The quality of workmanship all round impressed him but he was shocked to discover that a number of the women on the packing lines had earned a PhD at an American university. They explained to him that in Pune there was no other work, adding that working for Boots was a privilege. He heard similar views expressed by employees in Thailand. A driver told Benson that he had worked for Boots for forty years, while many of the women at the factory had been happy to work for the company for over twenty-five years.

Whenever he travelled with senior colleagues by car in the UK, they would try to call in on one or more facilities on their route by arrangement — and sometimes without any notice. One of the ways in which the company had expanded was by moving into the optician's business. The company speedily bought up several small chains of such shops and soon had the second largest UK chain. Inevitably, sometimes one of the acquired shops would prove to be running at a loss and to be incapable of improvement — even by experienced Boots employees.

Benson and two colleagues once decided at the last minute to drop in unannounced at one of their optician's shops in a small town. There were two members of the staff there and one of them, a woman, continued to talk to her colleague, ignoring the three unknown 'customers'. Eventually, one of Benson's colleagues interrupted her flow and said, 'We're from head office; could we see the manager, please?' She replied that he was out and that if they called back on Monday there would be nobody there, 'Because you've just shut us down!' *Exeunt omnes.*

Benson and David Donne, the chairman of Argos, received an unusual request from John McGregor, the Secretary of State for Transport. He was anxious for various good reasons to switch more traffic from road to rail, and asked them to conduct a trial. He knew that both their companies had good distribution centres — and that more would have gone by rail to or from those, but for the closure of many lightly used lines on the recommendation of Dr Beeching. In response to the minister's wish, Benson asked his Airdrie centre near Glasgow to dispatch one container by freight train to Swindon, a breakout point, and another at the same time by road. The road consignment arrived in the usual number of hours. The rail container was found three weeks later on a siding in Glasgow.

'It was a pleasure to be a director of Boots,' Benson told the writer more than once. The main reason was the quality of the staff. 'The executives were all very well qualified, steeped in the company tradition, very professional and intensely loyal to the company.' He had similar feelings about the remainder of the work force, and was particularly struck by their response to different bombs planted by the Irish Republican Army. Benson had experience of the aftermath of such bombs when MEPC premises were affected, but was to get more when with Boots.

Shortly before Easter 1993 the IRA planted a bomb between the two glass entrance doors of the Boots store in a shopping centre in Warrington, Lancashire.

When it exploded it killed two young boys and injured dozens of shoppers. The IRA announced that they had not intended to take any lives, but Benson found that hard to believe, given their device was planted to explode on the Saturday morning before Mothering Sunday in a most crowded location. He went to Warrington as soon as he heard the news but by then, obviously, all the casualties had been moved, some after first aid from the dazed Boots staff only yards from the blast. The staff all rallied round and the manager of the branch spent all of Sunday cleaning the blood marks off the floor.

Boots also suffered from the effects of the IRA bombing of civilian targets in Manchester (at the Arndale Centre — not a development that Benson had been involved with); at Bishopsgate and at Victoria in London; and in Coleraine in Northern Ireland. In the Manchester store a defect in the sprinkler system and the bomb combined led to the whole premises becoming covered with dust and filth. All the staff bar one turned up on the next morning, a Sunday, to clean off one million items of merchandise, to be sure that the store was open for business as usual on Monday. The missing member of staff was in hospital with pneumonia.

The Bishopsgate bomb had blown out the glass of the store in Liverpool Street. One elderly woman on the staff, old enough to have been in the wartime bombing of London, said resignedly to Benson, 'We've been through it all before, darling.' It was a point of honour with her and nearly all the staff he spoke to at the different damaged premises, that their shop would re-open next day, if at all possible.

Boots employees also demonstrated their team spirit by engaging in different charity fund raising events. Benson on one occasion had to fly to Land's End to start a staff charity cycle race from there to Airdrie by Glasgow. All sorts of cycles had been entered, everything from a modern racer down to an old sit-up-and-beg bike, with plain pedals and no toe clips. They all made the 580-mile journey.

The company encouraged members of the staff by having bonus and share schemes, and by rewarding those who came forward with innovative ideas. For example, one woman packer came up with the idea of improving Christmas gift packing. By adding a simple extra elastic band on some merchandise at a given point of the process, several thousand pounds were saved, and the packer received a handsome financial reward.

Benson's connection with Boots was severed in a sad way for him after his five years with the company and four years as chairman. After he had completed his first three years, he was invited by the board to continue for a fourth year. However, during the course of that year it became clear that his fellow non-executive directors did not wish him to continue as chairman once it had come to an end. Different reasons were hinted at, but nobody ever raised any serious point against him. Benson accepted the decision of his colleagues: they were fully entitled to make it.

At least one of the non-executive directors wanted Blyth to keep his job and to take on the chair as well. Benson did not approve of this idea, neither did Carol Galley of Mercury Asset Management, who wrote to him on 16 July 1993: 'I hope you do not mind me writing to you, but I am aware of some speculation in the press that you will be stepping down as Chairman of Boots and that the Board is considering combining the role of Chairman and Chief Executive. I thought you should know that my colleagues and I would consider a combination of the roles entirely inappropriate in the case of Boots.' Benson placed that letter before the Board and the idea of the combined post was not pursued. Lord Blyth told the writer that it was never his wish to hold both posts simultaneously, and that he was not aware of any director favouring such a move.

A search was commenced for a new chairmen, led by Benson with headhunters, and eventually Sir Michael Angus, then chairman of Whitbread and previously of Unilever, was selected to be deputy chairman immediately and to succeed Benson in the chair from the end of July 1994. Blyth succeeded Angus in the chair three years after that.

The last annual general meeting chaired by Benson was held on 21 July 1994 at the Queen Elizabeth II conference centre, opposite Westminster Abbey. One of the things that he said in his opening remarks was, 'As you know, this is my last meeting as your chairman.' The audience knew because he had mentioned that fact in his printed chairman's statement. He added that his successor would be Sir Michael Angus. After receiving the auditors' report, Benson pointed out that at the previous annual meeting there had been 'an unfortunate degree of disturbance which arose in connection with questions raised by some shareholders who hold strong views on animal rights issues.' After adding that the purpose of the meeting was to consider the annual report and accounts, he said that although the board's position on the use of animals had been stated on a number of occasions, he would nevertheless ask Sir James Blyth to state it again.

Blyth stated the legal requirements, adding, 'This company will continue to undertake animal tests to the extent that these are necessary to meet the requirements of the licensing authority.' At that point a near riot broke out and a very large number of strategically placed objectors would not let Blyth continue, despite his and Benson's pleas. Blyth related, practically unheard, how the company had reduced the amount of animal testing and pointed out that cosmetics and toiletries had not been subject to animal testing for almost twenty years. Despite those facts, he added, the company's chemist stores had been attacked by activists. 'Windows have been broken or damaged with acid. Locks have been glued up. Incendiary devices, real or hoax, have been placed in our stores, or sent through the post.'

He then turned to the most serious incident. 'You may have read of the most recent attack on our store in Cambridge. Let me tell you something about risk to life. I visited our Cambridge store with Gordon Hourston, who runs Boots the Chemists, last week. £2.5 m worth of damage has been done to that store. We were damn lucky that nobody was killed. It is only a matter of time, if this continues, before somebody is killed.' As Blyth spoke about the damage done by the rioters, Benson asked himself once more the recurring question: 'How many of these animal rights protesters refuse medical treatment for themselves and their children, because they cannot be given the assurance that none of the medicines have been tested on animals?' He also recalled that some of the animal rights extremists were not too clear about human rights. They cheerfully dispatched booby traps in jiffy bags, which were more likely to injure the post clerks or secretaries opening them, than the directors to whom they were addressed.

In accordance with standard practice for the conduct of public meetings, Benson invited questions from the floor. The next person to get up and make a speech was Nigel Watts, who while talking at length about Sun Alliance and Lord Aldington, made insulting remarks about Benson. He eventually, when pressed to do so, produced a question: he asked whether it would not be appropriate for Benson to step down and hand over to Angus. Since Watts knew perfectly well that he was shortly going to do just that, the question was clearly intended merely to add insult to insult. It came as no surprise to Benson when Watts interrupted proceedings again later, nor when the large number of animal rights protesters continued to try to wreck the meeting, with some success. Many bona fide shareholders attending the meeting were enraged and beseeched the hecklers to keep quiet and let the meeting continue with its business, but they were no more successful than the chairman or the chief executive with that request. In short, the meeting was in an uproar. However, Benson was determined to complete the proceedings and pressed on, eventually completing the agenda and closing the meeting.

Benson had enjoyed his spell with Boots, mainly because of the dedication of the staff. His fellow non-executive directors' views about his continued chairmanship had been disappointing, but Benson was realist enough to accept that in the business world you have to be prepared to take the rough with the smooth.

CHAPTER ELEVEN

Send for Benson!

Benson was a great admirer of the Costain Group, a leading British civil engineering and construction business that worked all over the world, earning large sums of foreign currency for the UK. The group was well-known for its excellent work in different fields, including directional drilling for oil and liquefied natural gas, and for top quality concrete work, including railway sleepers. As Benson was to regret for personal reasons later, it also built roads.

It was Costain, under its local director Peter Costain, which had completed MEPC's large Sydney Exchange development, after the original Australian builders had gone into liquidation. After that success it was placed on MEPC's short list of preferred contractors. When Benson was coming to the end of his time as chairman of MEPC, Costain was completing one the many projects it successfully executed for his company, a joint venture with IBM UK for the Bedfont Lakes business park near Heathrow. However, despite many large projects being successfully under way in different countries, Costain ran into a bad patch early in the 'nineties.

In the annual report of the group for 1992 Peter Sawdy, the chairman, reported: 'I wrote this time last year that I expected 1992 to be an extremely hard year. At that stage, however, we had no perception as to just how difficult it was going to be for the contracting and real estate markets worldwide. It is with great disappointment that I present to shareholders a second year of unacceptably bad results.' Although the turnover of the group had only declined from £1.32 bn to £1.24 bn, operating profit had dropped from £27.4 m to a mere £2.9 m, as large sums had been written off.

Peter Costain, by then the group chief executive, gave hope for the future when he reported that both major projects in Hong Kong in connection with its new airport were progressing well. Costain was in a joint venture with Trafalgar House to build the massive Tsing Ma suspension bridge, as well as another working on mobilising most of the world's cutter suction dredger fleets and undertaking the enormous challenge of creating the platform for the Chep Lap Kok airport. He added the great news that the international order book had increased by 350 per cent in 1992. However, that was of little use if the company ran any further into serious debt or indeed, bad luck, in the short term.

In view of the group's importance to Britain's economy, there was clearly concern in the City, including it would seem, at the Bank of England, that Costain might fail. Benson was approached by the group's concerned bankers, National Westminster. John Melbourn, the deputy chief executive of the bank, asked him whether he would be prepared to take over as chairman of Costain, adding, 'The Bank of England has been kept fully informed at all times at the highest level, with the full knowledge of the company.' Benson said he would be prepared to do so and when approached soon afterwards by Costain, agreed to become a director, with a view to taking on the chairmanship in June 1993.

Once in the chair Benson was regularly reassured by insolvency practitioners that the group was solvent and, despite various problem areas, need have no inhibitions about continuing to trade. After he had been in the chair for some eighteen months, two creditor banks, at different times, made threatening noises about enforcing their loan agreements. Benson each time went to see Eddie George, the Governor of the Bank of England, whom he knew quite well from various encounters, and pointed out that Costain was making good progress and that the banks should really not be concerned about their security. George listened sympathetically and presumably passed on his own views to the banks concerned, because they suddenly became more patient and made no more premature demands.

As he had done in his first years at MEPC, Benson had made a speedy assessment of the group's strengths and weaknesses, both in the UK and abroad. Financial problems clearly had to be addressed first and that involved, among other steps, the sale of unprofitable arms of the business. One of the divisions of work that was worrying was the provision of housing. One house building project that went awry was in Newport Beach, California. A development in Spain, near the Gibraltar border, was also hit by the recession. It was the kind of development popular with British and other European buyers: villas surrounding a golf course. As there was little chance of getting a purchaser to pay a reasonable price for the whole site, Costain decided to hold on to that property.

In his first annual statement as chairman, Benson was able to report: '1993 saw the restoration of the Costain Group's financial stability and, with it, resumption of its place among the industry leaders in the UK. The year began with gearing at an unacceptably high level, but a concentrated programme of disposals, the successful rights issue in the autumn and improved cash controls reduced this to 37 per cent by the end of the year.' He pointed out that the improvements had not all started after his arrival by adding:

Good progress had already been made when I joined, particularly the completion of the sale of our Australian coal-mining business. This and the subsequent sale of our UK housing business brought the total generated by disposals over a two-year period to more than £320 m. The rights issue, which received encouraging sub-underwriting support from existing and new shareholders, raised an additional £83 m.

The sale of the group's remaining holdings of peripheral commercial properties in the UK and Australia raised some more cash.

The group was not out of the woods yet, as Benson had to add that as a result of the disposals and continued difficulties of the UK construction industry, the turnover was down again, from £1.27 bn to £1.14 bn. Peter Costain added the good news that the debt of the group (including preference shares) had been reduced from £331m to £83m and that overheads in the UK had been cut by thirty per cent in fifteen months.

Costain had very extensive holdings of coal mines in the United States, mainly in Kentucky and West Virginia, which brought in useful profits. Despite that, Benson had an uncomfortable feeling when looking at the various reports and accounts relating to those ventures. He went to inspect most of them and felt even more uneasy. On his return he suggested to Peter Costain and Alan Lovell, the finance director, that they should inspect the mines and their accounts for themselves. They went and returned with similar misgivings. Anxious to avert any further minor disasters, the three directors decided that the US mines should also be sold.

Benson often travelled to see the various projects in the Middle and Far East. Costain had a great deal of work in the Gulf States, ranging from a hospital in Oman, to a ship repair facility in Bahrain and a naval base in Saudi Arabia.

As a result of his involvement in the regeneration of Docklands, Benson was particularly interested in two of Costain's contracts in the UK. The group was given the difficult task of the tunnelling and other engineering works underneath London Bridge railway station, for a new Tube station on the extension of the Jubilee line to Canary Wharf and onwards — at last! (This contract, together with later successful work for the railways, doubtless led to Costain being chosen as the lead contractor for the massive rebuilding of London Bridge station for the Thameslink project and also for the Crossrail surface route from Stratford to Shenfield.)

The other Costain development of interest to Benson was the building of the barrage to enclose Cardiff Bay. Because of his experience, he had been asked to give expert evidence to both the House of Commons and the House of Lords committee dealing with the proposed project. In the Commons he had only been asked a single question — but three times, and by the same MP: 'What about the

How to wear two hats

coal?' He had answered each time that coal was no longer shipped through Cardiff. The Lords committee hearing proved quite different: he was expertly grilled there by a number of peers with highly pertinent questions.

The Sun Alliance group, of which Benson was a director and then chairman, already owned premises in Horsham in Sussex and then Costain built another office complex there for it. As Costain built a total of five office blocks for the insurance group in that town, and completed about twenty-five projects for it in all, it is scarcely surprising that Sun Alliance was also Costain's lead insurer. Benson's old friend Michael Dew was the property director of the insurance group and invited him to top out the new Sun Alliance building early in August 1993. When Benson, the director of both the companies, arrived to do his duty, he was presented by Dew with a hard hat. One side was painted in Sun Alliance house blue and bore that company's crest; the other half was white and carried the Costain logo. Dew had found the answer to the age-old problem of how to wear two hats at the same time. When Benson met the chairman of the district council attending the ceremony, he recognised him as one of the former members of the Building Services Division of MEPC, which he had been obliged to disband, with regret. Fortunately he was by then a successful consulting engineer.

Benson, the dedicated traveller, enjoyed the visits to the American mines. At one Kentucky mine he found that many of the operators of the big coal cutting machines, deep underground, were women. One of them, on hearing that he was from England, asked if he knew Queen Liz. He said that he had met her, and was asked to be sure to see to it that she visited her and her colleagues 'down the mine' some time, rather than just attending the Kentucky Derby and studying the horses. Admiring the shirts of some of the male miners, Benson said that he must make a point of buying a hill-billy shirt while there. 'Whadya say?' one of them asked in a menacing way. Benson repeated his remark and was advised, 'You'd better call it a check shirt while you're here.' As he was driven between two mines, he noticed a huge number of small white sheds in different fields. They were too large to be beehives so he asked what they contained. 'Fighting cocks,' was the answer. 'Isn't that illegal here?' 'Yep.' 'Don't the police do anything about it?' 'Nope,' was the predictable answer.

It was ironic that with Costain's experience of building roads and improving motorways, it was a mere nine-mile stretch of road in Hampshire and Berkshire that caused the group — and Benson — the most grief, and also landed the unfortunate taxpayer with a bill of millions of pounds in extra costs. The road was the Newbury by-pass, which managed to attract more protesters than any similar road project. The reason for the scale of the protests was that the road was to pass through beautiful countryside, including three Sites of Special Scientific Interest, and to involve the felling of thousands of sound trees. A number of opponents had more specific objections, for example, conchologists were concerned about the danger to the habitat of the rare Desmoulin's whorl snail. As well as the large numbers of peaceful citizens exercising their rights of free speech and free assembly perfectly properly, the opposition also attracted some semi-professional protesters, possibly members of the Protest of the Month Club, who considered themselves entitled to do whatever they liked.

Early one Sunday morning Benson got up to find that his garden had been invaded by a number of men and women, who had climbed into his trees and had tied protest banners to their branches. A police inspector advised Benson and his wife to stay indoors, but Jo Benson said firmly that nobody was going to stop her going to church as usual. She was jeered but otherwise not molested in her own garden on the way out. The police were told by the demonstrators that they would leave after a while, together with their banners, one of which proclaimed: 'Benson's backyard is still green'. Benson was not sure whether they expected him to cut his trees down and concrete it over, or merely stop Costain's work, in breach of contract.

After they had gone, Benson had to climb into the trees to remove the banners they had left. The ex-sailor told the local newspaper reporter who called on him that he found 'the quality of their knots was very disappointing.' He also suggested that if they were true supporters of the environment, they should have travelled by donkey, rather than by the cars they had left around the corner.

The next visit by protesters was by a mixed party, which broke into his office while he was there. He recognised some of them as regular animal rights protesters from various Boots meetings. They broke into the filing cabinets of the company but stole only his personal file. Some of them later visited his house by night and left a message for him by his heavily soiled swimming pool: 'You won't want to swim in this pool after what we have done in it.'

The most violent protest that Benson ever encountered was at an annual general meeting of Costain, held at the Queen Elizabeth II conference centre in Westminster, just around the corner from the Metropolitan Police headquarters. As Costain had suffered so much from riotous behaviour, a woman police inspector in uniform attended the meeting. The protesters on this occasion stormed the stage, virtually wrecking it. One of the men swung a length of timber at Benson's head but missed. After the meeting was over, he asked the police inspector why she had not intervened. 'I didn't see anything life-threatening,' she replied. Benson was worried that the Metropolitan Police might have given up having eye tests.

The final interference with Benson was at Costain's annual general meeting in 1996, shortly after he had ceased to be a director. He thought that he should attend it as a matter of courtesy to the new chairman. He sat in the back of the hall but as he was leaving at the end, he was spotted by a woman he recognised from several earlier meetings as an animal rights protester. 'Oh, it's Mr Benson,' she called out loudly, coming towards him. He was immediately abused and jostled by a number of her colleagues, but managed to get out of the building, pursued by them. His former driver was standing by the new chairman's car, noted the danger and told him to jump in quickly — which he did. The driver was unable to move the car, as the woman lay down in front of it until the police removed her.

Benson introduced two men, whom he greatly respected, to the Costain board of directors. The first was Sir Terry Heiser, who had been the Permanent Secretary at the Department of the Environment during most of Benson's time at the London Docklands Development Corporation, and who had retired from the Civil Service. The other was Sir Francis McWilliams, a civil engineer, who had just completed his year in office as Lord Mayor of London. Heiser did not seem to enjoy his service on the board and did not stay on it long.

McWilliams had a great deal of experience of working in Malaysia and introduced some leading Malaysian industrialists to Peter Costain. As a result of the joint efforts of those two directors the Malaysians, who were clearly impressed by the solid nature of the group and confident about its future, became substantial shareholders. McWilliams and Costain also managed to attract significant investment from Kuwait and the United States. Once they had control of the group the majority shareholders did not want to keep McWilliams on, despite his many talents. It was their loss, but even without him, the Costain Group went from strength to strength. Without Benson's firm action as chairman, the story might well have ended less well. Although the Malaysian, Kuwaiti and American shareholders owned almost seventy per cent of the company, on a split of roughly 40/20/10, they wisely decided to continue to treat the company as a British one, appreciating that the goodwill it had earned worldwide was attached to the UK.

Not long after Benson had left the Costain board, Sun Alliance proposed building an overflow office block in the City for N M Rothschild, who had offices immediately opposite the site owned by the insurance company. The lowest tender for the work was from Costain, but Sir Evelyn de Rothschild and some Sun Alliance directors were a little concerned about the group's financial state. Benson was able to reassure them all that Costain was once more on a sound footing and that there was no longer any cause for concern, so the contract was signed and the work was executed to the satisfaction of all parties.

The Saturday Profile in the *Daily Telegraph* on 3 August 1996, carried the heading: 'Costain's confidence builder', and a subheading that stated: 'Sir Christopher Benson, who calmly steered troubled Costain out of danger, talks to Clare Sambrook about his life with the accomplished understatement that is his trademark.' Sambrook quoted John Melbourn, the banker who had called him in to save Costain: 'Chris Benson doesn't see problems, he sees issues to be resolved, and challenges. If you take the view that glasses are half full rather than half empty, you can take people with you.' In his letter to Benson of 23 July, Melbourn wrote, referring to the company meeting on the previous day, 'Three years hard graft (without remission) deserved a vote of thanks.' He added, 'Many, many thanks for all you have done for Costain. We here at NatWest are very grateful. I shall not forget.'

The next company to send for Benson, during his time at Costain, was not wanting him either for his property skills or for his help with financial problems. On the contrary, the company was a young one, very efficiently run and so successful that it was planning to seek a listing of its ordinary shares on the London Stock Exchange. As a part of that plan it was offering some 78 m shares to the public so as to reduce its borrowings and to strengthen its balance sheet. Benson was asked to come aboard as he was needed for his good record and established position in the City. The company wanted to have four executive and four non-executive directors, with one of the former as executive chairman. Benson on this occasion accordingly accepted the role of a non-executive deputy chairman.

The Thorn Lighting Group owed its existence to Jules Thorn, who started his lighting business in England in 1928. One of the original products that made his business a success was the manufacture of light bulbs. Thorn died in 1980 but his name and his business lived on. In 1986 Hamish Bryce became chief executive and made significant changes. He and his colleagues decided to concentrate on the more lucrative side of the business, the manufacture of light fittings, for both indoor and outdoor use. The bulb manufacturing part of the business was sold off to the American General Electric Company. The decision was also taken to make the business more international, so as to take advantage of markets in Europe and elsewhere.

Specialist companies in Sweden, France and Australia were bought up, the latter one specialising in airport lighting. The plan succeeded in many countries: the indoor light fittings were bought extensively for use in buildings of all kinds, including hospitals, school and art galleries. The outdoor ones were successfully sold for use on roads, sports venues and airports. The lighting of the five kilometre bridge linking Sweden with the island of Öland was provided by the group, as was the relighting of the Sydney Opera House. In the UK a quarter of the market had been secured and in Europe the group had become the second largest supplier of light fittings.

Shortly before Benson was asked to join them, in August 1994 Bryce and his management colleagues joined with a group of investors and bought the Thorn Lighting Group (TLG) from its then owner, THORN EMI, which retained a 12% stake. Benson joined the board in the following month and stayed for four years.

He knew something about the business before he joined it but he was interested to learn how extensive its reach was and how efficiently it was run by Bryce and his colleagues. Like Costain, TLG was a British business that earned a great deal of foreign currency from its operations abroad. Like Costain, TLG was involved with the construction of the new Hong Kong airport, supplying the airfield lights and all the lighting for the vast new terminal building. It was, of course, not unusual to find British companies operating in Hong Kong, but China was rather different. Thanks to its joint venture with Jardines, the group also obtained contracts for the floodlighting of the Macau Stadium and the Mission Hills Golf Courses in China, the success of which confirmed that some Scottish missionaries had been successful.

Benson was very impressed by the way Bryce involved all his non-executive directors in the running of the company. He made a point of educating them in the ways of the company and the range of its products, both at meetings and elsewhere. Benson still recalls the careful lesson they received from Bryce about the company's interest in airport runway lights. The company exhibited regularly at the Frankfurt Fair and Benson attended it there twice on Bryce's suggestion.

In Europe TLG advanced slowly eastwards after the Iron Curtain had gone for scrap. Benson visited the group's new robotics line in Sweden with some of his colleagues. The group also obtained work in Norway and Finland and then opened up in Hungary, the three Baltic states and in St Petersburg, to serve the Russian market. It was greatly to the credit of all concerned, and a tribute to the products, when the Hermitage Museum ordered TLG lighting for one of its galleries. No less than 250 special fittings were designed for the museum, and their light was diffused through skylights and made to look like daylight.

In 1997 Benson visited late Sam Wanamaker's Globe Theatre on the South Bank and saw the newly installed Thorn floodlights in action. He was sorry that the originator of the project was not there to see the completed theatre.

Apart from chairing the remuneration committee of the group and serving as a member of its audit committee, Benson's role was essentially one of an adviser with all-round experience in the City and in business generally. Before each monthly board meeting Bryce, as executive chairman and Benson as deputy chairman, spent an hour going through outstanding matters. Bryce told the writer: 'His advice was genuinely sought. I found him very helpful.' Benson's name helped to confirm the company's entitlement to recognition as a major player in its field, but he is the first to concede that his executive fellow directors, under the leadership of Bryce, coupled with the efforts of the workforce, deserved all the credit for the success of the Thorn Lighting Group.

Benson's link with the company ended when it was sold to another English company, which passed it on to a large international enterprise, the Austrian Zumtobel Group. If a successful company like Thorn had to end up outside the UK, it was perhaps fitting that it should be in Austria, where Jules Thorn was born, received his technical education and set up his first lighting business.

CHAPTER TWELVE

Two More Quangos

The London Docklands Development Corporation, which Benson had chaired for over four years, though undoubtedly the most important quasi autonomous non-governmental organisation (quango) he ever served on, was not the first. He had earlier been a member of the Property Advisory Group and the New Towns Advisory Group, which advised the Department of the Environment. Both were time-consuming in attendance, travelling and paperwork, but their burden was somewhat reduced when the New Towns Commission was wound up in 1984. In August 1982 he had been appointed as a member of the Property Advisory Group, with the remit: 'to keep under review changes to the land and property market, advise on matters concerning the development process and advise the Department generally on property issues.' After two years as a member he then served for another two as the unpaid chairman of the group.

In July 1988 he also served on an ad hoc committee of six under the chairmanship of Sir John Sainsbury, set up by the Prime Minister, Margaret Thatcher, who was concerned about the time taken by Inspectors appointed to hear major planning inquiries. She was particularly concerned about the inquiry into the proposed new nuclear power station, Sizewell B in Suffolk, chaired by Frank Layfield QC. Benson felt that Layfield, who was one of the top planning lawyers, had done a good job and had taken no more time than was necessary, having regard both to the importance of the plan and the number of witnesses, including experts covering complicated matters. The Prime Minister asked the committee to make suggestions for the speeding up of the appeal process, pointing out that High Court judges were routinely able to deliver judgment immediately, or soon after the conclusion of a case, no matter how complicated.

The committee submitted its findings in a report of over a hundred pages to Mrs Thatcher. At a final meeting with her in March 1989, Benson saw that she had clearly read the report carefully as she had scribbled comments on most of the pages that she referred to in the fairly brief discussion. Mrs Thatcher announced early on in the meeting that the whole thing was 'encapsulated' on one of the pages, whose number she gave. That was possibly a slightly over-simplified conclusion, but the report certainly did not recommend any major changes to the system, other than to stress the urgent need for computerisation. It was therefore filed away, doubtless marked: No further action.

During his time with the Docklands Corporation, Benson had acquired a healthy respect for the housing associations and their work in providing below market price housing for those in need. As mentioned earlier, he had suggested that their accounting systems should be brought into line with commercial insti-tutions, with proper annual accounts, so that they could obtain loans, and the government had agreed with the appropriate changes being made. He was pleased to be invited to chair the Housing Corporation in 1990, as he knew some-thing of its valuable work from his earlier connection with housing problems, and a little more from his wife Jo, who was then just completing a six-year term as a member. Her appointment had been attributable to her extensive experience of local government and of council housing. He later said: 'I was keen to join the Corporation because I knew there was a major task to be performed in the provision of social housing.' On another occasion he explained, 'The problems of unemployment and racism in the East End are very real indeed. That was partly why I took on the chairmanship of the Housing Corporation. I wanted to try and repay some of my own good fortune to those who need help so badly.'

The housing finance scheme that Benson took on was a completely new one, introduced by the Housing Act 1988 and the Housing and Local Government Act 1989. It required housing associations to borrow on the open market to finance new homes. According to David Edmonds, who had been the chief executive of the Corporation for seven years, 'A massive change of culture was needed.' The housing associations had to get used to the idea of needing accoun-tants to establish their ability to borrow and repay loans from rents — which often needed to be increased above the level of rents pegged by local authorities. Understandably, association members were reluctant to increase them. The rising value of housing association properties made them more attractive to lenders. However, as Benson felt obliged to warn some of the more eager associations, they could only use their properties as security once.

Among other changes introduced by the 1988 Act, the tenants of associations lost both the benefits of the fair rents scheme and their protection under the Charter of Rights under the Housing Act 1980. To mitigate the effects of those losses the Corporation had drawn up a new Tenant's Guarantee in consultation with the associations. All bodies wanting to be approved had in future to satisfy the Corporation on four points:

(a) That they operated on a 'sound and proper' financial basis;
(b) that they had the skills for managing tenanted property;
(c) that they agreed to let at rents 'which can be afforded by those in low paid employment'; and
(d) that they adopted a satisfactory equal opportunities policy.

The new housing finance scheme led, apart from anything else, to an increased amount of money going out to the English associations at a rate which took the chief executive by surprise and had unintended consequences. As a result there was an overspend of £100m in Benson's first year. Needless to say, the Treasury was not best pleased: this was one of the costliest events since the government's hopeless Tanganyika Groundnuts scheme had failed in the immediate post-war years.

The overspend was not the sole fault of Edmonds, who was a very competent chief executive, but the buck stopped with him. In view of that and his long service in the post, Benson decided, with great reluctance, that it was time for a change and that he should be replaced. What followed was an example of Benson's thoughtfulness towards those who worked for him. Edmonds immediately heard from a firm of headhunters, who introduced him for the job of property manager for the National Westminster Bank group. He noticed that the firm's address was in the same Park Lane office building as the headquarters of MEPC. Benson had been obliged to sack him but had at once got him another good job.

Edmonds had come to the Corporation from the Department of the Environment, where he had helped to set up the London Docklands Development Corporation for Michael Heseltine. He told the writer that in his opinion Benson built up a very good relationship with the ministers concerned with the Housing Corporation. He also felt that he always listened and responded to advice.

Anthony Mayer, who took over as chief executive from Edmonds, was well qualified for the difficult task ahead. After a successful career in the Civil Service, he had worked at Rothschild for six years, the last four of them as a managing director of their Asset Management business. His experience of both Whitehall and high finance made him the right man for the Corporation after it had been entrusted by Parliament with enlarged powers and substantial funding.

By the time Benson took over as chairman, the housing associations owned, managed and maintained some 600,000 houses or flats. They were also providing more that 50,000 hostel beds. That meant that they were providing accommodation for well over a million people. As a result Benson was able to claim in the Corporation's action plan for the years 1991–96, published as Homes for the

90s: 'Housing associations are now the main providers of new social housing. They are central to the government's housing strategy.' He went on: 'Over the next three years to 1994–95, just short of £6 bn will be invested by the Corporation in housing association schemes targeted at homeless families and others in housing need. A total of around 150,000 homes for rent and sale will be delivered from this programme which will draw in nearly £1.5 bn of private sector investment.'

An important task for Benson, whenever he was chairman of a public body, was to explain its statutory basis and the nature of its work, to various audiences. He always worked hard on the preparation of his talk and never relied on one standard one. He obviously often asked for points that his chief executive or other staff members wanted him to put across. He was extremely unlucky on one occasion when he addressed members of the Chartered Institute of Housing in Harrogate. One of the Corporation officers, Ken Bartlett, had suggested a last minute change to Benson's carefully crafted speech, and was asked by him to add a note in handwriting to the typed pages. All went well at the meeting until Benson got to the handwritten note and said out loud, 'Ken, I can't read your writing.' The audience of some 1500 may have been given the false impression that an unknown staff member called Ken had written the speech in manuscript, and that the speaker had not bothered to read it through in advance. 'One of my most public pratfalls!' says Benson.

One of the principal tasks of the Corporation was the regulation of the associations. That involved, apart from anything else, ensuring that its regulatory powers were used to good effect when dealing with any association having financial or other management problems. A good illustration was afforded by the case of a black and ethnic minority association in the Midlands, which had run into financial and governance problems. Benson was determined to ensure that a highly qualified inspector should be appointed to investigate the matter, one who would prove acceptable to the members.

Mayer suggested Patricia Scotland QC, who later became the first woman and the first ethnic minority member to serve as Attorney-General. Benson agreed to her being appointed as he had met her at the Middle Temple and had been impressed by her. She accepted the appointment and in due course, after hearing from many witnesses, produced what Benson has called, 'An immaculate, first-class report which offended no-one; it was hugely professional and solved the problem.' As a result the Corporation had no need to exercise any of its drastic powers, such as striking the association off the list of registered bodies. A good outcome to that inquiry was important on general grounds. As the action plan had stated: 'A single act of financial imprudence can adversely affect the reputation of associations overall.'

Baroness Scotland, as she now is, told the writer that Benson had clearly appreciated the difficult times that some housing association members had in adapting to a new professional approach, and that some had difficulty in understanding the rules. He appreciated the distinction between deliberate fraud and unintended mistakes. The former Attorney-General added: 'He really cared about fairness and being just.'

Benson and Mayer had a good working relationship, based on the understanding that the chief executive could be trusted to get the work done. Although Benson had a gentle manner, Mayer thought he was 'as hard as nails'. He told his chairman soon after they met: 'As I understand it, you want to leave it to me as the chief executive to run the place, but if I make two mistakes that embarrass you, I'm out.' Benson had confirmed that was so. 'His under-stated, relaxed and always good-humoured manner,' Mayer added, 'belied an almost ruthless determination to get what he wanted. He invariably did.'

Mayer told the writer that he thought that Benson's contribution to the success of the Corporation's work could be put under three heads. The first was his response to the overspend, which had 'shattered' everyone there, according to Mayer. He came in and quietly and without panic put the Corporation together again. He was highly supportive of his chief executive; together they re-jigged the executive team and gave it back its brio.

The second was that Benson gave the Corporation back its credibility with the government. He was a private sector man who was taking it forward with confidence. That was particularly necessary as it was a delivery organisation, like the London Docklands Development Corporation, that actually did things.

The third was his proposal for the modernisation of the accounts of the Housing Associations. They needed to be simplified and made more transparent — and that was done. As a result, under his leadership, associations were more easily able to borrow on the open market, a crucial improvement. Sir George Young, the Minister of State at the Department of the Environment, told Benson that he thought he would be 'crucified' by the associations for the changes he had introduced, but he was proved to be quite wrong. On the contrary, the members who dealt with finance were quick to see the huge opportunities for leverage that the changes afforded.

Apropos simplified and transparent accounts, Benson will never forget an occasion on which he and Mayer were invited to meet the chairman of the now notorious United States Federal National Mortgage Association (FNMA), better known as Fannie Mae. They were told how the homeless could be helped much better if they were only to follow the good old US example. That example led the the American taxpayer having to stump of billions of dollars, and contributed largely to the world financial crisis. Benson and Mayer decided, *nem con*, that they would sooner not adopt a course that might end in prison.

As Benson was often asked by friends and others, how he managed to cope with so much work in different areas almost simultaneously, it is interesting to note that Mayer volunteered the fact that he was 'time efficient'. They regularly went through matters orally and did not need position papers. His chairmanship Mayer described in one word, 'magic'. Benson got on well with the staff, with 'no shred of pomposity'. When staff numbers had to be reduced, he was always generous with those taking 'early retirement', the Civil Service euphemism for redundancy.

One of their joint achievements of which Mayer is proud, is the fact they spent 99.9 per cent of the Corporation's funds every year and never lost the taxpayer a single penny of taxpayers' money. That added up to a large number of additional or improved homes.

Benson has especially warm recollections of the deserving community schemes in Liverpool that the Housing Corporation was able to help, thanks in large measure to the efforts of its local representative there, Max Steinberg, himself a Liverpudlian. Apart from anything else, those schemes were not unlike those that he had been concerned with in the London Docklands, but above all they demonstrated what a determined local community could achieve.

The residents of the Vauxhall area, just north of the Liverpool city centre, had for years endured appalling housing conditions. The City Council's general plan was for the clearance of its most depressed areas, coupled with the decanting of their populations into new tower blocks built in different suburbs with which they had no connection. The residents of Eldon Street (the Eldonians) and their neighbours became increasingly opposed to their communities being split up and began to consider cooperative housing schemes. They received the support of the Roman Catholic Archbishop Derek Worlock, as many of them were descendants of Irish immigrants, warmly and enthusiastically supported by his colleague, the Anglican bishop, David Sheppard. The leader of the community was Tony McGann, their dedicated architect was Bill Halsall, and their professional adviser in early days was a Canadian, Jack McBane, whose moving and inspiring book, *The Rebirth of Liverpool: The Eldonian Way*, was published in 2008.

The most exciting project arose out of what was a disaster for the local community, the closing of the Tate & Lyle sugar refinery in Vauxhall in 1981, with a loss of 1700 jobs. The large site was acquired by English Estates, a government agency.

Michael Heseltine, who was largely responsible for the creation of both the London Docklands and the Liverpool Regeneration schemes, persuaded the chairman of the historic sugar company to give £400,000 for the demolition costs. The site included a section of the Leeds and Liverpool canal, owned by British Waterways, which had been filled in — and was later to be reopened as an amenity, like some of the lost stretches of water in the capital. However, British Waterways put a high price on its neglected section of canal. McGann scurried round and found well connected friends to lean on the chairman, Sir Leslie Young, who was then prepared to waive the price and give the land to the community.

Plans were drawn up for 145 houses to accommodate the local residents who had resisted the blandishments and implied threats of the City Council, and had decided they wanted to remain together in new houses on the refinery site. Money was the next hurdle. McBane has written of Steinberg:

> As part of the Housing Corporation, Max was directly involved in the funding of a range of initiatives by the Eldonians. He is one of those professionals who was so impressed by the Eldonians that he became a long-standing supporter and friend. As with many of their friends, the Eldonians named a court after Max as their way of saying thank you.

The government had set up the Merseyside Special Allocation and passed the funding for housing schemes over to the Housing Corporation, one of those schemes being the Tate & Lyle site. The Corporation approved a grant for the Eldonian Village, as it became known, in principle in 1984, and accepted the finals costings in 1987.

The City Council, which had earlier built a school near the site, refused planning permission for the village on health grounds: noxious fumes from adjoining works made housing unsafe. The community was outraged and went to appeal. Jeremy Sullivan QC (later Lord Justice Sullivan) appeared for the would-be 'villagers'. The Council's Director of Public Health explained at length, with the help of a much-marked map, why the prevailing winds would bring the noxious fumes onto the site and make it unfit for human habitation. Sullivan asked him whether he would be concerned if the wind came from the opposite direction. In that event, the witness said, he would have no concerns. Difficult though it may be to believe, Sullivan then pointed out to this highly qualified expert witness that his map was upside down. Collapse of stout party and of the City Council's case. The appeal was allowed.

The newly constructed Eldon village was opened by Prince Charles in May 1989. Later efforts on the part of the community, with the Housing Corporation's help, led to the construction of sheltered accommodation and community facilities for all generations. As happened in London Docklands, private developers decided that formerly run down areas could safely be built in by them, once a significant number of decent houses had appeared there as trailblazers.

Benson received a letter from Tony McGann in 2014 on notepaper with the heading ELDONIAN Community Based Housing Association; at its foot was its Housing Corporation registered number.

> Dear Christopher, It was great to hear from you again after all these years. I remember vividly those difficult days when I seemed to be yo-yoing back and forth to London to meet you. The Eldonian village is 25 years old this year and still looks as good as the day the first tenant moved in. I can't thank you and Max enough for the trust and support you gave our community and me personally; you both helped me through some very dark times. If you saw the village today I hope you would agree that that support was well founded. I hope you do get a chance to visit Liverpool as Max suggests; you wouldn't believe the changes that have occurred and the improvements that have been made.

He enclosed a copy of McBane's book. Max Steinberg is now chief executive of Liverpool Vision, the city's economic development agency, which is continuing the process of building up the city to its former place among the leading cities of the country.

This is perhaps a suitable place to mention a matter ancillary to housing associations. The plight of the young homeless in London was something that regularly troubled Benson. He was able to help some relevant charities in different ways. One was by helping with the Westminster Christmas Appeal Trust as its appeals chairman, supported by many others, including numerous companies linked to the property world. For example, in 1982, after a carol concert attended by 900 people in St George's, Hanover Square, half of them adjourned to Sotheby's where an auction was conducted by Benson, who had learned to auction livestock in his younger days. He found the bidders rather easier to please than the farmers had been. He had the unusual pleasure of being able to auction a donated car twice, as the first successful bidder had given it back. Those two sales alone raised £12,500.

In 1984 Benson persuaded two MEPC colleagues to undertake the project management of the conversion of a house in Ladbroke Grove, which had been bought by the Notting Hill Housing Trust, so as to provide accommodation for sixteen homeless young persons. The architects, surveyors, engineers and solicitors of the project all gave their services free. The appeals regularly raised large six figure sums annually.

'Joy to the World' concert at the Royal Albert Hall

In 1989, when he was chairman of the 'Joy to the World' Appeals committee, money was raised with the help of a Carol Service at the Royal Albert Hall. The charity that year was the Save the Children Fund and the event was in the presence of Her Majesty The Queen, Patron of the Fund, accompanied by The Princess Royal, its President.

After four years chairing the Housing Association Benson took up, without a break, the chairmanship of the new Funding Agency for Schools. That meant a significant change, from matters concerning the Secretary of State for the Environment to those covered by John Patten, as Secretary of State for Education. The Agency had been authorised by Parliament in the Education Act 1993 and Benson's appointment was announced by Patten in the October, although the Agency was only to come into being six months later. The *Times Educational Supplement* published an account of an interview with him by Biddy Passmore as early as 22 October. She asked him to comment on Patten's statement at a

143

Conservative Party meeting that he intended the new Agency to take an active role in cutting wasteful council spending, by 'getting in there and mixing it with some local education authorities.' Did Benson intend to 'mix it'?

The peaceable Benson replied with a laugh, 'If mixing it means meeting and talking to find a way ahead then that's fine. If it means standing in the blue corner waiting for somebody to hit me from the red corner, that's not what I am in it for. I can't see the point of having a fight if a fight isn't necessary.'

At the launch on 11 April 1994 Benson said: 'Self-governing status has been welcomed by all those who have embarked on it. The Funding Agency for Schools has been established to help these and all newcomers to the sector continue with their achievements.' There were many opponents in local government, schools and elsewhere, to the idea of schools opting out of the long-standing control of education by elected local authorities and choosing to become grant-maintained, that is, funded by central government. Benson made it clear that he was not intending that the Agency should turn its back on the local authority schools. 'I am looking forward to the Agency establishing a close working relationship both with the grant-maintained sector and local education authorities. I see our future as a partnership to provide the best education possible in our schools. We are not being created to take away the autonomy of self-governing schools.'

John O'Leary, who interviewed him for *The Times* at the time of the launch, or possibly a sub-editor, headed his article: 'Mr Quango takes the reins.' He then made the mistake that a number of journalists made, of assuming that Benson was a Conservative and would act as such, because the board of one or more of the companies he chaired had made donations to that party. In fact, Benson had turned his back on politics, as he personally, unlike many another, could not reconcile political allegiance with membership of a non-governmental body. Benson had accepted this particular office because he had come to the conclusion that opting out from local council control and changing to grant-maintained status, could be helpful to certain schools. However, he was not fanatical about it. As the article put it:

> Nor does he see himself as a standard-bearer for opting out, although he would not have taken the job if he did not believe in the system. 'It is not for me to be evangelical: that would be offensive. But I do feel there is a great deal of merit in it because I think that flexibility and choice are very important for parents.'

The correspondent suggested that even the grant-maintained schools viewed the new body with a degree of suspicion, fearing that any gains made from their escape from local control could be cancelled out by centralised regulation. Benson assured him that, even if that was true, he had no such plans: his aim was to create an accessible and comprehensible system that left maximum authority with the schools.

The Independent carried a critical article by Judith Judd, who after a reasoned criticism of quangos generally, wrote: 'Quangos under both Conservative and Labour governments have always had their placemen, but the wholesale packing of bodies with government supporters is new. There is not one local authority head on the Funding Agency, although it is supposed to oversee both local authority and opted-out schools.' In fact, so far from the government packing the Agency with its supporters, Patten had given Benson complete freedom of choice to select his own team, and he had personally chosen a cross-section of education experts, including four head teachers, together with some outsiders to the field, but on a non-partisan basis. An accurate point was made by some critics, that four members seemed, from their description, to favour grant-main-tained schools. That was true, as Benson wanted to have heads who favoured the idea, rather than opponents who might want to block the work of supporting opted out schools. The outsiders included Stanley (later Lord) Kalms, the chair-man of Dixons, who became chairman of the Agency's finance committee; Shailendra Adwalpalker, the finance director of Gillette International; Lee Karu, a barrister; and Robert (later Lord) Balchin, chairman of the Grant Maintained Schools Foundation, who had played a major part in the creation of the move-ment.

Patten had, almost inevitably, given that Benson was his choice, said kind things about him at the launch: 'We are extremely fortunate to have attracted somebody of the calibre of Sir Christopher to serve as its first chairman.' Of more value, perhaps, was Benson's praise for his first chief executive, Michael Collier, after they had worked together for some years: 'My first job was to find a chief executive and in Mike Collier we hit the jackpot first time.' He was also able then to praise John Codling, the finance director, who had helped Stanley Kalms to devise a seed money scheme for schools. In conjunction with the schools they also devised a scheme for better financial monitoring, which was so successful that the next Labour Secretary of State, David Blunkett, recommended it to all schools as best practice. Kalms was the very busy chairman of a large electrical goods chain. He noticed that Benson was able to fit a great deal into each day, commenting, 'He is a man who is in control of time, much more than the rest of us.'

There is an old saying that if you need something done, you should ask a busy man. At the launch of the Agency, Benson was approached by Susan Daniells, the chief executive of the National Deaf Children's Society, who had been speaking to Jo Benson. She said: 'If you believe all you have just said, you should become one of us. After all, you are deaf in one ear.' So Benson joined the Society, which had Queen Elizabeth The Queen Mother as Patron and the Duke of Devonshire at its President. One of the trustees whom Benson greatly admired was Jack Ashley, the profoundly deaf member of both Houses of Parliament in turn. Benson was pleasantly surprised when he was later asked to succeed the Duke as President. He is currently working on the project for a second 'Listening Bus', which will take the most modern hearing technology and learning techniques to deaf children in different parts of the country, the first bus having proved a great success.

After the Agency had found its feet, Benson and his colleagues, together with Collier, drafted a very long sentence to guide their work.

> The purpose of the FSA is to carry out functions as efficiently and effectively as we can, and while meeting all the requirements of our accountability to the Secretary of State, enable schools to flourish, to develop long term plans with confidence and to optimise their freedom to meet the needs and preferences of parents and children and to produce the best possible outcomes.

Together with Collier and different members of the Agency, Benson visited all the grant-maintained schools and he was regularly appalled by the physical condition of their buildings. Much to the annoyance of the Secretary of State, he commissioned a condition survey, which revealed a number of serious problems. A shocked Benson ordered that they be categorised from 'Immediately dangerous' to 'In need of repair'. The cost of repairs was high but had to be carried out. Benson wondered about the condition of the 24,000 schools still the responsibility of local authorities.

Over the next three years the Agency supported grant-maintained schools successfully in different ways, helping them to raise standards. One way was to help fifty-one of them to create or extend their sixth forms. The Agency also helped the creation of sixteen new grant-maintained schools from former independent schools: seven Roman Catholic schools, three Jewish, two Muslim, one Seventh Day Adventist, together with three others. Whenever the number of grant-maintained pupils exceeded ten per cent in any local authority area, the Agency acquired a shared responsibility with the local education authority for ensuring there were sufficient school places and planning for them. Once the proportion of grant-maintained pupils exceeded seventy-five per cent, the Agency assumed sole responsibility.

The idea of any pupil being removed from local authority control was anathema to the teaching unions as well as to many politicians. Mike Collier told the writer: 'We were subjected to continuous hostility from the Education trade press and most local authorities with whom we had to work, not only in the planning role but in relation to annual maintenance grants.' Benson on one visit encountered extreme hostility from an audience of teachers and school governors — though his description of the event may be slightly exaggerated. 'I only agreed to attend what we knew would be a hostile meeting, because my aunt was in a hospice in Stafford, and I thought I might as well kill two birds with one stone. Well, it was this bird that nearly got killed!'

When it became clear that the three-year term of office of Benson and his colleagues would fall at about the same time as the next General Election in May 1997, their term was extended by a few months. The Labour victory then led to Blunkett coming into office as the Secretary of State for Education. As the Labour Party in opposition had been against opting out for grant-maintained status, it was clear that the Agency would be wound up or drastically changed. Blunkett sent for Benson and ordered him to get rid of the Conservatives on the board, adding that he personally would be free to apply for the job of chairman. Benson did not see the point of applying for his own job when it was clear that it would be changed fundamentally. He had no wish to preside over the running down of a scheme that was working well, so he did not apply, giving Blunkett and Stephen Byers, his Minister of State, his reasons.

The grant-maintained idea was not wholly abandoned by the new government. Collier is of the opinion that both Blunkett and Byers grew in their appreciation of the strength of the model, and that the Labour government would not have introduced Academy schools without its inspiration. More recently the Coalition government has added another type of self-governing school, the Free School, under an Education Funding Agency. That is a government agency rather than a quango. One result of this difference from the Funding Agency for Schools, according to Collier, is that 'It does not benefit as readily as we did, from the valuable perspective we gained from Sir Christopher and his non-executive colleagues.'

Collier found Benson 'an excellent chairman to work with: he was always very clear about what he wanted. I learned lessons from him which have helped me in my subsequent roles as a chief executive and then as a chairman.' Despite his other interests, he made himself available whenever Collier needed him:

> Sometimes meetings between us took place in the back seat of the Boots Rolls-Royce as he travelled from one appointment to another. He was always businesslike, did not waste time with a great deal of small talk, yet always charming.

CHAPTER THIRTEEN

Science Old and New

In 1851 Arthur Albright began the manufacture of phosphorous at Oldbury near Birmingham. Five years later he went into partnership with John Edward Wilson and in 1892 they formed Albright & Wilson Ltd (A&W). Their company provided a wide range of chemical products for industry in peace and war. The principal business was the manufacture of phosphorus and its products, including phosphoric acid made by burning, or 'thermal acid'. The peacetime users of the products included the manufacturers of a wide range of domestic items of food and drink, and of cleaning materials. The company could justly claim to have put the bubbles into millions of fizzy drinks. In the 1914-18 war A&W-filled smoke shells helped to save the lives of thousands of infantry-men by hiding them for a while from the eyes of the enemy machine-gunners; in the 1939–45 war their provision of chemicals for equipment such as flares and beacons, helped the rescue of aircrew crash-landing in the sea.

In 1948 the company went public and in 1955 it bought a business in Cumbria that was making phosphates by the 'wet acid' process. That introduced it to the manufacture and sale of surfactants, which were used in the manufacture of its wide range of personal and domestic cleaning products. The company also developed some special chemicals.

An American conglomerate, Tenneco, became interested in the products of A&W and first bought shares in the company in 1969. When Tenneco acquired the remainder of the shares in 1978, A&W obviously ceased to be a publicly quoted UK company. Its new name was Tenneco International Holdings Ltd but it reverted to A&W in January 1995. It may be that the American directors realised after a while that the product range they had acquired, though still profitable, was becoming out-dated and overtaken by new discoveries and developments by rival enterprises. Sixteen years after acquiring the company, they decided to sell it and float it off on the London market. They may have had more than one reason for wishing to dispose of it.

The reason given in the 1995 prospectus was as follows: 'Tenneco has decided to float Albright & Wilson as part of its strategy of focusing on its three selected growth platforms (packaging, automotive parts and natural gas) and proposes to utilise the resources released from the flotation of its chemical business to concentrate on these platforms.' No less than 313,500,000 ordinary shares were on offer at 150p per share. The company by then employed 4000 people and had manufacturing operations, some on a joint venture basis, in sixteen countries.

The American chairman resigned and Benson was appointed to replace him. The company's name was still a highly respected one in the UK. In April 1995 Benson was able to confirm that by writing:

> Welcome back! That is the greeting that I, as chairman of your company, have enjoyed from a remarkably broad audience of investors, City commentators and ordinary citizens who remember Albright & Wilson when it was last a publicly quoted company.

It was nevertheless clearly desirable to have a chairman with both extensive experience and a good reputation to lead the company. Benson's statement confirms the fact that one of the roles of a chairman of a company is to act as its ambassador.

In his report on the company's first full year, 1995, Benson was able to report that turnover was up from £641.6 m to £703.2 m, and that profit before tax was up from £44.4 m to £55 m. The report of the experienced chief executive, Dr Robin Paul, was bullish. Although the sharp increase in the price of input materials had caused difficulties both for the company and its competitors, he thought that particular problem was over. Success with new products led him to claim that the company was on target to achieve the objective by 1998, of having a fifth of its global turnover being generated by products introduced in the previous five years. He added that a new plant had been commissioned to produce a newly patented product for flame retardants and water treatment chemicals, which placed the company 'in the forefront of technological development in this sector.'

Benson, as usual, made a point of visiting the world-wide sites of his new company, starting with North America. Production of phosphorous in Newfoundland had ceased, but the company had obviously been required to clean up the former industrial site. That had involved extensive use of environmental measures so that the site could be left both safe and green. Benson noted that a newly created lake was stocked with fish, and saw a fox ambling around its shores. It occurred to him that the company's acquired skills of cleaning up industrial polluted sites could perhaps be marketed profitably. Something on the lines of, 'If we clean up, we can clean up.' However, his suggestion fell on barren ground and was heard of no more.

In his first year Benson also visited plants in Charleston, South Carolina and Aurora, Colorado, as well as all the European facilities. On a later visit he was most impressed by the new plant of one of the company's partners in Mexico. It was efficiently and cleanly run. All the technicians who had not learned it earlier, had been given the opportunity by their employer to learn English — and a number of them carefully explained their particular tasks to him in detail.

Benson enjoyed visiting China for A&W. He first travelled to Shanghai, to see a local phosphorus business with which a possible link up had been discussed. He was very disappointed to find that health and safety standards were not applied at all. He was horrified by the number of potentially dangerous tasks that were being carried out by hard-working men and women, without a single item of protection for eyes, hands, body or feet. He left the site as soon as he could, ruling out any idea of a joint venture with that business, being conscious of A&W's excellent record in the safety field. In his chairman's statement introducing the annual report for 1997, he referred to the staff focus on maintaining high standards both in the health and safety field and in environmental matters. He added: 'The Group has achieved its lowest level of lost time accidents ever in 1997 and is one of the better performing members of the UK Chemical Industries Association.'

There had in fact been a potentially dangerous incident, fortunately without any injuries, in 1997, but A & W were cleared of any blame. In October of that year there was a massive fire at the company's Portishead premises, near Bristol, the acrid smoke from which had closed the Severn bridge for many hours. Benson was soon on the spot and learned that some highly flammable material imported by the company, had been wrongly labelled by the consignors. When opened the container burst into flames; there was nothing to put the consignees on notice.

On the same visit to Shanghai, when he was enjoying a leisurely walk along the famous Bund, he bumped into a family of Chinese friends from Hong Kong. After a chat, which included the usual comments about the smallness of the world, they asked him whether he had been to the Barber Shop. Benson felt his chin, and was reassured that he had remembered to shave that morning, so he asked what they meant. They strongly recommended a restaurant with that intriguing name. He took their advice and found that it had good food and, somewhat surprisingly, an excellent New Orleans style barber shop jazz band.

The visit to A&W's supplier in Changsha proved fascinating. The company's main supplies of phosphorous came either from there, or from Morocco. Benson found a very efficiently run plant, which was kept supplied by a sturdy conveyor belt from a mountain source. When he asked how long the belt was he was given the startling but true answer: twenty-four kilometres. Full of admiration, he inquired who its makers were, only to be told matter-of-factly, 'We made it.' Their own engineers had designed it and had made many of the parts as well.

In his statement covering the annual report for the year 1997 Benson was able to confirm that the company was still making progress, but the strength of sterling had affected both the turnover and the profits to some degree. The new chief executive, Paul Rocheleau, who had been with Tenneco, was cautiously optimistic in his review at the same time. However, the two of them shared some misgivings about the future.

Not long after that, when clouds were beginning to appear over the horizon, Benson visited Singapore for a conference attended not only by the local staff, but also representatives from Malaysia and Indonesia. He sat on the front edge of his table and gave them a truthful account of the future as he saw it. In short, he said that the company was facing hard times. A young woman stood up and said that as A&W had been very good to them all, they would be prepared to take a pay cut. She was applauded by her colleagues from the three countries. Benson had not mentioned a cut — and indeed none was ever imposed — so he was very touched by that display of loyalty.

By the time that the accounts for 1998 were published in the following year, the company's position had altered to such an extent that an offer of a takeover from another US company was being considered by Benson and his colleagues. In his chairman's statement on this occasion Benson tried to explain what had happened. 'Events of the past few weeks have demonstrated the complexity of the world in which we live and the rapid change that is taking place in the chemicals industry. Against a fairly hostile market environment we have been striving to position the Group for growth across its world-wide operations. However, the effects of currency, particularly the strong pound, and the global slowdown in the intermediate chemical industry, have made it extremely difficult for us to show any real progress in financial terms.'

The chief executive gave details of some of the problems caused by the strength of the pound and the weakness of the currency in some of the customer countries. One of the products sold to Indonesia had been dicalcium phosphate, used as the abrasive in toothpaste. Because of the fall in the value of the Indonesian rupiah by over eighty per cent, the customer had stopped buying the product from A&W and had switched to using chalk instead. The value of exports to Asia had fallen from some £50 m in 1997 to about £30 m in the following year. Rocheleau had to concede that the prospects for 1999 did not look significantly better.

As the overall prospects indicated that however hard the company and its 4000 employees tried, even with increased productivity, they were unlikely to attain any significant improvements in sales or profits. The hard decision was accordingly taken by the board and the majority of the shareholders in 1999 to sell this — not once-proud but twice-proud — British company to a US corporation with deeper pockets that was prepared to make a reasonable offer. Benson was desperately unhappy that Mr Albright's and Mr Wilson's creation had failed twice to survive as a home-based corporation — and that he had been unable to save it on the second occasion. Sadly, there was one more British company to follow that route, though in much happier circumstances.

———

In 1992 an unusual trio of scientists combined their talents at the University of Bradford. Peter York, the Professor of Physical Pharmaceutics, had for some years been working on the physical characteristics and particle structures important for the activity and performance of pharmaceutical compounds. He and Glaxo plc shared an interest in the comparatively primitive technology used for the production of micron-sized particles, needed for inhalers for asthma and similar conditions. (A micron is one millionth of a metre.) Glaxo offered Professor York a studentship for a scientist to do 'blue-sky research' at Bradford on a better way to make such particles.

The studentship was awarded to Mazen Hanna, an Iraqi Kurdish refugee, who had fled from Saddam Hussein's Iraq, where he had been a research chemist. In his interview with York, Hanna told him that he had been working at Leeds University with supercritical fluids. Neither York nor his university had worked with supercritical fluids, but he realised that they might provide a solution for his and Glaxo's problem. In due course Hanna discovered a way to configure equipment so that it would allow the formation of micron-sized crystalline particles, and also allow control of the crystalline form of the asthma chemical, salmeterol. It was Hanna's invention but developed under York's supervision at the University of Bradford. They were both in need of advice about patents and other legal formalities.

York approached the third member of the trio, who had only joined the University earlier that year. Dr Gwyn Humphreys had always worked in microbiology and molecular biology, but had moved into the area of technology transfer and the commercialisation of technology. At Bradford his role was to look after all the industrial collaboration, technology transfer and business development activities of the university. Humphreys called in the university's patent agent and also kept Glaxo involved. Once the patent application had been filed, extensive discussions took place with the company about an appropriate licence for use of the technology. Glaxo accepted that the university was entitled to conduct research in the wider field, for which increased funding was needed.

After the licence had been negotiated, York and Humphreys were free to talk to other pharmaceutical companies. In August 1994 they were visited by a representative of Genentech of San Francisco, who later moved to Inhale Therapeutic Systems Inc. SmithKlineBeecham and Astra also showed interest and sent representatives to Bradford. After dinner with the Astra team in October, York, Humphreys and Hanna felt very optimistic about what they had to offer. They stood discussing the future in the restaurant car park in drizzling rain and decided to form a company to exploit Hanna's invention, with the university having a financial stake. They next discussed the matter with the university. The Vice-Chancellor, his Deputy and the Registrar were all supportive, but the V-C was anxious for the University of Bradford name to be included in the title of the company. They compromised on Bradford Particle Design (BPD). The company started with £1000 capital, with the shares divided so that any two of the trio would have a majority; the three of them took twenty-six per cent each and that left twenty-two per cent for the university.

The company took on premises on the science park adjacent to the university and not only continued research there but manufactured supercritical fluid kits, which it sold to the pharmaceutical giants at £95,000 each. In April 1996 Humphreys left the university and began to run the business full-time. The turnover for the first full year ending 31 May 1997 was £570,000 and the operating profit £117,000. During the year it had become increasingly clear to the trio that a significant amount of capital was needed to make the most of the opportunities that were appearing. The university, understandably, was anxious not to get involved in any high finance solutions. In February 1998 Tom Quinn, a friend of a friend, came to see York and Humphreys. He suggested that Christopher Benson should be approached as he was looking for interesting ventures. Benson visited Bradford in March and discussions with him continued in London in April. At the second meeting he agreed to join the company as its non-executive chairman. As Humphreys later wrote, 'The future growth path of BPD was assured.'

It was clear to Benson and his fellow directors that the business would benefit from the infusion of a large amount of cash. An accountant with experience of major financial deals was needed for BPD, so Benson suggested that Carole Nicholson should be approached. She had been the treasurer of MEPC, who had personally dealt with the financing of the takeover of Oldham Estates. Nicholson readily agreed to work part-time as financial director. Humphreys has written: 'The rapport between Carole and Sir Christopher and their City contacts proved a major asset to BPD over the next 18 months.' He added to the writer that Benson had also been useful in getting the university to see the wisdom of being more cooperative with the company; apart from anything else, it stood to gain financially as well as in prestige.

The year to end of May 1999 showed turnover of £1.3 m with operating profit of £72,000. The directors had no thoughts of selling the company; they wanted to build up the business, which clearly had huge potential. A private placing of shares in 1999 raised over £1 m from private individuals, mostly City financiers, whom Benson knew from his previous activities. Most of the capital was employed in the building of a pilot plant to produce pharmaceutical compounds for clinical trials; this was opened in early 2000 by Stephen Byers, by then the Secretary of State for Industry. A large overdraft was a problem for Humphreys and Nicholson for a time, but apart from that, money proved to be much less of a problem once Benson was on board. All that was needed was obtained from different sources in the City, including £3 m from Investors in Industry, and a lesser sum from Benson personally.

In August 2000 Humphreys and a colleague made a routine call on Inhale Therapeutic Systems in California, with whom they had had various discussions over the years. It was only intended to keep the relationship ticking over. They showed their American friends a video CD of their new pilot plant, but the Inhale computer they used was very poor and without its sound. Despite that, Humphreys felt that they were impressed by the mime show they had seen. Six days later Ajit Gill, the chief executive officer of Inhale, arrived in Bradford to discuss joint ventures, but nothing came of those talks, mainly because by that stage the two companies were in reality competitors.

In September, York and Humphreys ran a course in Virginia on the importance of particle science in pharmaceutical development, and arranged to meet Gill again for further talks. They continued their discussion in October in San Francisco and later in the month in London, a meeting that Benson also attended. The final negotiations took place at Newark airport, where Gill made Humphreys a firm offer to buy BPD. The price offered by Gill could be called satisfactory. It was to be $200 m, $20 m in cash, the balance in Inhale shares — and the offer caused a sharp inhalation of breath on the part of Humphreys. In addition, $40 m options were to be made available for distribution to the BPD staff, together with a £3 m cash bonus for the staff over two years post-acquisition.

Inhale's offer was accepted, so the company was lost to the UK but it earned a considerable sum for its founders, early investors and the University of Bradford. Benson was pleased with the success of BPD for the sake of its founding trio; he was not displeased with the return on his investment, which he had made because of his belief in the soundness of the project and because he always invested a significant stake in any company of which he was a director.

The University of Bradford expressed its satisfaction by awarding him the honorary degree of Doctor of Science. Professor Brenda Costell, the former Professor of Neuropharmacology, who as Deputy Vice-Chancellor had supported the BPD venture, said of the new graduate at the graduation ceremony:

> Sir Christopher likes people. He must be the most networked person I have ever met. He does not forget a face or a name and makes people feel valued. Whilst being an outstandingly successful businessman he becomes a friend wherever he works. He brought this personal gift to Bradford Particle Design and made all of us value our achievements.

Benson's interest in science and medical health has continued. He has sponsored two research scholarships in the medical faculty of Southampton University; is closely involved with the planned immunology Facility; and is an Honorary Fellow of the University.

CHAPTER FOURTEEN

The Middle Temple

From an early age Benson had an interest in the law. In the Merchant Navy he learned that the ship was a self-contained community, whose captain's word was law; in the Royal Navy he learned the elements of naval law, Queen's Regulations and Admiralty Instructions. As mentioned earlier, he had even written to one of the Inns of Court to inquire about the possibility of his embarking on a career as a barrister. Later, in his civilian career, he was often in touch with solicitors, and less often with barristers, in connection with problems of commercial, employment and land law.

His wife Jo was appointed a magistrate in 1970, the year in which she was elected Mayor of Salisbury, and sat regularly on the bench there until 1999. She was very enthusiastic about the work and often came home with interesting stories to relate. Benson envied her the experience but ruled out a similar one for himself, as he simply had no spare time available. In 1981, when he was managing director of MEPC, he decided that he would have to make enough time and applied to become a Justice of the Peace for the City of London. His application was successful, he underwent the requisite training and then served on the bench until 1985. In that year the Clerk to the Justices insisted that Benson should sit on alternate Monday and Friday afternoons.

On every Monday afternoon, unless he was abroad on business, Benson presided at the MEPC head office over his managing director's committee of directors and senior staff, to discuss the current developments and their problems. It was the most important meeting of the week and so he could not comply with the clerk's demand. He offered instead to sit on every Friday, a day when many magistrates preferred not to sit, as they wanted to start their weekends early. His offer was declined point blank by the clerk so Benson had no option but to resign. By 1998, Benson's life had become less hectic and he was able, somehow, to get back onto the bench and then to serve for a further five years, until reaching seventy, the compulsory retirement age for magistrates.

From 1986 Benson served in the not very onerous post of a Deputy Lieutenant for Greater London. He had for some time been a trustee of the proposed

Metropolitan Police Museum with the Commissioner, Sir Peter Imbert, who was later to become a peer and the Lord Lieutenant, and who appointed Benson a Deputy Lieutenant. Their search for a suitable site for the museum unfortunately came to nothing. They cast their covetous eyes on Bow Street Magistrates' Court, opposite the Royal Opera House, once it ceased to be a courthouse, but the powers that be — or were — considered the premises too valuable for a museum, and so they were allowed to rot instead. Bow Street was, of course, the obvious site for the museum, as it had given birth to Fielding's Bow Street Runners, the predecessors of Peel's Metropolitan police force.

During his first stint on the City bench Benson quite often sat with a very astute woman magistrate, Joan (Lady) Ackner. Through her he got to know her husband, Sir Desmond Ackner, whom he had already encountered occasionally. Ackner was a brilliant barrister and QC who had served as chairman of the Bar Council from 1968 to 1970. In the following year he had become a High Court judge and in 1980 he was promoted to the Court of Appeal. Six years later he became a Lord of Appeal in Ordinary. In 1984, when he was still in the Court of Appeal, Ackner was elected Treasurer, or head, of his own Inn of Court, the Middle Temple. He had since 1965 been a Master of the Bench (or Bencher, for short), as the governing members of all the four the Inns of Court are called, and had regularly expressed his concern about the lack of professional accommodation for members of the Bar, whose numbers were increasing annually. In that connection he spoke and wrote, sometimes passionately, about the need for residential accommodation in the Inn to be converted to barristers' chambers, and for more accommodation generally.

In his chapter in *History of the Middle Temple* (edited by Richard Havery, 2011), on the Inn in the twentieth century, the present writer included a section headed 'Bursting at the Seams' to cover those accommodation problems. It contained the following passage: 'Master Ackner, a former Chairman of the Bar Council, was always ready to take up the cudgels on behalf of barristers, whether in the Inn, the House of Lords or elsewhere.' During his year as Treasurer, Ackner asked Benson whether he would be prepared to give free advice to the Inn on property matters and he agreed to do so. He then gave the Treasurer and the Inn his opinion of the true value of two properties in Essex Street that became available for purchase. Subsequently, Ackner nominated Benson for election as an Honorary Master of the Bench of the Middle Temple.

Despite his later connection with the Thorn Lighting Group, Benson had never met Jules Thorn, its founder, who had died in 1980. The following passage from the chapter mentioned may nevertheless be of interest.

Distinguished members of the business community were elected from time to time, and were able to advise the Inn on matters relating to the estate and investments. For example, Sir Jules Thorn, the Chairman of Thorn Electrical Industries Ltd, was called to the Bench in 1970, and was a good friend of the Inn, both before and after becoming a Master. He first advised the Inn about the lighting of the Hall and Library, then generously paid for electrical improvements and finally left the Inn a substantial legacy for scholarships. Similarly, Sir Christopher Benson, a surveyor and property company director, who was made a bencher in 1984, gave valuable advice to the Inn and particularly to the Estates Committee in connection with the major acquisitions in Essex Street and Fleet Street.

Later in the chapter the writer added: 'The two largest expansion opportunities of the century came up near its end, and very close together, so that it was distinctly possible that only one could be afforded.' It was partly thanks to Benson's experience and contacts, that both complicated and expensive schemes were successfully completed and financed at a rate the Inn could afford, adding nearly 200 places for barristers to the Inn's estate.

The Middle Temple had owned 8 Fleet Street for some years, but it was an almost useless property. It could only be entered from an adjoining property, with which it had been jointly let out. At some stage the staircase of nr.8 had been removed by the lessees, but the floors, which provided only 5000 square feet of accommodation, were still usable, thanks to that access. During repairs to its listed old buildings at the top of Middle Temple Lane in the 'nineties, the Inn's surveyor opened up a doorway into the Fleet Street building and had it bricked up again, just in case it might at some stage be needed for linking purposes. The Estates Committee of the Inn decided that the site might as well be sold. A developer from Singapore became interested in building a 60-bedroom hotel on the site of 7–15 Fleet Street, and wanted to buy number 8. The Inn applied for permission to develop it, and that was granted, trebling its value. Fortunately, nothing came of the hotel plan, so the Inn remained the owner of its foothold in Fleet Street.

Benson's advice was next sought in connection with the Middle Temple's acquisition of one of the several properties in adjoining Essex Street, which the health group BUPA owned and was selling. It was at 24–27 Essex Street and called Provident House. It was attractive as it was a fairly modern property that contained nearly 17,000 square feet of space that could be used by barristers, after essential alterations and improvements had been made. As it was in the south-eastern corner of the street, it could easily be provided with an entrance into the Inn. Despite the fact that the required buildings works would be expensive, the Inn went ahead with the purchase. Although those works had not been quite completed, Blackstone House as it was then named, was opened by the Treasurer of the Inn, Sir David Calcutt QC, on 14 October 1998.

On the same day the Estates Committee discussed the idea of expanding into Fleet Street. By then numbers 7–15, including number 8, had been empty for some time. The idea of using the latter property for student accommodation, complete with a new staircase, had been ruled out, as conversion could only have provided thirteen rooms at the cost of almost £100,000 each. The Singapore developer who owned the other properties had decided not to proceed and was prepared to sell them for £4.6 m. The Inn reserves, including shares at near their peak, before the major downturn of share prices, just covered the purchase price. The property was bought, but construction work was going to require loans totalling £12 m. One reason those costs were going to be high, was because several different adjoining buildings were involved, and they included some superb architectural features that had to be carefully preserved. The City planners also insisted on a shop being included in the development, but that could provide useful rental income. As with the Essex Street property, the architects were able to provide an entrance, at the back of the Fleet Street block, into the Temple, albeit into the Inner Temple's Hare Court rather than directly into the Middle Temple.

It was with the acquisition of suitable loans that Benson's help proved most important. He was able to use his various connections to obtain some viable options. At one stage there was a major crisis, when it looked as though the scheme would fall through, but Benson was able to save the day. The properties were expertly converted and provided a significant addition to the Middle Temple's ability to provide professional chambers for barristers. The large set of commercial law chambers that took the whole of the Fleet Street premises as tenants, might well have moved out of the Temple and out of the area, had they not been acquired by the Inn.

Ackner later commented about this, the Inn's most important acquisition ever:

> Once again Benson's advice was sought. The purchase and refurbishment were both extremely complicated. Many senior Benchers were nervous of the project and without the calming and reassuring advice, I doubt whether the purchase would have gone ahead.

Benson was later invited to join the Inn's Scholarship committee and became the donor of two annual awards. The Middle Temple, like the three other Inns, tried to give some financial assistance to as many as possible of its own students in the final year of their studies. He was a happy man when both his sons, after attending university and the Inns of Court School of Law, were called to the Bar by the Middle Temple, Charles in 1990 and Julian in the following year; and again when, 20 years after becoming a barrister, Charles became a Queen's Counsel. In 2009 Benson was appointed as one of the members of the Council of the Inns of Court Disciplinary Tribunal.

The most interesting and challenging appointment was an educational one, at a time when Benson was still the chairman of the Funding Agency for Schools. The four Inns of Court had founded a joint law school in 1852, when they set up the Council of Legal Education with five professors, to be controlled initially by two Benchers from each of the four Inns. Twenty years later the Bar introduced mandatory law examinations for would-be barristers, though for a long time after that it was not necessary for applicants to be graduates.

By 1997, students wishing to be called to the Bar had to obtain a law degree, or a non-law degree followed by an appropriate one-year legal 'catch-up' diploma course, and then to pass the Bar's vocational training course. In short, either four and five years of study were required, before call to the Bar, which had to be followed by a year's pupillage with an experienced barrister. Many universities and other educational bodies offered law degree and diploma courses, but the Inns of Court School of Law for a while had a monopoly of the Bar vocational training course. That School of Law, which had physically moved from Lincoln's Inn to Gray's Inn in 1967, was an important law school but one of many. It became a corporate body only in 1996, with Mr Justice Hooper as chairman of the governors; he had started his distinguished career as a law teacher and ended up in the Court of Appeal. He had met Benson in a court case when he was still a practising QC and knew him to be an honorary Bencher of the Middle Temple. He invited him to become one of the governors, an invitation Benson accepted at once.

In 1997 the Council of Legal Education was wound up and its assets were transferred to the Inns of Court School of Law. However, it became clear to Benson and all others intimately involved with it, that the School was too small to survive in the highly competitive legal education field. Furthermore, the School was going through an internal crisis of confidence. Morale among the lecturers was low; Benson was not alone in being concerned that the students might suffer as a result. Management changes were made in 2000 and, somewhat to his surprise, he was appointed Principal of the School.

He next made inquiries about a possible future home for the School. He had a meeting with the Treasurers of all the four Inns and explained why, in his opinion, a more drastic move had become necessary. They were all fairly angry with him for wanting to take 'their' School away from them. He had the invidious task of pointing out to these four distinguished lawyers that, in law, the Inns no longer had any claim to it: it merely bore their name. Fortunately for him, he

Outside the Inns of Court School of Law

was backed up by another ex-chairman of the Bar Council and leading advocate, Lord (Robert) Alexander QC, the Deputy Treasurer of the Middle Temple, who was to be its Treasurer in the following year. The four Treasurers finally agreed to wave farewell to the school, whose exams they had all passed many years earlier, and Benson continued with his search. Once again, he had the excellent services of a personal assistant, Linda Witts, whom he regarded as an essential link between the governors, the lecturers and, to a lesser extent, the students. In due course she was to follow him to Crossrail, when he was appointed as the first chairman of that venture. He was also greatly assisted by the finance officer, Graham Hamer, who patiently and skilfully did all the 'heavy lifting' during the later negotiations.

One of several providers of legal education to whom Benson spoke about a possible new home for the School was Professor Graham Zellick, the Vice-Chancellor of the University of London and a Bencher of the Middle Temple. His federal university already had five of the top law schools and could have accommodated a sixth. However, in a meeting with Zellick, Benson concluded, possibly erroneously, that the Inns' School, of which he had become very proud, would be in danger of simply being subsumed into the University of London and of losing its identity, if that were to be his choice.

Subsequently he pursued discussions with City University (also in London), which was prepared to guarantee the School's integrity and separate identity. As a result they agreed that the Inns of Court School of Law should become its law faculty. The new Dean of the Inns of Court School of Law, Adrian Keane, and other academic staff members, moved with it to City University, where the new faculty was also headed by Keane. It retained its name until 2008 when, in response to complaints from competitors that the reference to the Inns might give the university an unfair advantage in attracting Bar students, the school stopped using the name of the Inns of Court and changed it to the City Law School. Benson's short life in the academic world had come to an end with the transfer to the City University, which awarded him an honorary Doctor of Science degree in 2000.

In view of his many links with the City of London, the award of the degree was gratifying but, especially in view of the earlier reaction of the four Treasurers, even more welcome was the letter Benson received in June 2001 from Lord Justice Mummery, the President of the Council of the Inns of Court, on which all four of them served.

> At the meeting of the Council last week, everyone present expressed great admiration for the way in which you have managed to turn round the Inns of Court School of Law and prepare it for merger with City University. As a member of the School's Board of Governors, I of course know better than most how much you have achieved.

The fact that the Middle Temple and the other three Inns had lost the School of Law did not mean that their educational functions came to an end. They merely changed direction from the education of students undertaking the Bar examinations, to an increase in the important post-qualifying instruction. The Middle Temple led the way with advocacy courses for young barristers, coupled with other courses for new practitioners and continuing professional development for the more experienced ones.

At the Middle Temple Benson found the help of the Under-Treasurer, Brigadier Charles Wright, invaluable at different times. Apart from anything else, Wright responded to his request to meet the Bar students shortly after their qualification as barristers and during their pupillage year, so that he could speak to them about life outside the law and other topics.

In 2002 Benson was appointed High Sheriff of Wiltshire. One of his duties as the holder of that ancient and distinguished office, was to look after the High

Court judges when they came on circuit. As he had many dealings with Salisbury Cathedral, of which he had been a lay canon since 2000, he felt honoured to be allowed to have the annual Sheriff's legal service there. Such ceremonial events are usually attended by the High Court judges coming on circuit, as well as by some of the local court judges and magistrates. The legal profession and police are also usually represented. Benson had his new sheriff's uniform on, complete with a sword, not much bigger than a midshipman's dirk.

It is not difficult to imagine the pride felt during that service by Benson and his wife Jo, who apart from being a former Mayor of the city and a magistrate was also a Deputy Lieutenant for Wiltshire. Most unusually, and clearly as a compliment to him personally, it was attended by both Lord Woolf, the Lord Chief Justice, and Lord Phillips, then Master of the Rolls (and a Bencher of the Middle Temple) together with other judges. Among the lawyers present in their robes were their sons Charles and Julian.

During his time as High Sheriff Benson became fascinated with the education of much younger students, possibly because he was aware of his own early educational shortcomings. He determined to visit as many schools in his bailiwick as possible in that year, speaking about his historic post and the courts, and presenting prizes in many of them. His overriding interest was in the primary schools, where head teachers regularly warned him that the children's attention span was about seven minutes only. In that case, he told them, he would speak for seven minutes and no more, but then take questions until the same one was asked a second time. The average time for questions turned out to be forty-five minutes, with most of them being sensible ones. Benson loved those sessions. The head teachers regularly told him that he should come and visit them on a Wednesday, when the children cooked the lunch — so he did.

The election of the Treasurer of the Middle Temple for the year 2006 gave Benson great pleasure. The new Treasurer was Derek Wood CBE, QC, who had been a valued member of Benson's Property Advisory Group at the Department of the Environment. Wood was a property law specialist, who had the advantage of having been both a practitioner and an academic in that field. He was the only lawyer member of the group and his advice had always proved very helpful and sound.

Lord Ackner served as a Law Lord from 1986 to 1992. After his retirement he sat, regularly and very actively, in the House of Lords as a cross bencher — though according to Harold Wilson's precept it would not matter where he actually sat. Early in the new century, after they had known each other for over twenty years, Ackner told Benson that he thought his all-round experience would be useful in the Lords. Would he consider putting his name forward for a life peerage? Always willing to oblige and help out, Benson agreed. He obtained the additional support of Lord Armstrong, the former Cabinet Secretary; Lord Ouseley, the former chairman of the Commission for Racial Equality; and Sir David Williams, who had been the first full-time Vice-Chancellor of Cambridge University. Ackner was both saddened and puzzled when his attempt to get Benson into the Upper House failed. He asked the chairman of its Appointments Commission whether Benson could put his name forward again, and was told that such a course was possible, but that it would be better for him to wait until he had done something significant.

That reply startled Benson, when Ackner relayed it to him. He wondered whether the Commission had actually read the CV he had provided. He was also puzzled for another reason: the chairman of the Commission, then still a commoner, had been on the London Docklands Development Corporation as a board member during all the years that Benson had been at its head. He wondered what his Lordship regarded as doing 'something significant', as he was also chairman of one the large banks that was struggling to survive and soon had to be bailed out by the government and taxpayer. Benson decided that he could not equal that significant example — and so remained a commoner.

Benson felt that he was unlucky to have missed the boat. Whereas the chairman of the Appointments Commission was censured in Parliament for his part in the banking fiasco, Lord Ackner was highly regarded and his backing should have carried considerable weight. In the House of Lords on 22 March 2006, Baroness Scotland QC, then Minister of State at the Home Office, briefly delayed dealing with the Terrorism Bill to announce to their Lordships that Desmond Ackner had died on the day before. She added:

> Throughout his legal career, he made a great contribution to the General Council of the Bar, serving in a variety of positions, including as chairman from 1968 to 1970. He was loved by this House. There is not one Minister who has had the temerity to represent and speak on behalf of the Government for Home Office affairs who had not been placed *in terrorem* by Lord Ackner.'

Despite that, she added, he had been her friend. Other peers also paid their tributes.

It is no coincidence that Sir David Williams, when President of Wolfson College Cambridge, appointed Benson an Honorary Fellow, in recognition of his contribution to its expansion and well-being. Both of his sons obtained their law degrees there.

CHAPTER FIFTEEN

Crossrail

London's need for one or more east-west rail crossings had been discussed for many years, to no avail. The Regent's Canal had been built north of the Thames, in a curving line from west to east, eventually emerging in Docklands, and in the nineteenth century its directors suggested a railway, possibly following the line of the canal in parts. Parliament approved the idea in 1880, but nothing came of it. In 1943 the Abercrombie Plan for post-war Britain suggested the possibility of two new tubes lines under London to provide adequate east-west links. That idea was also abandoned.

In 1974 the London Rail Study produced the seeds of what became Crossrail. It suggested two railway tunnels. The northern one would run from Paddington, via Bond Street and Liverpool Street to near Whitechapel — close to the line eventually tunnelled for Crossrail. The southern would run from Victoria to London Bridge, a proposal made almost superfluous by the construction of the Victoria and Jubilee tube lines. The report drew attention to the successful city railways constructed in Paris, Hamburg and Munich. The next proposals, fortunately for London and the south-east, are now going ahead successfully at last.

Apart from Benson's four-and-a-half years as chairman of the London Docklands Development Corporation, his most exciting time on a quango was his three-year period as the first chairman of the Crossrail project. Shortly after he became president of the London Chamber of Commerce and Industry in 2000, the Chamber was asked by Ken Livingstone, the leader of the Greater London Authority, to nominate someone to chair the Regional Development Authority. Benson's name was put forward. He later learned that London First, when asked by Livingstone, had nominated Sir John Egan, who had succeeded Lord Blakenham as chairman of MEPC.

As it happened, neither man got the post but Livingstone, by then the first democratically elected Mayor of London (as opposed to the incumbent of the ancient post of Lord Mayor of the City of London), asked Benson to give him a list of six experienced people who could prove an asset on his new Transport for London board. A little later Benson answered his phone at home and was told,

With Ken Livingstone at the start of Crossrail

'It's Ken.' 'Ken who?' 'Ken Livingstone, of course.' He complained that Benson had not included his own name on the list he had supplied. When he replied that he would never put his own name on such a list, the Mayor protested, 'But it's you I wanted.' Not unreasonably, Benson countered, 'Why not ask me?' He was then invited and agreed to serve on Transport for London, which was chaired by the Mayor himself.

After a very interesting year on that body, dealing with London's multiple transport problems, Benson was invited by Livingstone to be the first chairman of the board of Cross London Rail Links Ltd (CLRL). That was the joint venture company set up in 2001, and owned on a 50/50 basis by Transport for London and a national body, the Strategic Rail Authority. Its purpose was to promote and develop Crossrail lines 1 and 2. The press release wording demonstrated the relevance of Benson's experience in Docklands and with Canary Wharf. It stated that the new company had been asked to report on the feasibility, costs and financing of Crossrail options by early 2002, a ridiculously optimistic date in view of the complexity of the issues, despite the fact that the government had provided substantial funding to the new company. The release continued:

> These options should meet the three main objectives of Crossrail: supporting the development of London as a World City and its role as the key financial centre of the UK and Europe; to support London's economic growth and regeneration; and to tackle the lack of capacity and congestion on the existing network.

Bob Kiley, the Transport for London Commissioner, announced Benson's appointment, adding: 'Sir Christopher has the vision and credentials to deliver this major railway project for London and the South-east.' Very flattering, but matters were so arranged that the three directors from Transport for London (including Kiley) and the three from the Strategic Rail Authority each had a vote. However, incredible though it may be, the chairman had none! Benson wondered whether he should ask to be issued with a referee's whistle and a red and yellow card. Instead, he commented:

> Crossrail is an incredibly exciting prospect as it will link London's business and economic centres from both east and west, as well as connecting to Heathrow Airport. I am delighted to be driving forward the biggest rail development in London since the Underground was first built.

One of the first steps for Benson was to find a suitable chief executive. He was keen to get John Armitt, a very distinguished engineer who had been chief executive of the Costain Group shortly after Benson had left it. However, Armitt was offered the same job at Railtrack and then at Network Rail, which he accepted, so he was ruled out. Fortunately, another equally well qualified candidate was found, Norman Haste, who had been the project director of the Second Severn Crossing and then at Terminal Five at Heathrow, which had just been completed. The deputy chief executive selected was Keith Berryman, who had worked on the Hong Kong Mass Transit Railway, the company chosen in July 2014 to operate Crossrail once it is completed. With their crucial advice and assistance, Benson managed to construct a team of some 200 engineers and other professionals, all with impressive experience and skills, who threw themselves wholeheartedly into their important tasks without delay.

Crossrail 1 was always going to get priority over Crossrail 2. The first line was going to cross London from west to east, splitting into two at the eastern end and possibly in the west also. Crossrail 2 was intended to run roughly from southwest to northeast London, cutting across the first line and thus creating a huge cross, and giving Crossrail a double meaning. That second line was first talked about as going from Wimbledon to Hackney and, later, to Alexandra Palace or New Southgate, and out into Hertfordshire. As far as Benson was concerned, Crossrail 2 was put onto, and remained on the back burner.

By March 2002 the short list of alternative east-west route corridors had been identified. Local authorities and other stakeholders had been asked for their views. In January 2003 the new Secretary of State for Transport, Alistair Darling, asked the company to investigate the possibility of terminating a southern branch of the western half, not at Richmond, as requested earlier, but at Kingston. Benson was aware that there were already strong objections to Richmond as a destination; adding Kingston was only going to make things worse. Other towns were later suggested by the minister, who seemed not to realise the amount of effort, time and money that had to go into each detailed engineering inquiry.

By dint of extremely hard work on the part of his dedicated teams, in September 2003 Benson was able to present to Government the business case for Crossrail (the number 1 was understood, as Crossrail 2 was not being discussed any more at that stage). The various alternatives suggested by the minister increased the work so much that Benson told the writer:

> We were all fed up with indecision and vacillation. I was amazed by the fortitude of the engineers when told to go and survey and do total engineering tests — knowing they had the certainty of being rejected.

One of Benson's assets is his calm personality: not a single person has spoken of his losing his temper, but he was made really angry by the minister's changes of mind, which caused his staff that extra work. At the time he referred more than once to Darling dithering, or to his being the Secretary of State for Indecision. At one point Benson commented bitterly that one of Darling's few firm decisions was to 'strengthen' his board with an official from his Department, 'whose prime function seemed to have been to ensure that no serious public money should be allocated to construction, but that private sources should be found'.

The Crossrail Business Case Summary was submitted to the Secretary of State in July and published in September 2003. The need for Crossrail was demonstrated first. Overcrowding (called crowding for short in the summary) was serious during peak periods on both the National Rail network and its London termini, and on the Underground. An increase in crowding was antici-pated, partly because of the plans to develop the London economy, as well as the Thames Gateway (on both side of the Thames) and the London-Stansted-

Cambridge sub-region. 'Transport infrastructure is seen as a significant component in the strategy for delivering growth in the Thames Gateway.' The earlier
improvements to transport in Docklands were useful, but did not help much
with the needs further east. Crossrail, it was submitted, could help in three ways:
by reducing crowding; by increasing capacity to and in the central area; and by
increasing accessibility to the central area from new centres of population.

The summary pointed out that some important changes had taken place since
Crossrail had first been tentatively mooted in the 'seventies. 'Critically, since
then, Docklands regeneration and growth ambitions have come to fruition and
have now been extended into the wider Thames Gateway area.' The proposed
Crossrail service pattern was explained, a main point of which was that 24 trains
per hour should go through the central tunnel section, with 200 metre long trains
made up of ten carriages, each of which would have two double doors each side
for the speedy loading and unloading of passengers. Time repeatedly leads to
changes of plans, especially where competitive tenders are concerned. That point
was illustrated in early 2014 when Bombardier was approved as the train manu-
facturer for Crossrail, and demonstrated that better and cheaper provision could
be made by their proposed nine carriage model. With nine longer carriages,
together slightly longer than 200 metres, three sets of doors could be fitted to
each one, speeding up dwell times in stations.

The calculation of anticipated costs was, as Benson well knew, as crucial as
with any major building project — the more so perhaps, as public money was
involved. The cost of tunnelling was estimated using the experience of the Jubilee
Line Extension. The base capital cost was estimated to be £7 bn at 2002 prices,
plus £3bn for contingency, included in accordance with Treasury guidelines. The
benefit:cost ratio of the scheme at that time worked out attractively as 2:1.(It may
well eventually turn out to be even better than that.)

The Business Case for the project was also prepared in accordance with
Government guidance, this time on major transport projects. Detailed forecasts
were included of the beneficial effects of the new line on the city and its sur-
roundings. The benefits for the mainline stations and the individual
Underground lines was discussed in detail. Apart from anything else, far fewer
passenger interchanges between railway and Underground would be needed. It
was estimated that Crossrail would create some 130,000 jobs.

In September 2003 Benson also launched the first phase of the consultation
programme. That was a public awareness campaign, explaining the proposals to
the public, and based partly on his experience of sounding out the community
in Docklands. Press releases and advertisements were used and over 300,000
leaflets were distributed at stations affected by the plan. The leaflets included a

Freepost card for comments. Local authorities and community groups were also informed about the main proposals.

Most of the responses were favourable. The Corporation of London commented:

> London needs Crossrail today. Improving the transport system is the number one concern for City businesses and it is essential for the capital's future that we can deliver these improvements.

Michael Snyder, the Corporation's Policy and Resources committee chairman, added: 'Crossrail is the most important rail link in the last 30 years and the only line that can be built for the next 20 years. Crossrail will bring billions of pounds in economic benefits and unlock powerful regeneration forces for the capital and the South East.' The Canary Wharf Group wrote enthusiastically, in words that could have been written by Benson:

> Crossrail is probably the most important investment decision that London faces in this decade. The opportunity of linking the combined financial and business districts of the West End, City and Isle of Dogs to Heathrow in the west and Stratford in the Thames Gateway in the east, creates unparalleled opportunities for London.

Fortunately, it was not just the City interests that responded in that enthusiastic manner. Brendan Barber, the General Secretary of the TUC, stated:

> The TUC fully supports Crossrail as an essential part of an integrated transport network, not just for London, but the entire South East. And we welcome its capacity to redress historic imbalances of transport provision, economic opportunity and quality of life between communities to the East and West of London.

In the following month further information was made available to the public, including schools. Because of the diversity of the population along the proposed route, publicity was printed in the eleven most appropriate languages and also in braille. Letters were sent to the owners of any property likely to be directly affected, inviting them to meet a specialist adviser. Almost forty per cent of over 7000 people who visited the specially set up information centres, responded on reply cards. Three out of four made favourable comments, but all remarks were sifted and alterations were made to the plans where appropriate. Comments were also invited by phone or email. The consultation exercise proved very worthwhile. Benson was pleasantly surprised by the intelligent response obtained from most commentators, who appreciated that they were being offered additional transport links and, for some, increased property value as a further bonus. He found very few replies on the lines of 'Not in my backyard.'

Benson and his team also canvassed every school in London, asking junior schools to produce colourful posters to promote Crossrail and to assist passengers at stations. Senior schools were invited to provide ideas for the interior design of the new rail coaches. Benson has described the response as 'incredible and of high quality, to the extent that some of the coach interior designs were sent to Bombardier for evaluation. The result was that some were so good that they should be used.' Commercial television helped to sponsor that initiative and gave all the prize winners and runners-up a day at a TV studio, with opportunities to meet celebrities. The whole enterprise was a huge success and reinforced Benson's belief in the ability of young people to respond to challenge and opportunity.

The Business Case was submitted to the minister was on 11th July; three days later he announced the appointment of a body to review that submission, headed by Adrian Montague, a former member of the Strategic Rail Authority. The minister asked particularly for an assessment of the extent of government funding that might be justified, together with a forecast of how much could be raised from other sources. He also asked the review body, somewhat unrealistically, to consider 'whether there were any other means of delivering a Crossrail project that might offer better performance than CLRL's proposals.'

The review was very thorough and published in July 2004. As an illustration of the detail of the comments, one related to the proposed trains and 'the impact on dwell time of the proposed two doors per side design.' That point was clearly picked up by the designers of the Bombardier train eventually selected. As far as the number of trains per hour in the central section was concerned, the review doubted that twenty-four hours per train would be achieved.

As to the likely costs, the review pointed out that some savings could be made by, for example, a reduction in the size of stations. More generally, there were a large number of uncertainties to be resolved about costs. The reviewers concluded that some estimates were too low and others too high, but that they almost cancelled out. The total cost was likely to be higher than the figure given in the Business Case, but not by more than an additional £1 bn. On the issue of value for money the review stated: 'The Business Case for the Benchmark Scheme is robust and could provide good value for money. It is, however, critically dependent upon the extent to which expected population and employment growth in London materialises.'

Benson was gratified to see praise of his hard-working staff. 'The Review wishes to pay tribute to the quality of the work that CLRL has undertaken in developing the Benchmark Scheme. Its professionalism and dedication has provided a strong basis for the Review's analysis.'

Shortly after the publication of the review, Benson learned from a senior London Gateway official that he and his colleagues were just about to put in a planning application for major works on a site in East London. When Benson asked for the exact location it turned out to be almost precisely on the designated place for one of his Crossrail tunnel portals. He told Norman Haste, who was horrified by the news, and they both went to the Thames Gateway offices armed with the relevant plans. Fortunately, they were able to prove their point and the proposed planning application was abandoned. When Benson later complained to the Secretary of State that there should have been consultation between the different parties to avert such conflicts, he replied that it was not his remit.

Darling, the Labour Secretary of State, probably heard via the Whitehall grapevine what Benson thought of him. He sent for him, and after expressing a preference to have 'one of ours' as chairman, dismissed him. Benson was afterwards at a meeting attended by Darling at which a possible explanation for the delays became apparent. The speaker, the new chairman of CLRL, said in the presence of the Secretary of State, that he had put it to him that he was against Crossrail. According to him, Darling had replied that he had been against it originally, but had changed his mind later and was by then in favour of the project. Neither at that meeting, nor at any time later did Darling dispute that description of his earlier state of mind.

It is still Benson's belief that if the original satisfactory plan had been allowed to go forward by a supportive Department of Transport, the central London core of Crossrail could have been completed in time for the Olympics in 2012, instead of being deferred, though partly for financial reasons that only raised their ugly head later, to 2018.

The Crossrail Act was passed in 2008 and work started in the following May. Benson learned with pleasure that the first pile was to be driven was at the site of the new Canary Wharf station, which is to be joined in due course to another in Docklands at Custom House. The western end of the line will be at the newly modernised and enlarged railway station at Reading, instead of Maidenhead, the earlier terminus; and there is to be no spur to Richmond or Kingston, two of the destinations that had wasted so much of his engineers' time. However, on 7th August 2014 the Secretary of State for Transport mentioned, for the first time, the possibility of a north west spur to Watford and Tring. Benson, who greatly valued his three years on the project, was sorry that he was no longer involved, saying to the writer: 'I believed Crossrail one of the greatest projects of the century and enjoyed working with highly professional men and women. I wanted to be involved as long as possible.'

It is easy to understand Benson's great interest in Crossrail. Apart from anything else, it rounded off his education and experience in the transport world.

Not many men can claim to have had so much personal experience of sea and air travel, coupled with road and rail building.

Benson is still the proud possessor of Ticket nr 000 001 which states unequivocally: 'This first edition ticket entitles the bearer Sir Christopher Benson to be the first passenger to travel on Crossrail Line One' — but he is not holding his breath.

CHAPTER SIXTEEN

In the Wake of Captain Coram

When Benson's time as chairman of Crossrail was terminated by the Secretary of State at the end of October 2004, he was aged 71, and although he had no intention of retiring, he was content to contemplate a future without any major employed role. He considered himself to be a very fortunate man to have had such a full and rewarding career, and welcomed the opportunity of having more time available for various good causes. Some of them, including the National Deaf Children's Society, have been mentioned in passing earlier, so only four of those that concerned him in the next decade will be discussed briefly in this chapter.

In 2005 Benson was approached by David Goldstone, whom he had known for many years as the chairman of the Regalian property company, and asked whether he would care to take over from him the role of President and chairman of the governors of the Coram children's charities. Benson knew a little about the ground-breaking Foundling Hospital, set up in 1741 in north London by former shipwright and sea captain, Thomas Coram, but knew nothing about the various subsequent initiatives for the welfare of children, such as fostering and adoption, that had been developed over the years. Benson always had a concern for children, particularly in their housing and education, and so agreed to replace Goldstone. He was not made aware of the fact that the institution had substantial problems of its own.

Some of Coram's earlier problems, and the steps taking to solve them, have been summarised by Dame Gillian Pugh, its distinguished chief executive from 1997 to 2005, in her history of Thomas Coram and his Hospital: *London's Forgotten Children*, which was published in 2007, during Benson's time at the helm. The high value of the charity's various art treasures, and especially of paintings donated by William Hogarth and his contemporaries in the early days of the Hospital, had proved to be both a blessing and a problem. In the early 1990s it became clear that expensive conservation work was required both for those paintings, and the building on the original Hospital site in which they were kept, 40 Brunswick Square. The building had been closed for some years, owing to the risk of theft and the cost of insurance. As money charitably donated for the benefit of children could not be used to provide the substantial sums needed, the public had lost sight of those treasures.

The governors understandably did not wish to sell the art collection and managed to find a solution with the help of the Charity Commission. Coram was split: a new charity, the Foundling Museum was set up to run the art collection and to support Coram's work with children. The collection remained the property of Coram, but was lent to the Museum for twenty-five years, on the basis that it would gradually raise sufficient money, in that period, to purchase it all. A grant from the National Heritage Memorial Fund ensured that the repairs to the building and essential conservation work could be executed, and that the public could once more see the collection.

The Attorney-General, Lord Goldsmith QC, who had responsibility for charity law matters, made it a condition of his consent to the new arrangement, that Hogarth's *The March of the Guards to Finchley*, should be sold by Coram to the Museum. The price of £3.9 m was put up in 2002 by the same Fund and, with luck, sufficient further donors will ensure that the remaining precious items will be bought by the Museum in the remainder of the twenty-five-year period. (Hogarth had painted The March in 1746, twelve years after completing *The Rake's Progress* series, one of the greatest assets of the Sir John Soane's Museum, for which Benson had helped to raise £2m for repairs and improvements.)

These complicated arrangements caused no problems for Benson, but another charity law point did. Before he took over the chair, two separate donors had each given a substantial sum, earmarked for particular charitable purposes, which were clearly expressed by them. It goes without saying, that they both expected to receive an account in due course, explaining how their particular funds had been used. Benson was disturbed to hear from the Mercers' Company and from Roger de Haan, the former head of Saga, that they had not been informed about what had happened to their substantial gifts.

Benson was unable to obtain any satisfactory explanation from Coram's relatively new chief executive (Gillian Pugh's immediate successor) and so had to undertake considerable research personally, much of it with the help of the Mercers' Company charity specialist. It turned out that, in breach of the law, the money had been used by Coram, but not in accordance with the expressed wishes of the donors. Benson was relieved that there was no question of any of the money having been stolen. However, he felt acutely embarrassed by the whole affair, the more so as he was left with the impression that, despite the fact that he personally had no connection with the charity at the material time, de Haan 'still thinks I'm a crook.'

There was another major problem. When Benson first inquired about the forward strategy of the organisation, the chief executive was unable to tell him what it was. When he insisted on her producing her plan for the future, none was forthcoming. A few members of the staff had their own concerns about the running of the organisation at that time. Christine Kelly, the head of human resources, along with her finance colleagues, was aware of the difficulties the organisation was facing; she was pleased when Benson arrived and immediately grasped the essential points and tried to remedy the shortcomings that he found.

Having investigated the running of the organisation thoroughly, with the benefit of advice from his deputy at Coram, David Bramson (the retired senior partner of a firm of City solicitors), Benson came to the conclusion that drastic steps were necessary. Although the chief executive was academically well qualified as a social worker, it was not her talent to run such an important charity, with its substantial staff and large sums of money to control. He accordingly negotiated a settlement with her, which enabled him to seek a replacement. He had just arrived in Corfu on holiday, when he received an urgent message to the effect that some of the senior social work staff were up in arms, as they were supporters of the departing chief executive, and that the junior staff were concerned for their jobs. Benson returned from Corfu immediately. He saw the senior staff first and heard their views, but was not deflected, and explained to them why a replacement at the top of the organisation was essential. They listened to him courteously and seemed to understand his reasons. Not one of the senior staff resigned over the issue. When he saw the remainder of the staff, he made it clear that their jobs were safe.

Benson acted for a short time as interim chief executive, and set in motion the search for a new permanent one. Kelly gave the writer a description of Benson at work, one that resembled the comments of others who worked with him, and which have been discussed earlier.

> He was very clear about what he was doing. He was not afraid to make decisions. He was a strong and brave leader — but he allowed people to do what they did best and was good at recognising their contribution. You felt valued by him.

She mentioned one instance when Benson had announced an important decision he had made. She told him that she disagreed with him on a sensitive point, giving her reasons. After thinking about the matter he conceded that her view should prevail.

Kelly felt that Benson had arrived at a time when the organisation was incredibly dysfunctional and that he had pulled it together with a steady hand. That being so, she had felt able to stay on — and is still there. When Benson recently asked her whether she would be prepared to pass on her recollections to the writer, Kelly readily agreed, adding: 'It's also an opportunity to say how much you helped put Coram on its feet. For my part, it always felt safe knowing you were there.' Benson's successful intervention at Coram reminds one of what was said about his early days at the troubled Housing Corporation, by its chief executive, namely, that he came in and quietly and without panic put the Corporation together again.

Benson's choice of John Hart, a retired Royal Navy Commodore, to succeed him as interim director, was an inspired one, as he quickly gained the respect of the staff, and restored morale. Both Benson and Hart seem to have impressed Jeanne Kaniuk, who knew Coram well, as she was in charge of its important adoption work. On 18 March 2007 she wrote to Benson:

> I am writing to thank you for the courageous way you have handled Coram's problems over the past year. It was a most inauspicious and unenviable situation. However you faced the problems squarely, and I hope your courage and determination will be vindicated. I do think John Hart's appointment was propitious and I believe he leaves a legacy of optimism and of constructive planning built on healthy foundations. He has tackled a range of problems in a forthright manner, and re-established trust and a cooperative spirit across the organisation. None of this would have been possible without your determination to make a difference, and your active support. I see you and John as very worthy guardians of the Coram legacy.

After an extensive search and selection process, the post of chief executive was filled by Dr Carol Homden, who brought verve, talent and ambition for Coram's success and the expansion of its caring role. Fortunately, Dr Homden, who in 2013 was awarded a CBE for her work, is still there. Benson stayed a little while longer, until things had settled down. After three years in the posts he had taken over from Goldstone, he decided that, having been the instigator of major changes, it was appropriate for him to step down. In 2006 he had suggested that Edward Hartill should be appointed as his vice-chairman. Hartill was the very experienced former City of London Surveyor and succeeded Benson as chairman in 2008. As a result of a review of the governance of the institutions that Benson had initiated, the role of President of Coram and chairman of the governors was split; Benson remains an Honorary Vice-President and a governor.

In 2007 the Dean of Salisbury, the Very Revd June Osborne, discussed her Cathedral's lack of a permanent font with Benson. For some reason the earlier font had been sent to Australia in Victorian times and not replaced. The Dean

The new font

had been looking for a sculptor who could do justice to the Cathedral and its stunning architecture, and had succeeded in finding one. He was William Pye, who specialised in water sculptures, which are now located on many different sites. He might justly be called, like the Pope who had fountains erected all over Rome, Fontifex (instead of Pontifex) Maximus — though without any irony in Pye's case.

Pye's beautiful modern design was duly erected in the Cathedral and funded by the Bensons together with the Jerusalem Trust, one of the Sainsbury Family charitable foundations. The new font was consecrated by the Archbishop of Canterbury, Dr Rowan Williams, on 28 September 2008, the 750th anniversary of the Cathedral. When the four corner spouts of the font are not spouting, the water surface becomes so still that it looks like a mirror. Some thoughtless visitors placing their cameras or handbags on what they thought was merely a handy polished surface, have had a well-deserved surprise. Fortunately, most visitors to the Cathedral respond to the font with respect and admiration.

———

Jo Benson had for a long time involved herself with national and local charities, but one hospital visit affected her so deeply that she told her husband they must

178

do something about a problem she had encountered. On a visit to the Salisbury District Hospital's maternity unit, she found that mothers who had given birth to stillborn babies, or who had lost their baby shortly after a live birth, shared a ward with happy mothers enjoying the company of their babies. She felt heartbroken and Benson instantly understood his wife's distress. He spoke to Dave Cates, the head of the 'Stars' appeal for the hospital, who suggested they might like to fund the fitting out of a separate bereavement suite for the mothers who had suffered such a loss, where they could mourn for their child with its father — and their other children, if they wished. The Bensons agreed to do so.

On the day the new suite was opened by the Bensons (22 April 2013), Christopher said: 'No one can doubt the quality of service and the dedication of caring staff at Salisbury District Hospital, but at certain times in life, all one wants is a place of peace and the company of loved ones. We hope that this suite will be such a place for people at a time of great tragedy. Jo and I feel very honoured to have had the opportunity to help a little.' Benson has recently added wryly, 'Sadly, the suite has been in regular use ever since.' On one of his visits he noticed that a small area of land adjoining the new suite had been left uncultivated, and offered to provide a flower garden there. His offer was turned down for a touching reason: some of the mothers decided that they wanted to plant a garden there themselves.

The Australian Ballet Gala concert that Benson had arranged for MEPC to sponsor in July 1988, for the benefit of both the Royal Opera House and the Australian Ballet, was partly celebrating the latter's twenty-fifth birthday. However, it also marked the bicentenary of the arrival, in January 1788, of Captain Arthur Phillip in what is now Sydney harbour, in command of the First Fleet of convicts and others. He arrived there just in time to forestall a landing by the French explorer La Pérouse, who disappeared without trace soon afterwards. Despite Benson's love of both the sea and Australia, at that time he did not pursue his superficial interest in the Captain, who had been appointed as the first Governor of New South Wales and later, an Admiral in the Royal Navy.

Phillip had to leave New South Wales for England because of ill health in December 1792, but during his five years as Governor, he had managed to lay the foundations of what became the modern Australia. As early as 1800, the English translator of the French book, *Voyage in Search of La Pérouse*, was able to contemplate the possibility of a future when '... great nations in the immense

The Benson Suite

region of New Holland may send their navigators, philosophers, and antiquaries, to contemplate the ruins of ancient London and Paris, and to trace the languid remains of the arts and sciences in this quarter of the globe. Who can tell, whether the rudiments of some great future empire may not already exist at Botany Bay?'

The year 2014 marked the bicentenary of the death of Phillip. Benson, who had for a long time been a friend of Australia, as well as a chairman and then vice-president of the Britain-Australia Society, chaired the appeal for a suitable memorial to commemorate the first governor. He launched the appeal at a meeting at Australia House in London on 1st October 2013, which was also addressed by Michael Pembroke, a New South Wales judge, who spoke about his new biography of Arthur Phillip. That interesting book mentions that after a period at sea, shortly before his thirteenth birthday in 1751, 'Phillip commenced a more formal process of naval education when he was accepted for admission to the Charity School of the Royal Hospital for Seamen at Greenwich.' As mentioned earlier, Benson had started his own naval education at the age of thirteen in *HMS Worcester* on the Thames at Greenhithe — quite close to the hospital.

Initially, Benson made a relatively modest request to Westminster Abbey, for permission for a commemorative plaque to be placed on a suitable section of

Remembering Captain Phillip

wall or column. Fortunately, the Dean of Westminster, the Very Revd Dr John Hall, read an earlier account of Phillip's history and made the very welcome suggestion that he merited rather more, such as a memorial stone in the floor of the centre of the nave of the Abbey. With the help of others, especially Pauline Lyle-Smith, his deputy chairman, Benson raised sufficient funds for a memorial stone to be placed in the floor of Westminster Abbey, close to the Grave of the Unknown Warrior; also for a bronze armillary on a stone base in Bath, in the grounds of the Assembly Rooms and opposite Phillip's last home.

The Abbey memorial was formed, from a piece of specially imported Sydney Cove stone, by the sculptor Ken Thompson. The scientifically correct armillary, with its internal globe, is the work of the sundial designer and maker, David Harber. Its stone base, which includes a representation of a quayside bollard, was designed and carved out of Bath stone by Nigel Fenwick. Any surplus and future funds raised will be used to finance scholarships, bearing Arthur Phillip's name, for British and Australian students wishing to study for a Master's degree, or to serve an apprenticeship in, say, marine or aircraft engineering, in the other country. Benson has several times emphasized that he is more interested in the success of those educational ventures, than in the commemoration of the past.

The Duke of Edinburgh, the Patron of the Britain-Australia Society, attended the service in the Abbey for the dedication of the memorial on 9 July 2014, where

Westminster Abbey memorial

he laid a wreath. He did not speak at the ceremony, but his earlier supporting remarks were included in the Order of Service:

> As the Captain commanding the First Fleet and then as the first Governor of New South Wales at a crucial period in the development of Australia, his selfless service fully deserves the memorial stone which the Britain-Australia Society Education Trust will lay in Westminster Abbey, and the memorial which it is intending to establish in July in his home city of Bath.

Leading the many distinguished Australians attending the service was the Governor of New South Wales, Professor Dame Marie Bashir, who gave an address. The Hon Alexander Downer, the High Commissioner for Australia, read one of the lessons, as did Vice Admiral David Steel, the Second Sea Lord, Royal Navy. To mark the fact that Captain Phillip had firmly planted the Common Law on the other side of the world, and encouraged the application of its principles, the Attorney General for Australia, George Brandis QC, and his colleague for England and Wales, Dominic Grieve QC, also read a lesson. Benson spoke simply to ask the Dean of Westminster, who conducted the service, to receive the memorial into the safe custody of the Dean and Chapter.

For Benson personally the occasion was a moving experience, as it combined several of his main interests: a love of the sea and the Royal Navy, his attachment to Australia, and his interest in education. While he was delighted that Vice Admiral Steel had represented the Senior Service, the support and attendance of his favourite Admiral of the Fleet, the Duke of Edinburgh, made it a perfect day. It seems fitting that his first decade of semi-retirement, which had started with his work for the charity launched by Captain Coram in the eighteenth century, should be rounded off by the commemoration of Captain Phillip and his achievements later in the same century.

It is not clear what Benson's next contribution to the welfare of London and the wider community will be. One thing can be stated with confidence: whatever Christopher Benson takes on, he will tackle with dedication, efficiency and hard work. His years of experience in a variety of settings have demonstrated that he has an unusual combination of aptitudes and personal qualities. After learning about his various achievements, it is easy to understand why on different occasions, when faced by financial, management or other major problems, the chief executives or advisers of troubled corporate bodies have urged: Send for Benson!